Literary Intelligence: a Virtue Theoretical Analysis with Special Reference to its Educational Implications

Cover design: Maedium, Utrecht
Lay-out: Jan-Jaap van Peperstraten

ISBN 978 90 8728 105 2
NUR 730 / 840

Literary Intelligence

a Virtue Theoretical Analysis with Special Reference to its Educational Implications

Jan-Jaap van Peperstraten

Leiden University Press

Promotor

Prof. dr. W. Humes (University of the West of Scotland)

Copromotor

Dr. C. Holligan (University of the West of Scotland)

Manuscriptcommissie

Prof. dr. F. Inglis (University of Sheffield)

Prof. dr. P. Neil (University of the West of Scotland)

Table of Contents

Abstract

In this dissertation it is argued that the concept of "literary intelligence" as used and developed by Frank Raymond Leavis and other members of his *Scrutiny* circle is a viable theoretical and educational notion and is long due a reappraisal. Their thesis that reading quality texts intelligently assists our personal and moral development is taken up and subjected to philosophical analysis.

It is also argued that a theory of intellectual virtue is best suited for such a reappraisal. Literary intelligence is then found to be best interpreted as a form of Aristotelian practical intelligence.

This interpretation allows us to theorize the moral salience of literary experiences. This theorization is achieved through an in-depth analysis of relevant articles written by Leavis, Harding and Bantock, assorted writings on the relationship between life and art as envisaged by a number of thinkers, as well as a sustained analysis of the theory of intellectual virtue.

In particular, recourse is taken to the theory of intellectual virtue as drafted by American philosopher Linda Trinkaus Zagzebski.

Consequently, a number of educational implications of the above theories are identified and commented upon. Also, it is shown that the above-mentioned theoretical insights fit in well with the consistent findings of research into reading.

Finally it is argued that if the capacity to read well is best approached as a moral trait, then reading education cannot be legitimately conceptualized as one 'competence' among others. On the contrary: reading education ought to form the moral kernel of the curriculum. A sustained and socially sanctioned emphasis on the fostering of reading and the creation of a culture of literacy will widely expand the social, cultural and moral horizons of children and adults alike.

Acknowledgements

I gratefully acknowledge the assistance of the following people: First of all, my supervisors at the University of the West of Scotland: professor Walter Humes and dr. Chris Holligan, whose assistance has been invaluable. I also express my gratitude to professors Fred Inglis (Sheffield) and Peter Neil (UWS) for their critical examination of this dissertation. I also wish to thank the staff at the University of the West of Scotland, both academic and ancillary, who did so much to make me feel at home in the three years I spent in Scotland. I would especially like to mention Professor John Atkinson who has been an inspiration. Of the Ayr staff, I would particularly like to mention Catriona Alexander, Louise Barrett, Paula Cowan, Jennifer Ellis, Charlie Fielding, Morag Giblin, Lynne Grant, Bryce Hartsthorn, , Diarmuid McAuliffe, dr. Lisa McAuliffe, Jim Maclean, Grace Paton, Noel Patterson, dr. Anne Pirrie and professor Ian Smith.

Also I would like to express my gratitude to scholars from other institutions who spared no effort to be of assistance. Particularly I would like to mention Prof. Dorothy Leal (Ohio University), Dr. Richard Storer (Leeds Trinity University College) and Prof. Jim Bradley (Memorial University Newfoundland). Finally, this dissertation is dedicated to my parents without whom I could not have committed a single word to paper

Chapter 1 : Introduction

In what sense can it be said that reading literary texts is good for the reader? Does reading a great volume of quality literature make one a 'better person'?

A literary education is often valued, and sometimes derided. Its advantages are sometimes seen as merely utilitarian, as an acquisition of symbolic capital. On the other hand, in traditional liberal-humanist circles the existential formative power of the arts finds staunch defenders: nonetheless they too find it often difficult to persuade others that the humanities do, in fact, humanize. Although extensive reading praxes are widely valued among parents and teachers there is also a great deal of misunderstanding and little theoretical foundation to the understanding of the relationship between literary education and moral formation.

It is obviously difficult to justify that there is a direct and causal relationship between being well read and being morally good. There are many people that may be considered morally good without being well-read. More worryingly, there are also people who, though well read cannot be considered good persons. The spectre of the concentration-camp Commandant who wiles away his leisure hours with a volume of Goethe is not easily exorcised. (Eagleton 1983)

Nonetheless, there are strong arguments for a relationship between literary and moral formation. In this dissertation it will be argued that a strong case may be made for such by reappraising the concept of 'literary intelligence' as posited by F.R . Leavis and the circle of educationists and literary scholars which congregated around Leavis' periodical *Scrutiny*. It will be argued that their analyses of the epistemic and cognitive dimensions of the reading process may be fruitfully interpreted through virtue ethics. The thesis defended in this dissertation is that the link between literary education and moral formation may be upheld through an analysis of the cognitive process underlying the richly qualitative understanding of literary texts. This cognitive process, which by Leavis was dubbed 'literary intelligence' bears a striking similarity to the Aristotelian faculty of practical wisdom which is, in short, the capacity to judge well in unpredictable circumstances. *Phronesis,* or practical wisdom, is considered the cognitive lynchpin underlying all virtuous activity. (Zagzebski 1996)

By bringing 'literary intelligence', the art and capacity to appraise texts well, into the realm of virtue ethics new vistas are opened and a much more nuanced understanding of the relationship between literature and moral formation emerges. Such an understanding may well be important for our thinking about reading education, and the role of literature in the primary and secondary curriculum.

The argument will take the following form: In chapter 2 an analysis of the Leavisian concept of 'literary intelligence' will be offered. It will be argued that the different visions of literary intelligence used by Leavis as well as those influenced by him may be analysed in virtue ethical terms. This link is not far-fetched. On the contrary, it is already alluded to in Bantock's work, which has obviously been influenced by the epistemological work of John Henry Newman who, in turn, was strongly influenced by Aristotle. The link with Newman allows for an *ethical* approach to knowledge, making it possible to make the link between literary intelligence as a cognitive trait *and* as an intellectual virtue.

In chapter 3 the educational and literary thought of David Holbrook is compared to that of Leavis, and it is argued that Holbrook's approach to literary intelligence, though Leavisian in nature, is much more inclusive in scope.

An in-depth philosophical analysis of the concept of intellectual virtue, and how it may relate to Leavisian literary intelligence is offered in chapter 4 where it is shown that theoretical links between Leavisian literary intelligence and Aristotelian *phronesis* may be understood in a variety of theoretical ways. In particular, an understanding of the relationship between 'art and life' may be found in the philosophical work of Maritain, Nussbaum and Macintyre. All of them suggest certain forms of cultural or literary intelligence are not only necessary for the moral life, but may themselves be approached as intrinsically good character traits. It is therefore possible to think of Leavisian literary intelligence in terms of 'intellectual virtue'.

In chapter 5, recourse is taken specifically to the rather more formal theory of intellectual virtue as drafted by Linda Trinkaus Zagzebski. A number of issues are taken up, among others how virtues relate to skills and how we may understand the central, coordinating role of *phronesis*. Phronesis will be shown to be the most central intellectual virtue, the cognitive lynchpin of all other virtues. Considering that literary intelligence, the result of a literary education, is in fact a form of practical wisdom, this entails that literary education must of its very nature have a distinct moral dimension. It is argued that literary intelligence, if a virtue, is not just *any* virtue but must be understood in terms of being a form of the most central architectonic virtue present in the human mind.

What this means for education is analysed in chapter 6, where it is argued that empirical educational and psychological research suggests that what Leavis describes as 'reading capacity' shows distinct characteristics of a virtue. Analysing reading capacity, or literary intelligence, is then not merely grounded on theoretical observations. It may be shown that there are many practical and empirical reasons to assume such an interpretation is correct. This observation has particular consequences for how we think about literary education: as virtues cannot be taught but only fostered a need to move away from an overly technical educational discourse may be identified.

In chapter 7, a formal philosophical argument is offered as to why stimulation of literary education is not merely good but rather positively ethically mandated and some observations about the moral nature of literary education are offered.

Finally, in chapter 8 the dissertation concludes with a number of remarks about the moral dimension of a literary education.

Chapter 2: the Epistemic Dimension of the Concept of Literary Intelligence in *Scrutiny*

§2.1 Introduction

Through the educational work of FR Leavis (most notably *Culture and Environment: The Training of Critical Awareness* (Leavis 1964) and *Education and the University: A Sketch for an English School,* (Leavis 1961)) , his collaboration with Denys Thompson (who went out to found the National Association for the Teaching of English (NATE) and his decisive influence on educationalists such as Bantock, Holbrook, Inglis, and (indirectly) Cox and Dyson, we can safely say that his influence on the teaching of English literature in England has been enormous (Mulhern 1979). This influence, though widely recognized has not found universal approval, some going so far as to compare the legacy of *Scrutiny*'s educational campaign with 'a mortmain' (Mulhern 1979: 328). Some critics have raised even more powerfully phrased objections [1]

In this chapter, I will sketch the concept of 'literary intelligence' or the 'literary mind' as described in *Scrutiny* by, concretely, Leavis, Harding, Bantock and Holbrook.

I will argue throughout this theses that their concept of literary intelligence is structurally similar, or structurally isomorphic, to the intellectual virtue of *phronesis,* or practical wisdom. This virtue lies at the heart of Aristotelian ethics and epistemology. This observation has both philosophical and educational consequences.

I shall also endeavour to analyse both Leavis's conceptions of 'intelligence' and 'sensitivity'. It is this conjunction between literary 'sensitivity' – 'taste' even – and ethical development which has come under heavy fire. Terry Eagleton –with Mulhern and Raymond Williams – criticizes the *Scrutiny* circle for being relatively apolitical. Also, they equate ethically evaluative 'literary intelligence' with a kind of Platonic cultural elitism (a radical ethical cognitivism where 'being good' is equated with 'having propositional moral knowledge').

---

[1] Eagleton, T. (1983). Literary Theory, an Introduction. Oxford, Basil Blackwell. , Similar sentiments can be found in Carey, J. (1992). *The Intellectuals and the Masses: pride and prejudice among the literary intelligentsia, 1880-1939.* London, Faber & Faber.

In a salient example of such criticism, Eagleton states Leavis maintained that the moral dimension of literary intelligence must necessarily result in an ethical view in which being well-read equates being a good person:

> The strength of Leavisian criticism was that it was able to provide an answer (...) to the question 'why read Literature' The answer, in a nutshell, was that it made you a better person. (...) When the Allied troops moved into the concentration camps some years after the founding of Scrutiny, to arrest commandants who had whiled away their leisure hours with a volume of Goethe, it appeared that someone had some explaining to do.
>
> (Eagleton 1983:35)

However, such allegations are not justified. They cannot be drawn from any detailed understanding of Leavis's work or of that of the *Scrutiny* circle. Of course Leavis never said that reading *as such, inevitably* made one a better person but he *did* argue that having a strong background in the humanities and having a certain kind of reading capacity *is morally pertinent* in the sense of having an effect on character-formation.

So how do Leavis and the early Leavisites understand the epistemological and moral dimensions of 'literary intelligence'? I shall focus on the descriptions of 'literary intelligence' of Leavis, Harding and Bantock and Holbrook. The first three having been the contributors to *Scrutiny* who have made the most serious efforts to offer epistemological descriptions of 'literary intelligence' , it will be argued that their notion of literary intelligence can be interpreted broadly as a reworking of the Aristotelian concept of *phronesis*. David Holbrook in turn was strongly influenced by these three and reinterpreted the theory of literary intelligence in his own educational work.

§2.2 Leavis's concept of literary intelligence in *Scrutiny*.

Leavis's theoretical writings are littered with epistemological and cognitive terms such as 'Intelligence', 'Sense', 'Criticism', 'Consciousness' and 'Judgement'. The problem of how we come to justified cognitions of a literary work of art was central to his critical endeavour. An analysis of these cognitive terms is called for.

It has been argued, among others by Northrop Frye in his *Anatomy of Criticism,* that Leavisite criticism, in being evaluative, must necessarily be based on subjective strictures and that, as such, evaluative judgements in literary criticism lack content. Without dwelling on the merits of Leavis' concrete judgements of certain works of literature, this sections aims to show that the notion of literary criticism Leavis and his followers worked with *does* have a theoretical content.

As such, there is an epistemic foundation to what Leavis called 'the business of criticism' – and there are reasons for this business being, as Leavis put it, 'the business of life'.

Leavis saw himself as an anti-philosopher, yet this does not mean his terms are not open to philosophical study. He refused, as he put it, "to take the plunge into epistemology" (Stotesbury 2008: 35) but this does not enjoin us to subject the concept of literary intelligence to epistemological analysis.

Indeed Leavis' epistemic terminology is central to his endeavour to describe the all-encompassing, universal and affective 'literary' intelligence. Literary criticism cannot be, for Leavis, merely "a discipline of scholarly industry and academic method" (Leavis 1961, p.7) but is rather a "discipline of intelligence and sensitivity" (ibid.). So what does Leavis mean by 'criticism'?

Leavis initially defines 'criticism' negatively, in the sense of distinguishing it from number of related yet quite different, intellectual endeavours such as linguistics and 'scholarship' and at the same time takes great pains to dissociate "criticism" from:

> a glib superficiality, a 'literary culture' too like that of those milieux in which literary fashions are the social currency – milieux of which the frequenters cultivate quickness in the uptake, knowingness about the latest market-quotations, and an impressive range of reference, all that at the expense of real intelligence and disinterested understanding, or interest in anything but kudos
>
> (Leavis 1961: 120)

Also:

> It is hardly possible to insist too much on the training of sensibility as prior and irremissible. Literary study unassociated with it becomes, infallibly, 'academic' and barren – a matter of profitless memorizing, of practice in graceful or scholarly irrelevance, of scanning metrical feet and drawing graphs of plots or actions, or of 'discipline' at the higher navvying.
>
> (id.)

Whatever criticism, the art of reading intelligently, is: it is quite clear what it is not. It is not formal, it is not 'academic', it is not irrelevant, it is not abstract. It is, on the contrary; personal, evaluative, and relevant outwith the realm of the purely literary. At the same time, criticism as a discipline is a 'positive ideal', and the intelligence and sensibility which ought to result from the literary training envisaged will not result in a mere capacity for purely literary appreciation (Leavis in fact questions the possibility of a purely literary appreciation) but rather that this intelligence and sensibility will – by its very nature – associate itself with 'work in other fields' (ibid.). The emphasis on the *universality* of literary intelligence, and the insistence of the *evaluative nature* of said intelligence enables a link to be made between Leavis' concept of literary intelligence with the (neo-)Aristotelian concept of *phronesis* as practical wisdom.

Like *phronesis*, Leavis's *intelligence* is:

> an exercise of the sense of value, [and] is controlled by an implicit concern for a total value-judgement.
>
> (Leavis 1964:71)

Because the discipline of literary criticism is at the centre of the fostering of 'intelligence and sensibility' questions concerning the status of literary criticism as practised in the university (and it should be remembered that English was a relatively new degree course in Cambridge in the nineteen-twenties and thirties) cannot fail "to become a preoccupation with the problem of devising a humane education" (ibid. 34). This follows from the epistemic nature of literary criticism itself:

> [Literary criticism] trains, in a way no other discipline can, intelligence and sensibility together, cultivating a sensitiveness and precision of response and a delicate integrity of intelligence – intelligence that integrates as well as analyses and must have pertinacity and staying power as well as delicacy.
>
> (ibid. 34)

The concept of literary intelligence has a deep relation to what Leavis refers to as 'sensibility' which is a "scrupulous sensitiveness of response to delicate organizations of feeling, sensation and imagery" (ibid. 38), which can only be achieved through "appreciative habituation". (ibid)

Leavis, in discussing the importance of literary training, also introduces the term 'reading capacity' which seems to describe the same concept:

> The training of reading capacity has first place. By training of reading capacity I shall mean the training of perception, judgement and analytic skill commonly indicated as 'practical criticism'. Sureness of judgement, of course, implies width of experience.
>
> (ibid. 68)

However, reading capacity envelops more than mere 'sensitiveness' or 'intelligence' as it involves 'analytical skill' as well: We may therefore describe 'reading capacity' as the practical actualization of sensibility; in much the same way as we acquire skills to actualize our intellectual potential.

This reading capacity, although it requires skills is not itself a skill; it may require technique, but the sensibility underlying 'reading capacity' is ontologically prior to any technique used to actualize it. Leavis makes this abundantly clear:

> Everything must start from the training of sensibility, together with the equipping of the student against the snares of 'technique.' Everything must start from and be associated with the training of sensibility. It should, by continual insistence and varied exercise in analysis, be enforced that literature is made of words, and that everything worth saying in criticism of verse and prose can be related to judgements concerning particular arrangements of words on the page
>
> (ibid. p.120)

This sensibility cannot be dissociated from intelligence and is in fact a necessary component of intelligence:

> The relationship between 'intelligence' and 'sensibility' is not the simple distinction that is readily assumed. [A] defect of sensibility is a defect of intelligence.
>
> (Leavis 1932: 22)

And what is the literary mind to be sensitive *of* ? Of the concrete particulars of human existence:

> [A] certain fidelity to concrete particulars *is* required (...) And it may be hazarded of all thinking, however abstract, that is likely to invest those of us who are pre-occupied with the problems of living, that the criticism of it concerns its fidelity to concrete particulars, and the quality of these.
>
> (ibid: 24)

Leavis' educational proposals are then 'teleological' in that they have a certain ideal in mind. His ideal of an 'educated mind' is surprisingly open-ended:

> The goal of this proposed school is to produce a mind which exhibits a: 'scrupulously sensitive yet enterprising use of intelligence, that is of its nature not specialized but cannot be expected without special training – a mind, energetic and resourceful, that will apply itself to the problems of civilization, and eagerly continue to improve its equipment and explore fresh approaches.
>
> (ibid: 59)

The goal of the proposed literary-critical schooling is therefore not to perpetuate an already given and homogenous literary or cultural tradition but rather to foster a truly autonomous and creative individual within the given cultural context.
Leavis stated many times that the primary concern of such 'literary minds' ought to be their contemporary cultures. A superficial reading of an early work like *Culture and Environment* might lead us to believe that the Leavisian project is one of hidebound conservatism. This is not borne out by passages such as the following:

> An addiction to literature that does not go with an interest in the literature of to-day, and some measure of intelligence about it, goes with the academic idea of tradition – traditionalism, that is, in the bad sense. And a lack of interest in the present means usually an incapacity for any real interest (...) in literature at all.
>
> (ibid: 130)

Leavis's concern for 'tradition' is a bound up with the notion of sensibility leaving us with a concept of intelligence that is historically conditioned and deeply contextual:

> Sensibility and the idea of tradition – both concerns are essential. The latter is inseparable from the former; otherwise we have the academic sterility, the Humanist manipulation of the barren idea, the inability to conceive tradition as a matter of organic life. And no one could propose to foster the idea of living tradition by a study of literature that should ignore the present.
>
> (Leavis 1932: 32)

The concept of sensibility demands something objectively given to be sensible *of*. Leavis supposes that the attention of a reader's well trained sensitivity is directed towards literary works of art. That is to say, directed towards great works of literature which themselves enact their meaning.

These works are part of, and collectively form a living tradition. Conversely, without there being such a 'continuity of consciousness' - as incarnated in a living tradition – and without a cultural context to be deeply aware of, one cannot be said to be truly *sensitive*. Leavis's remark concerning tradition is important because it is not unlike Aristotle's argument that we cannot be charitable in a purely communistic state – we need something external to exercise our mental excellences, or virtues, on: if we cannot do so for whatever reason, we cannot achieve certain states of virtue. In a world without great works of literary art; we cannot come to develop literary intelligence. The presence of a cultural life is then a necessary condition for acquiring literary intelligence. In the absence of a genuine literary culture, our intelligence must eventually become stunted. The importance of this literary culture is consequently not so much its contingent historical givenness, but rather that it is the result of human nature working on itself and seeking to understand itself. Both a wider culture and the unique individual therefore find themselves in a dialectic relationship, the individual necessarily being born into the specific historical culture of his age and him- or herself working upon it in turn.

It may be argued that on a first reading it is already clear that Leavis' use of the term 'literary intelligence' denotes something that is quite unlike a method, or technique and very much like a morally relevant character trait, in other words: a virtue. Literary intelligence is not a technique, it is a universal operation of the entire mind, it is not neutral but is oriented towards a *telos,* it is aimed at some good which is non-exhaustively described, is acquired through 'appreciative habituation' and may only be said to function within a given socio-cultural context. It is at least a justifiable assumption that literary intelligence is then to be considered a virtue of the intellect, a kind of *intelligence* which is also a *virtue,* a character-trait that is both admirable and desirable, and good in itself.

If this is so, literary intelligence must be distinguished from other cognitive processes which do not have this moral dimension. If literary intelligence is a virtue, this does not mean that being intelligent as such is to be virtuous. Also, a literary intelligence which is affective, contextual, telistic, and evaluative will be unlike forms of 'intelligence' which do not share these traits. The task of distinguishing different forms of intelligence was taken up in *Scrutiny* by Denys Harding.

§2.3 Harding's critique of intelligence testing and its relation to the psychology of reading.

Denys Harding - one of Leavis's pupils and fellow *Scrutiny* contributor – himself combined his English studies with a Part Two in Moral Sciences Tripos, this not so much out of an interest in philosophy but rather because it was the only course in Cambridge where one could study psychology.[2] (MacKillop 1995: 110)

One of his contributions to *Scrutiny* was "The Cultural Background of Intelligence Testing" (Harding 1937a). In this article he does more than simply reiterate Leavis' theory of literary intelligence. Rather, he places it in a wider psychological context. By using Leavis' concept of literary intelligence as sensibility-laden and richly affective, he critiques the practice of IQ-testing, emphasizing the affective components of intelligence 'in the everyday sense' and squarely pitting himself against the reductionist notions of 'general' intelligence dominant in his day. (Harding 1937a: 149)

In "The Cultural Background of Intelligence Testing" Harding dissociates intelligence 'in the everyday sense' from the 'intelligence' that IQ-tests were presumed to measure.

The concrete historical context of Harding's writing was the contemporary debate concerning intelligence testing: specifically the debate between L.L. Thurstone and Charles Spearman regarding the existence of a singular general intelligence. Spearman affirmed the existence of such a general formal intelligence and described it in terms of a '*g* factor'. Thurstone, in opposition to this notion, identified seven distinct 'primary mental abilities'. Harding claims that what the tests measure is not so much 'intelligence' as a quite artificial problem-solving quality which Harding considered 'trivial' (ibid. 148).

The very nature of the tasks necessarily leads the testee to be placed in an artificial situation whereas, in contrast, 'real life intelligence' is a form of thought which has

---

[2] Harding proceeded to set up a psychological laboratory in the Philosophy Department of the University of Liverpool , serving as a lecturer in Manchester during the War, eventually becoming Professor of Psychology at Bedford College, University of London. (Costall, A. (2001). Pear and his peers. Psychology in Britain: Historical Essays and Personal Reflections. G. C. Bunn, A. D. Lovie and G. D. Richards. Leicester, BPS Books: 188-204.)

an 'affective background' that is to say its processes cannot be simulated in a clinical and emotionally sterilized environment – as is the environment in which intelligence testing takes place:

> It is an illusion to suppose that the technical conception of intelligence has merely made more precise, without at the same time emasculating, the everyday conception.
>
> (ibid. 153)

Harding consequently sides with Thurstone in explicitly aligning himself with the concept of intelligence which includes a strong affective component:

> "Conceived in the way Thurstone suggests, intelligence is bound to include sensitiveness to experience, to 'outer' experience and to one's own interests and desires and values. It follows that this capacity also lies behind the discovery and formulation (as distinct from the mere solution) of many problems of the greatest cultural significance. And it seems likely that of all technical theories of intelligence, Thurstone's would most commend itself to people interested in the subtler forms of experience
>
> (ibid. p. 151-152)

Harding's concept of intelligence, which is conformable to Leavis's, is also evaluative, non-formal and non-reductive.

Lacking reference to sensibility as a component of intelligence, I.Q. tests cannot be said to measure the kind of intelligence which makes one sensitive to new problems rather than given ones, it does not open anyone to contingencies, let alone allow for the kind of self-criticism that is one of the cognitive precondition for personal autonomy.

Ironically, this fundamental failure of intelligence tests also explains the social importance of intelligence testing as a selective procedure:

> [The] limitations of the tests do not invalidate them as selection tests for education as we know it (school certificate etc.) or for industry. The great mass of people – the great mass who produce the high correlations – are not required to be sensitive to new problems; the duties they must perform and the problems they must solve are thrust upon them ready-made.
> Self criticism is a hindrance to advancement. The success or failure of their work is not a matter for their judgement: external authority sets the standard and external indications show whether they have reached it or fallen below (...).
> This is probably true of any work concerned at all directly with the satisfaction of material desires. It is not true of the more highly developed cultural activities which in a different society might be an important part of social life.
>
> (ibid. p.153)

Harding's critique of intelligence testing in general therefore derives not merely from his contention that the underlying notion of intelligence is deficient, but also that the widely accepted concept of 'technical' intelligence is dependent on the intellectual context of industrial society. Industrial culture, seen as a condition of mass uniformity, then demands a uniform, generic and technical concept of intelligence to go with it.

As stated above such a concept cannot possibly serve as a cognitive foundation for personal autonomy as the achievement of personal autonomy requires a cognitive sensitivity that a technical notion of intelligence cannot conceptualize or reflect. Such a development is not harmless: it creates a cognitive context in which 'real' intelligence or 'literary' intelligence may find itself to be inhibited. In Leavis's words: "the Cartesian ghost may disable a notably vigorous intelligence" (Leavis 1977: 35).

Harding did not only write about intelligence testing. On the contrary: he also developed a rich psychology of reading which also serves as a model for forms of intelligence Harding *does* consider to be more praiseworthy.

In "The Role of the Onlooker", (Harding 1937b) he treats the psychology of the onlooker, the evaluating spectator[3], as a basic psychological mode for the reading of fiction. The novel reader, in "The Role of the Onlooker.", is not engaged in passive entertainment – rather he "makes a full imaginative response to a fiction". Literary intelligence is the cognitive faculty of making the appropriate responses.

Even though the reader's response does not render the reader directly *operative* in the empirical world, he *comprehends* the text and engages in an *evaluative* response to it.

The reader, like the spectator, is very much involved in what he reads or witnesses. The response is active and evaluative, because:

> [Though] they make no operative response, they still assess the event in the light of all the interests , desires, sentiments, and ideals that they can relate it to; and they feel it to be noteworthy, commonplace, agreeable, or disagreeable, tragic, funny, contemptible, heroic – to mention a few of the cruder responses.
>
> (Harding 1937b: 250)

By becoming readers, literary spectators, we become onlookers at a scene crafted by an author. We engage not only with the experiences set out for us by the author, but also engage with the wider membership of readers and spectators: the audience. And it is this membership which makes evaluative communication between performer and audience, and between individual members of the audience possible. Literary intelligence is then structurally related to the 'real-life' intelligence Harding described in "The Cultural Background of Intelligence Testing." (Harding 1937a).

The presence of an audience makes social sanctioning of artistic products and endeavours possible, and it is indeed the performer, or author in the case of literary products, that in having his work published *seeks* endorsements for his point of view.

---

[3] There is a fascinating similarity between Harding's notion of 'being an onlooker' as an archetypical model of moral cognition and Adam Smith's theory of the *judicious spectator* as described in his *Theory of Moral Sentiments.* I have not however found any references to Adam Smith in Harding's publications.

This observation too bears a remarkable similarity to Adam Smith's theory that individuals seek approval of what Smith calls "the judicious spectator". By being drawn into the author's narrative artefact, we engage the product, and indirectly the author, with what Smith would call 'sympathy' and Harding 'engagement' and it is this productive cultural relationship between author and audience which stretches itself out over many cultural and social activities.

In a very 'Smithian' fashion, Harding identifies the same dialectical relationship between author and spectator even in the way a gossip and his audience relate to each other:

> [The] essential fact in gossip as in entertainment is that the speaker who raises a topic is presenting what he takes to be an interesting situation – actual or possible – in what he regards as an appropriate light. He expects his hearers to agree on the interest of the situation and the fittingness of his attitude, whether in the hushed fascination with which he talks of cancer or his truculent satisfaction at the nation's increased armaments.
>
> (Harding 1937b: 257)

What the novelist does is not essentially different. He too posits his work for an audience and wishes his work to be endorsed – but at the same time the work of the literary 'performer' also aims to critically challenge his audience:

> [The novelist] invites his audience to agree that the experience he portrays is possible and interesting, and that his attitude to it, implicit in his portrayal, is fitting. (…) In the representational arts, most obviously in literature, the author invites his audience to share in an exploration, an extension and refinement, of his and their common interests; and as a corollary, to refine or modify their value judgements.
>
> (Harding, 1937b: 258)

It follows that the relationship between reader and author is much more multi-faceted, and richer, than the relationship between, say, a Football player and spectators. The reader *shares* in the experience of the author, performing what Booth would call coduction (Booth 1988*:* 71**)** At the same time, spectatorship is emphatically *not* vicarious experience. Like Smith, Harding posits his onlooker to be involved (Adam Smith: 'sympathetic') but yet distinct (Adam Smith: 'impartial'). The reader is not *submerged* in the experiences of the author: Rather, the relationship between author and reader is rich and communicative. Eliciting an intensely evaluative response to a shared reality and, indeed, also deeply pedagogical. The author seeks, through the sharing of his experiences, in a literary form, to *extend* and *refine* the value judgements and experiences of his readers.

The richness of the work elicits a rich response and this is where we find ourselves back in the realm of literary intelligence. After all, not every response is appropriate or good. We apparently need some degree of judgement to come to an appropriate response to a rich and evaluative work.

So, in Harding as in Leavis and, as we shall see, in Bantock, cognition and evaluation go hand in hand and cannot be treated separately. There is therefore no 'neutral' literary intelligence because all reading is wound up with existential value judgements. This observation is central to treating literary intelligence in terms of an intellectual virtue.

Harding returns to his earlier considerations, and questions concerning the psychological nature of the reading experience, in an article published much later in his life. His "Psychological Processes in the Reading of Fiction" (Harding 1962)[4] continues his analysis of the concept of spectatorship, and relates it to a psychology of reading.

This text is particularly valuable as it heralds an extension of the notion of literary intelligence – making the difference between reading great and popular literature only one of degree. In the "Psychological processes of the reading of fiction" Harding builds on his previous observations made in Harding 1937a & b.

---

[4]Harding, D. W. (1962). "Psychological Processes in the Reading of Fiction." British Journal of Aesthetics **4**(2): 133-147.

He still considers reading a form of spectatorship, and spectatorship demands an evaluative intelligence:

> Attentiveness on any particular occasion implies the existence of an interest, if we take that to mean an enduring disposition to respond, in whatever way, to some class of objects or events. The response almost instantaneously becomes (or is from the start) evaluative, welcoming or aversive. And in a complex, experienced organism, an evaluative attitude is usually one expression of a sentiment, if we take that to mean an enduring disposition to evaluate some object or some class of objects in a particular way; an event or situation is then assessed in the light of its cognized significance for the object of a sentiment.
>
> (Harding 1962: 134)

In reading fiction we engage in an imagined spectatorship, which nonetheless like real spectatorship, engages identical psychological functions. If one reads a book, one is a spectator to events befalling imaginary *personae* . The fact we find it difficult to recognize that fiction is a convention using the psychology of spectatorship (ibid: 139) is a strong argument for the psychological power of fiction.
According to Harding, fiction represents: "possibilities of human experience" (ibid: 138) and it may do so by describing situations which are physically impossible. Even physical impossibilities themselves, according to Harding, find a use:

> "as vehicles presenting realities of experience. In many fairy-tales the wonders are of importance chiefly as providing the least laborious, most compressed, and vivid means of representing some quite possible human experience."
>
> (ibid: 139)

Fiction then is a cultural convention which allows for a widening of the scope of human experience, for "enlarging the scope of the discussions we have with each other about what may befall". Contingency is the stuff of fiction, and the stuff of narrative.

This is why a purely formal 'intelligence' is not suited to respond to these discussions, as Harding noted in "The Cultural Background of Intelligence Testing." – a purely technical sense of intelligence cannot respond to new and unexpected situations. Formal intelligence is closed to contingency because of its formality. This is a not unimportant observation. Those experiences of contingency, of "what may befall", generated by and directed at the fictional *personae* may include "empathy, imitation, admiration, or recognition of similarities" (ibid: 141), or the opposite. This is another reason why Harding would desist from describing reading experiences as 'vicarious', for we do not 'identify' ourselves with the personae as such. We do emphatically *not* become fellow-whalers on the *Pequod* but rather *witness* their actions, empathize with them – or not as the case may be – and as such, a recourse to the concept of vicariousness adds little but theoretical confusion.

By centring the psychology of reading on the notion of spectatorship, Harding comes close to demolishing the distinction between 'high' and 'popular' reading.

If all reading is a form of spectatorship we cannot simply relegate the reading of literary work of lesser quality to the level of primitive wish fulfilment as, say, Q.D. Leavis was prone to interpret it. Harding interprets the wish-fulfilment fantasies permeating some forms of popular literature actively, as *statements* of desire. "[Defining] the same time as it offers hallucinated satisfaction [and expresses] interests and affirming desires for which ordinary life offers small scope." (ibid: 143) So, in contrast to what Q.D. Leavis had to say about the matter, even reading for wish fulfilment describes certain desires vividly and is *as such* of worth. Popular literature's combination of desire-definition and – at some level – desire satisfaction carries a good deal of valuable social and cultural information:

> What is sometimes called wish-fulfilment in novels and plays can, therefore, more plausibly be described as wish-formulation or the definition of desires. The cultural levels at which this works may vary widely, but the process is the same. It is the social act of affirming with the author a set of values. They may centre round marble bathrooms, mink coats and big cars, or they may be embodied in the social milieu and *personae* of novels by Jane Austen or Henry James; Cadillacs and their occupants at Las Vegas or carriages and heirs at Pemberley and Poynton. We may lament the values implied in some popular forms of fiction and drama, but we cannot condemn them on the ground of the psychological processes they enjoy. The finer kinds of literature require the same psychological processes, though putting them to the service of other values.
>
> (ibid: 144)

Some books may be shallow and badly written in comparison to others, and responses made to popular literature may be inappropriate in relation to more challenging texts, but popular literature operates fundamentally on the same psychological level as 'high' literature.

This insight forms is a strong argument that 'literary intelligence', whatever its form and whatever the degrees to which it may be acquired, can fundamentally be acquired by everyone.

Texts do, of course, differ in quality but in Harding and – as we shall see – in Leavis, it is the values which the texts *enact* which are fundamental to the text's worth, and this makes ethical criticism unavoidable. The teasing out of the appeal which certain values are making on the reader through the *personae* demands a well-developed ethical sensibility. But what makes the *reading experience qua reading experience* special is that it allows us to experience human lives to which the reader otherwise would not have access. This makes a reading practice a valuable extension of any person's social and experiential scope that he would not have been able to achieve otherwise. "The mode of [psychological] response made by the reader of the novel", Harding concludes, "can be regarded as an extension of the mode of response made by an onlooker at actual events" (ibid: 147) . The experience of the reader is therefore 'structurally isomorphic to the spectator's point of view' (Nussbaum 1990: 339). This means that:

> A dubious issue in the real-life moral sphere can legitimately be pinned down by appeal to literary experience. The experience of readership is a moral activity in its own right, a cultivation of imagination for moral activity in life, and a test for correctness of real-life judgement and response.
>
> (Nussbaum 1990: 339)

The observation, that the psychological response made by the reader of the novel is structurally isomorphic to the mode of response made by an onlooker at actual events then forms the basis of my analysis of treating literary intelligence as a form of *phronesis.*

Phronesis, or practical wisdom, can only be acquired through morally salient experiences, both through witnessing the lives of people and their interactions and through engaging with others. In so far as reading fiction is not unlike witnessing the lives of real people and their interactions, reading fiction is one particularly promising and valuable way in which we may come to acquire *phronesis.* Also, the same psychological operation operates both in 'high' and 'popular' literature, albeit at different levels. This gives the lie to the idea that literary intelligence is simply another way of equating moral knowledge with cultural status and is as such existentially the preserve of a 'minority'.

Harding's notion of spectatorship has played a pivotal role in the later development of Reader-Response Theory, most notably in Wolfgang Iser's variation of this aesthetic theory. Indeed, for Iser it is the consciousness-expanding function of the reader's spectatorship in the act of reading fiction which gives it its salience. As soon as we seek to transcend the 'Cartesian minimum' of consciousness of self the reading of fiction is 'not unimportant':

> Wenn aber die Gewißheit des Subjekts nicht mehr ausschließlich in seiner Bewußtsein gründet, ja noch nicht einmal in jener kartesianischen Minimalbedingung, daß es das ist, als was es sich im Spiegel seiner Bewußtheit wahrnimmt, dann gewinnt die Lektüre fiktionaler Literatur (...) eine nicht unwichtige Funktion im 'Bewußt werden'[5].
>
> (Iser 1994: 256)

Harding, like Leavis, is then part of the wider project of 'exorcism of the ghost of Descartes' (Leavis 1977: 229). As such, he is an interesting theorist of literary intelligence.

---

[5] But when the certainty of the subject is no longer founded exclusively on its own consciousness, indeed not even in any Cartesian minimal condition, that is it that, as what it perceives itself to be in the mirror of its consciousness, then the reading of fictional literature gains a not unimportant function in "becoming conscious". (my translation, JJvP)

§2.4 Bantock and Literary Intelligence

Geoffrey Bantock is another primary representative of the *Scrutiny* tradition in education. It is obvious that Bantock was shaped deeply by Leavis' intellectual project. Bantock does not seem to share any of Leavis' perceived 'anti-theoretical' bias.

In fact, his reception of the epistemological work of J.H. Newman points towards an attempt to come to a further theoretical deepening of the concept of literary intelligence sketched by the early Leavis and Denys Harding.

With the exception of publishing a single work of literary criticism[6], all of Bantock's writings were preoccupied with educational questions, his efforts culminating in the publication of the two-volume *Studies in the History of Educational Theory* after his retirement as Professor of Education at the University of Leicester. In this section, I will focus on his early writings, later published in *Freedom and Authority in Education*[7] (hereafter *Freedom and Authority*). This selection is also interesting because three of the more prominent papers had been published before in *Scrutiny*[8]. When *Freedom and Authority* was published, *Scrutiny* was still in existence and it will become clear that Bantock's earlier writings on education are outspokenly 'Leavisite'. Bantock claims in the foreword to the second edition that upon publication *Freedom and Authority* had a certain *'succès de scandale'.*

However, even though we see the recurrent referencing to George Bourne, D.H. Lawrence, and Matthew Arnold, Bantock has a wider theoretical scope than Leavis. This wider scope shows itself in Bantock's writing about the educational work of John Henry Newman[9] and T.S. Eliot[10]. I shall, however, focus on Bantock's reading

---

[6] Bantock, G. H. (1956). *L.H. Myers, a critical study.* London, University College Leicester Jonathan Cape.

[7] Bantock, G. H. (1965). Freedom and Authority in Education: A Criticism of Modern Cultural and Educational Assumptions. London, Faber & Faber. , the first edition was published in 1952.

[8] Bantock, G. H. (1947). "The Cultural Implications of Planning and Popularization." Scrutiny **XIV**(3): 162-170. ; Bantock, G. H. (1948). "Authority and Method in Education: Some Reflections on Mr. Ford's Rejoinder." Scrutiny **XV**(4): 289-309. ; Bantock, G. H. (1948). "Some Cultural Implications of Freedom in Education." Scrutiny **XV**(2): 82-97. ; Bantock, G. H. (1951). "Matthew Arnold, H.M.I." Scrutiny **XVIII**(1): 32-44.

[9] Bantock, G. H. (1965). Newman and the possibility of 'order'. *Freedom and Authority in Education.* London, Faber & Faber.

of Newman, as his Newman-reception offers a distinct but powerful avenue towards interpreting literary intelligence in virtue-ethical terms.

[10] Bantock, G. H. (1970). *T. S. Eliot and education*. London, Faber.

§2.5 Bantock's *Education and the Literary Intelligence*

In his paper *Education and the Literary Intelligence,* (Bantock 1965a) Bantock follows up on Leavis's position with regards to 'literary intelligence' and conceptualizes it as a form of intelligence antagonistic to what he calls: 'rationalism'. He describes 'rationalism' as a form of intelligence which is 'separated from the emotions' and concerned to 'bring everything to the bar of his judgement'. The likeness to Harding's critique of 'abstract' or 'analytical' intelligence is clear.

Like Leavis and Harding, Bantock's preoccupation is basically epistemic. His interest lies in the cognitive aspects of reading literature and in doing so critiques the same 'rationalism' which Harding had critiqued earlier in his work on intelligence testing. (Harding 1937a). Bantock's critique has, much like Harding's, political implications as well. The central cognitive process in 'rationalism' is perceived to be 'analysis': analysis implies abstraction, which is a simplification of the complex of social existence.

It therefore necessarily implies a denial of basic psychological processes for the sake of a presumed "objectivity". This critique mirrors Harding's statement that the normalization of analytical intelligence somehow falsifies and inhibits the exercise of 'real-life'-intelligence. But the rationalists' flight from the affective life is in vain, for they do cannot undo their own basic humanity. So, the rationalist cannot be said to be without emotion, indeed "there is usually an emotional basis to the analytic enterprises – part indignation, part assertion" (Bantock 1965a: 34)

The rationalist's feelings "are coarsened in that they are usually directed externally to the bare *facts* implicit in the process of analysis and synthesis rather than as partners in the act of discovery" (ibid: 35). Cognitively detached from his emotional life, the rationalist is quite literally the 'ideologist' *pur sang,* "very much at the mercy of ideas" of whatever ilk.

Bantock describes other politically pertinent characteristics: "[a] concern for perfection and [b] tendency to eschew variety". Both of these characteristics are politically pertinent because it is these characteristics which lead rationalists to think about social problems in terms of categories in which "the repercussions of a little juvenile misbehaviour becomes 'the delinquency problem' "(ibid, p. 36).In place of this rationalism, Bantock emphatically states that he does not advocate any form of irrationalism or intuitionism.

Rather, again like Harding, he considers the intellect is incomplete without an affective component and needs to be refined by "what of feeling can afford it depth and concreteness" and this is where literary education is seen as of prime importance:

> [The] close conjunction of intellect and feeling which issues in that imaginative insight (...) is our most profitable way of thinking about human 'sciences' and (...) is peculiarly the function of literature to help to train.
>
> (ibid: 37)

It is worth noting that his argument, although of political consequence is essentially *epistemic.* In short, his critique of utilitarian, outcome-based education is founded not so much on an explicit ideology but rather on the epistemic argument that a utilitarian outcome based system of education must base itself on restricted epistemological grounds which will never be able to value literature as being morally salient in its own right. Bantock considers literary education to be valuable because it may foster a refining of reason through emotions, thereby achieving:

> a wholeness of conception, an embedded quality of idea in temperament and circumstance which we find nearer to the actual behaviour of human beings in political circumstances than we would guess at from the writings of political theorists.
>
> (ibid: 40)

Bantock further states that by making delicate and precise discriminations of experiences "there is an evaluative aspect which comes to wear very much the appearance of a moral concern". Bantock, like Leavis, would therefore claim that the importance of literature transcends the merely literary. The literary artist: "*engages* us in his experience through his handling of language, through metaphor and rhythm, in order to bring into play a full and delicate perceptiveness, engaging both the intelligence and the emotions – the 'feeling intellect' " (ibid: 40). Bantock does not offer a theory of spectatorship, but like Harding centres on the *activity* of the responding literary intellect. This makes this intelligence's exercise first and foremost a *praxis.*

These cognitive feelings are not, however, relevant, as *mere* feelings. Rather, writers – as should mature minds – make "discriminations among experiences". They are relevant *as* feelings because they are evaluative. They are 'moral sentiments' and hence the stuff of which moral discriminations are made and communicated through. The author communicates his sense of moral reality to us, not in a didactic or homiletic fashion, but his sense of what is important follows from the structure of the narrative itself. Indeed it is this narrative which allows for the process of spectatorship described by Harding. The writer's account of human interactions and conflicts never remains ethically neutral because:

> our sympathies have been *actively engaged or repelled in terms of concrete particularities behaviour by which we have been led to discriminate between the different values of various types of conduct*
>
> (ibid: 41)

So, if literature truly affords privileged insight into the human condition, how is this relevant for the field of education? Bantock argues that the educationist: "needs the profoundest penetration possible in the nature of human existence before his claim to education 'for life' can be accepted as valid". Any curriculum that claims to go beyond a merely cerebral development of the pupil, which can never be *good in itself* - should therefore be based on the creative strains and frictions in the exercise of the literary intelligence.

It is clear that this training of the literary intelligence is the 'great labour' which Eliot warns is needed for the acquisition and – eventually – transmission of any the cultural tradition. At the same time, the kind of consciousness fostered by a literary creation, though not purely cerebral, is certainly conducive to the exercise of practical reason, and as such is conducive to mental development and the growth of rationality.

In fact, the literary intelligence is in singular ways *more* rational than the exercise of abstract intelligence. The former is open to contingency, to cognizing our human condition, for properly coming to an understanding of our socio-cultural environment. Furthermore, because the literary intelligence is universal in scope, or at least stretches out beyond the appreciation of the merely literary, it has relevance beyond individual contemplation.

It cannot be seen as a luxury or a privilege but has a wider social relevance which transcends the merely conformist political demands of 'good citizenship'.

The literary intelligence, undetached and evaluatively committed, "enables us to achieve a degree of imaginative projection which is of the greatest usefulness in any concrete situation" (ibid: 50).

It is this phrasing which strongly invites an Aristotelian reading of the concept of literary intelligence. For practical wisdom, *phronesis,* is exactly that – the capacity of judging what is right in a contingent, unique, and unpredictable situation – and we cannot exercise *phronesis* without the use of the imagination. Aristotle's *phantasia* plays much the same role as Bantock's *imagination*: "[Aristotle's] *phantasia* [is a capability] of focusing on some concrete particular, either present or absent, in such a way as to see (or otherwise perceive) it *as* something, picking out its salient features, discerning its content" (Nussbaum 1990: 77). This is why moral or social procedures can never be substitutes for a mature, judging mind, and once more, an emphasis on abstract intelligence prevents us "from thinking about the real capacities of children". (Bantock 1965a: 50). The uniqueness of every child can only be discerned imaginatively, and not methodically.

Bantock also treats this question on how the proper exercise of the cognitive faculties relates to fictional literature in his articles "Literature and the Social Sciences" (Bantock 1981c) The emphasis is, once more, both explicitly epistemic and firmly in the Leavisite tradition:

> "Leavis has always seen in literature a supreme expression of the human – and humane – consciousness; and it is this high consciousness I need."
>
> (Bantock 1981c: 24)

What does he need it for? For another epistemic goal, the critique of positivist models of social understanding. They are the contemporary incarnation of abstract intelligence, of the Cartesian mind so utterly rejected by Leavis, of the intelligence that seeks to understand human beings quantitatively, and hence marginalizes a properly mature, richly affective cognition of the human condition as would be exercised by a literary intelligence.

A literary intelligence is not merely good for understanding fictional texts but is *universal.* If this is so, then it should offer an epistemic advantage in explaining at least certain social occurrences and trends. This, according to Bantock, is exactly what a literary intelligence does, literature is for him:

> "an exploratory instrument which offers, among other riches, revelation of the complexities of consciousness"
>
> (ibid. 29)

And indeed in the social sciences, or the *humanities* we cannot epistemically justify approaching people's social existence as if they were mere variables, 'units' or 'social atoms'. It can even be argued that the objectivity that we ought to aim for in the study of society cannot possibly be achieved through positivistic means. The very object of the nature of the literary intelligence, the human condition, means that only a 'deep' qualitative consciousness may satisfactorily enter into an understanding of this object. For social science to become more objective it may actually need to adopt 'literary' methods:

> [It] may well be that the sort of 'objectivity' that social science research can seek will ultimately turn out to be an objectivity nearer that of literature that that of science. (…) The fact is that the social world only achieves limited objectivity; it is itself the product of the minds that go to make it up, and these minds differ in intensity, and penetrative power – 'a fool sees not the same tree that a wise man sees' etc."
>
> (ibid: 49)

Bantock's admonitions may well have been prophetic, in contemporary social theory, there is a great deal of interest in the use of narrative especially for case-studies. The Danish sociologist Bent Flyvbjerg especially has been very active in redeeming the cognitive dimension of narrative for the social sciences. (cf. Flyvbjerg 2001)

§2.6 Bantock's reception of John Henry Newman's epistemology.

In *Freedom and Authority in Education,* Bantock positions himself vis-à-vis three canonical writers on education: John Henry Newman, Matthew Arnold, and D.H. Lawrence. It is hardly surprising to find Bantock writing on Matthew Arnold in *Scrutiny:* Bell (1988) calls Leavis 'the principal twentieth century descendant of the English critical tradition in which Dr. Johnson, Wordsworth, Coleridge, and Matthew Arnold are among his most notable predecessors.' The Matthew Arnold of *Culture and Anarchy*, the Matthew Arnold who held that 'poetry[11] is the criticism of life' is undoubtedly close to Leavis and hence to Bantock. Moreover, Leavis' interest in Lawrence is well known and as such it is not surprising that Bantock shares this interest. However, his choice to devote a sizable article to the thought of John Henry Newman is surprising.

Hirst tells us that education, involves "a commitment to reason, nothing more and nothing less" (Hirst 1974: 84f). However we must ask ourselves the following questions: what is the nature of reason, second, how can we be committed to reason, what commits us to it? If we understand reason as a merely formal or abstract affair, it is difficult to see how we can be committed to it, as it lacks evaluative content. One cannot be committed to what is morally neutral. One must at the very least consider something to be *morally good* before one can commit oneself to it.

However, a richer conception of reason may well be a form of rationality which we may feel committed to. The Aristotelian conception is undoubtedly rich, and singularly evaluative: *phronesis* being essential to one's attempts to lead a successful *eudaimonic,* or good, life. But can reason commit to itself? Purely abstract reason does not seem capable of committing the cognizing subject to itself. It is this observation that forms the kernel of J.H. Newman's *Essay in Aid of a Grammar of Assent.*

[11] 'poetry' here used in the widest sense, including all forms of literature.

And this a text which drew much attention from an unlikely reader such as Geoffrey Bantock.[12]

It will be argued in this section that Bantock's reading of Newman is an extension of the *Scrutiny* circle's critique of the notion of 'pure' unalloyed 'logical' intelligence and points at a notion of intelligence which envelops and legitimises the cognitive dimensions of the emotional life. This implies that the educational process has to entail a development of the entire person and this insight has far reaching consequences for Bantock's educational thought. To begin with, his conceptual analysis of the notion of intelligence leads him to critique contemporary educational thought and policy.

First of all it is pertinent to ask why it is that Bantock held such an interest in Newman.

One answer is that Bantock's reading of John Henry Newman is focused on the problem of the role of emotions in cognition. Also, Newman's concept of an *illative sense* provides the theoretical backbone for Bantock's 'literary intelligence'.

It forms one more possible avenue to conceptualize literary intelligence as a form of *phronesis,* as Newman's *illative sense* and Aristotelian *phronesis* have strong structural similarities. Even though Bantock's article, "Newman and the Possibility of Order" (Bantock 1965d)[13] looks like an autonomous piece of redeeming criticism, defending Newman against charges of 'irrationality' and 'emotionality' laid against him by Sidgwick and others, it is obvious upon closer reading that Bantock aligns himself with Newman. He regards him as an emblematic character whose notion of personality and rationality proves pivotal for his own thought. Bantock's later work also show a great regard and concern for emotional development. In a cognition-driven curriculum a larger role for emotional development can only be legitimized by teasing out the cognitive dimension of the emotional life. Newman, in his *Grammar of Assent,* actually seems to be on a parallel course in this, and is hence of interest to Bantock.

---

[12] At the time, Newman's later theological and philosophical writings were not widely read outside of Roman Catholic circles. Bantock does not identify himself as being or at any time having been a Roman Catholic.

[13] Bantock, G. H. (1965d). Newman and the possibility of 'order'. *Freedom and Authority in Education.* London, Faber & Faber: 106-132.

Bantock's interest in Newman's work also allows a link to be established between his notion of literary intelligence and the Aristotelian notion of *phronesis*: connections between Newman's 'illative sense' and Aristotelian phronesis have been made by Dunne (1993) and Aquino (2004).

Newman's *Essay in Aid of a Grammar of Assent* (1870) is considered to be Newman's seminal work. Although the object of the *Grammar of Assent* was to provide an epistemological foundation for Christian apologetics, it is obvious Bantock's interests lie elsewhere. Bantock considered Newman's conception of rationality much more promising than the naïve empiricism of both the Utilitarians and Rousseau. In his rejection of abstract 'rationalism' Bantock seeks in Newman's *Grammar of Assent* an alternative epistemic foundation for educational theory and the cognition of the literary work of art.

Central to Newman's epistemology lies the concept of assent by which he means the cooperation of will and reason. 'Assent' occurs when we accept something to be true. Newman distinguishes 'notional' from 'real' assent. In his *Grammar of Assent* he gives a few examples of the two and how one may change into the other.

The following example is particularly illuminating:

> [Great] truths, practical or ethical, float on the surface of society, admitted by all, valued by few, exemplifying the poet's adage, "Probitas laudatur et alget," until changed circumstances, accident, or the continual pressure of their advocates, force them upon its attention. The iniquity, for instance, of the slave-trade ought to have been acknowledged by all men from the first; it was acknowledged by many, but it needed an organized agitation, with tracts and speeches innumerable, so to affect the imagination of men as to make their acknowledgment of that iniquitousness operative.
>
> (Newman 1955: 78)

The 'notional assent' is the *mere* acceptance, at an intellectual level, of the truth of a certain proposition or statement. However, rendering that 'acknowledgment operative' asks for 'real assent'. The object of a real assent is always a *res,* a reality, whereas the object of a notional assent is a concept. We can never therefore commit ourselves *merely* to a concept, something more is needed. Real assent is also distinguished from notional assent in that certitude is not reached by demonstration or inference, but rather by the exercise of the illative sense which Newman explicitly aligns with *phronesis:*

> [Aristotle] calls the faculty which guides the mind in matters of conduct, by the name of *phronesis*, or judgment. This is the directing, controlling, and determining principle in such matters, personal and social. What it is to be virtuous, how we are to gain the just idea and standard of virtue, how we are to approximate in practice to our own standard, what is right and wrong *in a particular case*, for the answers in fullness and accuracy to these and similar questions, the philosopher refers us to no code of laws, to no moral treatise, because no science of life, applicable to the case of an individual, has been or can be written. Such is Aristotle's doctrine, and it is undoubtedly true.
>
> (ibid:277)

Whereas notional assent leads to merely theoretical judgements, judgement *proper* demands real assent. No real assent can be given without the exercise of the illative sense, which, if Newman is correct in considering it his counterpart to Aristotelian *phronesis,* must commit the entire person rather than merely its faculty of abstract intelligence.

This also explains why reason, if it is formal, abstract, or theoretical cannot commit the entire person. Giving 'real assent' is an existential act, committing the entire person. Newman's epistemology, like Aristotle's, is holistic. Newman's concern for mental 'holism', in the sense that human consciousness and sensibility are to be fundamentally united in the person rather than set against each other, vouches for a positive cognitive role for the emotions appeals to someone who seeks to redeem forms of knowledge and judgement which are not dependent on the desiccating operations of the purely rational mind. Newman is therefore important to Bantock mostly for his psychology and this has distinct epistemic implications.

Real assent, as the coalescence between an Object existing *a se* and an active Subject involving itself existentially in the epistemic endeavour, involves the imaginative faculties. Newman, in Chapter 4 of the *Grammar of Assent* goes so far as to state that the active use of the imagination as a mental faculty is essential for the transformation of notional into real assents:

'The iniquity (...) of the slave-trade ought (...) was acknowledged by many, but it needed an organized agitation, (....) so to affect the *imagination* of men as to make their acknowledgment of that iniquitousness operative.' (ibid: 78). This emphasis on the central position of the imagination is not restricted to Newman. His position concerning the imagination shows a broadly Aristotelian influence. Aristotle's *phantasia*, as Nussbaum puts it, has its emphasis exactly on the selective and discriminatory character of the imagination. "Its job", according to Nussbaum (1990: 77) is more to focus on reality rather than irreality".

Assent requires the operation of the imagination; for it entails a dialectical meeting between subject and object. Rationalism, on the contrary, knows of no tension between subject and object and behind the empiricist model of the receptive mind, allowing itself to be passively imprinted by Nature, we actually find a rationalistic mind individually reading its own epistemic structures on reality. It is then, according to Newman, following Aristotle, the imagination which allows for the individual to come to an intimate understanding of realities.

Assent, being itself an act of will moving the person, it is itself closely linked to the imagination and cannot operate without it:

> Strictly speaking, it is not imagination that causes action; but hope and fear, likes and dislikes, appetites, passion, affection, the stirrings of selfishness and self-love. What imagination does for us is to find a means of stimulating those motive powers; and it does so by providing a supply objects strong enough to stimulate them. The thought of honour, glory, duty, self-aggrandisement, gain, or on the other hand of Divine Goodness, future reward, eternal life, perseveringly dwelt upon, leads us along a course of action corresponding to itself, but only in case there be that in our minds which is congenial to it. However, when there is that preparation of mind, the though does lead to the act. Hence it is that the fact of a proposition being accepted with a real assent is accidentally an earnest of that proposition being carried out in conduct, and the imagination may be said in some sense to be of practical nature, inasmuch as it leads to practice indirectly by the action of its object upon the affection.
>
> (Newman 1955: 81-82)

Also, a notion of Assent may explain how, possibly, Leavisite literary intelligence may be considered a virtue. After all, for any character trait to be a virtue, we must be, at some level, responsible for it. But how can we be responsible for our thoughts, beliefs and judgements? Real assents, committing the entire person, cannot be brought about by processes of inferential reasoning alone. By definition real assent involves an act of the will. Assent is a personal and therefore contextual act. This has as its consequence that that epistemic judgement is, in its fullness, presupposes and an integrated personality that is both creative and at the same time historically situated.

The notion of mind as active and creative was held by Newman but his insistence on personal involvement and creativity in the epistemic process does not lead to mere subjectivism.

Assent is a creative act of will deciding to accept a certain interpretation of reality. It assumes that there is no such thing as a reality which 'imposes itself'. To claim that a reality may do so without an act of epistemic reception, as the 'scientific rationalists' hold, is considered erroneous.

The 'detachment of mind' of 'Benthamite sceptics' then fails to commit 'the whole being' and leads, ironically, to an 'inflation of self' - because in the end the rationalist can only take 'their own human kind' as standard. (id.) Any judgement which commits our being, is an act of real Assent and as such involves the will, even if our formal epistemology does not allow for a notion of Assent – we are still responsible for our judgements and beliefs.

So too, for our judgements and beliefs concerning education: for Newman as for Bantock, an abstract and formalized approach to education 'fails to commit the whole being and thus leads to an inflation of self' (Bantock 1965d: 115)

In reflecting on Newman he re-iterates *Scrutiny*'s critique of purely formal and abstract notions of intelligence (cf. Harding 1937a, Harding 1937b) and looks to Newman for a model, which is essentially *phronetic* , which *may* commit the whole being to the business of knowing: "What it is to be virtuous, how we are to gain the just idea and standard of virtue, how we are to approximate in practice to our own standard, what is right and wrong in a particular case" (Newman 1903, 347)

In critiquing contemporary utilitarian intellectual tendencies, Bantock makes for an educational approach alien to direct and contemporary economical 'needs'.

If true knowledge is to be achieved through the exercise of virtue, then knowledge is a good thing in itself. This is not merely because through knowledge we can become good (and indeed we need a certain kind of moral knowledge to be good), but because truth and knowledge are in themselves good, and they are good-making qualities of a person as such because "there is a relationship implied between me and my knowledge" (Bantock 1981f: 77)

If knowledge is good, it is good to aim for knowledge and indeed, for Newman, the *telos* of the human mind is to seek truthful knowledge: "Truth of whatever kind is the proper object of the intellect" (Newman 1948: 53) Everything considered then, the intellectual quality which Newman describes as the *illative sense* is closely linked to Bantock's own understanding of 'literary intelligence'.

In turn, the illative sense is modelled on the Aristotelian virtue of phronesis: It is a universally working intellectual trait which as a capacity of mature judgement is relevant for all intellectual endeavours, and a necessary condition for us leading a good life.

For Newman, in calling his version of the notion of practical judgement the "illative sense", concedes it is "a grand word for a common thing" (Newman 1973: 375) and, as Zagzebski (1996) will do later, considers it the "architectonic faculty" (Newman 1962: 187) of judgement and conclusion in its perfection. *Phronesis* is, indeed, as Newman puts it, a "living *organon*" (Newman 1955: 230).

Newman explicitly aligns his *illative sense* as with *phronesis* and by doing so makes it clear that his ideas on the matter were modelled on the intellectual virtue first described by Aristotle.

In his *Grammar of Assent* Newman actually gives one of the most well written definitions of what *phronesis* is:

> What it is to be virtuous, how we are to gain the just idea and standard of virtue, how we are to approximate in practice to our own standard, what is right and wrong in a particular case, for the answers in fullness and accuracy to these questions, the philosopher[14] refers us to no code of laws, no moral treatise, because no science of life, applicable to the case of the individual, has been or can be written (…) An ethical system may supply laws, general rules, guiding principles, a number of examples, suggestions, landmarks, limitations, cautions, distinctions, solutions of critical or anxious difficulties; but who is to apply them to a particular case? Whither we can go, except to the living intellect, our own, or another's?
> What is written is too vague, too negative for our need. It bids us avoid extremes; but it cannot ascertain for us, according to our personal need, the golden mean. The authoritative oracle, which is to decide our path, is something more searching and manifold than such jejune generalizations as treatises can give, which are most distinct and clear when we least need them. It is seated in the mind of the individual, who is thus his own law, his own teacher, and his own judge in those special cases of duty which are personal to him. It comes of an acquired habit; though it has its first origin in nature itself, and it is formed and matured by practice and experience (…) it is a capacity sufficient for the occasion, deciding what ought to be done here and now, by this given person, under these given circumstances.
> (Newman 1955, 277-278)

Bantock states that Newman's 'dislike of paper logic' was therefore not essentially an outward sign of inner intellectual poverty but rather 'based on a profounder psychological understanding of the processes by which opinions are come by." (Bantock 1962: 107) And this profounder understanding is conformable to that of Knights' 'uncompartmentalized sensibility' (Knights 1945) and Leavis' insistence that:

[14] Meaning Aristotle, JJvP

> "The relationship between 'intelligence' and 'sensibility' is not the simple distinction that is readily assumed. [A] defect of sensibility is a defect of intelligence."
>
> (Leavis 1932)

Dunne is then correct to say that Aristotle resonates throughout the work of Newman (Dunne 1992: 35) Practical knowledge, if we follow Aristotle and Newman is of an entirely different epistemological nature than scientific knowledge. There is no 'abstract' practical knowledge and such an abstracted 'code' must necessarily be of limited value to praxis. Because practical knowledge, knowledge of individuals, their behaviours, their choices and their moral states, stems from practice and experience, this renders a literary education morally relevant, as a locus of practical experience.

Of course this is not to mean practical knowledge is not somehow theoretically approachable, but it is practical because its object is properly human *praxis.* (Dunne 1992: 51) An Aristotelian approach to Newman and a fortiori to Bantock is therefore salient To conclude: for Bantock, Newman was the English filter through which he allowed himself to be imbued with Aristotelianism.

Chapter 3: Some Educational Implications of the Concept of Literary Intelligence: the Case of David Holbrook

In Newman's ideas on education we see further evidence that what he considers to be a refined intellect is a mind steeped in intellectual virtues. If knowledge is the result of a cognitive contact between the virtuous mind and reality, then the virtuous mind must be trained for that task. A virtue is, after all, not a natural capacity. There can be, in consequence, no such thing as 'spontaneous' knowledge:

> [Newman] stresses the need for training 'the eye of the mind, of which the object is truth, is the work of discipline and habit.'
>
> (Bantock 1965d: 128)

Habit, of course, because if a well-functioning intellect is, like *phronesis* a virtue of the intellect, it must be exercised structurally and systematically. It is unlike a skill, it cannot be acquired easily through training, and it requires the fostering of, among other things, the imagination. It is a deeply contextual and culturally grounded mental trait.

Also, a virtue must be a habit, it must be ingrained in the mind, and, though respectful of a person's individuality, the individual mind cannot in this reading be left to its own devices.

Virtue is not acquired without effort; and this goes for intellectual virtues as well.

The mind must be initiated in intellectual practices and, as Bantock puts it, the mind can only develop "if it works on substance of value outside itself".

Literature may be some such substance, and this argument is not incommensurable with Harding's dictum that the value of literature lies in the extension of the individual's experience. For Harding too the mind must be brought outside of itself, to grow.

Literary intelligence is to be understood as a virtue of the intellect, and should therefore be acquired as a virtue. That is: through initiation, example, habit, and training.

A literary education would then be one way of training the virtues. Leavisite ideas about literary education may consequently be found to be essentially correct, although I believe his exclusive emphasis on a cultural elite to be mistaken. Leavisite insights into the nature of literature and the literary mind cannot be said to end with Leavis but may indeed be developed more fully by other parties. A further development, in the work of David Holbrook, will be sketched in the next few paragraphs.

§3.1 Holbrook and the Poetic Function as Literary Intelligence

Next to F.R. Leavis and Geoffrey Bantock, a third educationist whose ideas I will analyze is David Holbrook. Born in 1923, he read English at Downing College, Cambridge, afterwards taking up teaching positions with the Workers' Educational Association and later at a secondary school in Bassingbourn, Cambridgeshire, before turning to full-time writing in the early nineteen-sixties. He has written prodigiously on educational subjects as well as having authored numerous volumes of criticism, fiction and poetry. In this section I will of course limit myself to a number of Holbrook's educational writings in which, as I will argue, one can find a notion of 'literary intelligence' which is closely related but is more inclusive than Leavis's.

This inclusivity is due to his focusing on the imagination as one of the central features of literary intelligence. As I have argued before, Leavis' theory of literary intelligence is theoretically viable if conceptualized as a form of Aristotelian *phronesis*. If we do so this precludes us from approaching literary intelligence as the exclusive domain of a cultural elite. Of course, every form of intelligence allows for gradations, so too *phronesis,* but it can never be the exclusive domain of a single group of people, as a virtue it is an excellence of the human mind, and it is only an excellence in relation to our natural capacities and as every person has a natural capacity to practical judgement, they are capable of acquiring the corresponding virtue.

Indeed, *phronesis* is arguably the most fundamental virtue. It is the architectonic intellectual virtue vouching for the relative *unity* of the virtues and is the main characteristic of a morally successful human life. The very fact that goodness cannot be circumscribed by social or intellectual status consequently makes for an inclusive interpretation of literary intelligence.

That Holbrook's *poetic function* (as described in Holbrook 1968) too is closely allied to *phronesis* is borne out by Gordon Pradl in his article "A Moral Approach to English". (Pradl 1995)[15] If the poetic function is unrelated to *phronesis* than there would be no connection, however tenuous between "the reading and writing of literature and the quality of public and private lives" (Pradl 1995: 93).

Pradl argues for the continuity between Holbrook's educational writings and the moral arguments for literature as made by Arnold and Leavis – as well as his support for the educational centrality of character development (Pradl 1995: 94). This same continuity is argued for in Abbs (Abbs 1995)[16]:

> This tradition [of a moral vision of English education] can be seen to run from Blake and Coleridge, to Matthew Arnold, from Matthew Arnold to George Sampson, from Sampson to F.R. Leavis and Denys Thompson and from Leavis and Thompson to David Holbrook, Raymond Williams, and David Hoggart.
>
> (id.)

Although Holbrook adopted the Arnoldian 'moral argument for literature' we see already in his later reception of Arnold the same trend towards inclusiveness which characterizes his reading of Leavis as well:

> I find, when I read Arnold now, that his concepts of "perfection" and "culture" are terribly narrow – classical and literary education. I enjoy his irony, but he seems to be too parochial, and propagandistic, and his emphasis is too heavily on culture as a source of moral good – and as a way of making people polite, elegant, and cultivated, rather than "mean, vulgar, or hideous" [17]

---

[15] Pradl, G. M. (1995). A Moral Approach to English. *Powers of Being: David Holbrook and his Work*. E. Webb. London, Associated University Presses: 93-111.

[16] Abbs, P. (1995). The Tradition of Poetic Humanism and the Teaching of the Arts. *Powers of Being: David Holbrook and His Work*. E. Webb. London, Associated University Presses: 112-124.

[17] Personal communication of David Holbrook to Gordon M. Pradl, (Pradl 1995, 95-6)

Arnold, then, it seems, is, according to Holbrook to narrowly preoccupied with eliciting conformist behaviour and a phronetic attitude to moral development would indeed preclude this. Goodness transcends manners radically. Goodness transcends conformism radically. *Phronesis* and development of the virtues cannot possibly be limited to social conformism or the eliciting of polite behaviour and though it could be argued that a *phronimos* will not go about being deliberately hurtful, at the same time politeness does not necessarily imply *phronesis.*

A second line of thought running through Holbrook's educational writings is the Leavisite notion of English as a *discipline* rather than a *subject.* Central to Leavis's notion of English as an educative venture is the fostering of the 'central coordinating intelligence' which is fostered by literature but not exclusively *literary* i.e. works on the entire human condition rather than merely with aesthetic concerns. A critical judgement is then always a *moral judgement.* I have of course put this insight at the centre of my attempt to conceptualize Leavisian literary intelligence as a form of *phronesis.* This too makes English, in so far as it is preoccupied with fostering this kind of intelligence more than a subject.

However, Leavis, though being essentially correct about the nature of literature and the relationship of critical and moral judgement, is criticized by Holbrook. He identifies two points in which he believes Leavis to have erred. "Leavis proposals reinforced a serious division within education. While education for creativity and the imagination might initially undergird the development of critical sensibility, increasingly minority culture came to stand for a defensive posture within the curriculum, one seeking to inoculate students against the evils of mass civilization." (Pradl 1995: 98)

This indeed is a major problem suffusing Leavis's educational thought – if literary education is to play a central role in educating the virtues, or at least educating for *phronesis,* then it cannot be satisfied in merely providing a minority education for a minority culture. This is one of the major problems of the strictly Leavisite approach to literary education. Bantock, however, recommends an educational course of action not unlike that sketched by Holbrook in his *English for the Rejected.*

In the chapter 'The Education of the Less Able Child', in *Education in an Industrial Society* we see Bantock distancing himself, much like Holbrook did, from the educational elitism of Matthew Arnold who, as Bantock put it failed to see that: "the culture of the minority can never be that of the majority as well" (Bantock 1963: 201) and in dissociating between minority and majority cultures what he seeks to do is emphasize that the less intelligent pupils should be offered an educational programme which is not modelled on that of their more academic peers, but rather one that is more distinctly appropriate for their own level:

> What I want is a schooling that will enable these children to realize their natures as much as in their own way our able children realize theirs through intellectual accomplishment
>
> (ibid: 221)

Bantock too strongly emphasizes the need for creative writing and extensive reading. (ibid: 215-216) Although Holbrook was deeply influenced by Leavis (Pradl 99) he distinguishes himself from the emphasis on minority culture which he considered authoritarian and broadened the notion of culture, deprecating those who would claim culture to be the preserve of a minority.

It was on the basis of this sentiment that Holbrook also started thinking about the theoretical underpinnings of the relationship between literature and moral formation, focusing especially of the process of self-realization elicited by the exploration and extension of the understanding of the human condition. For Holbrook as for Bantock and Leavis, the 'moral' of literature, as the 'moral' of the human condition is never a heteronomous given:

> I hope I will not be taken to mean by "moral" that poetry must be didactic, or that its moral impulses should exhort us to do good. But essential to a civilized people is the constant pondering in the spirit, in the feelings, of the nature of life, of possible patterns of living, possible attitudes to life, possible significances in it – How to live? And poetry is one essential means of maintaining continuity in the pondering and reconsidering in concrete, felt, terms this "why?" and "what for?" of human life
>
> (Holbrook 1962: 72)

Thus, of course, it must be according to a model of virtue theory, the inexhaustibleness of *phronesis* makes it impossible to frame in advance a model for good living which will be valid for generations to come. To be virtuous in different times is to be differently virtuous in a way we might not exhaustively predict.

In Hannah Arendt's terms, one of the tasks of education is to 'preserve newness', by establishing a 'continuity of consciousness' between past, present, and future and at the same time realizing that this continuity is not in Aristotle's words that "All people seek, not the way of their ancestors, but the Good" (*Politics* 1268a 39ff)

That the Holbrookian 'poetic function' cannot be "finally argued or fully conceptualized"

(Abbs 1995: 113) therefore renders it systemically similar to *phronesis.* The faculty of judgement too is non-reductive to any formal, abstract scheme or procedure.

Pradl (1995) mentions Holbrook's creative work as an example of such an individual creative attempt to negotiate the particulars of his humanity, and it is this coming to terms with ourselves and others which makes for the educational relevance of poetry.

Imaginative creativity is a central notion to Holbrook's thinking about literature and education: his emphasis is *less* on cultural continuity than on individual creativity, yet he too escapes from the more solipsistic forms of self-expression so vehemently combated by Bantock. But to emphasise creativity is not to disqualify tradition. Indeed, creativity for Holbrook as for Leavis, happens in a dialectical transaction between self and others, presence and past:

> Our role is that of fostering a life flame which is already going, and this we can do by offering the child all kinds of cultural resources which are "lying around" in our civilisation. These he will make use of as he chooses , as he finds them relevant or not, to take his personal culture and employ him there , in the quest for an identity. Many of these artefacts will be the products of man's reason: but many will be symbolic and mythological expressions of "inner reality" including both bodily existence, and the signs of meanings of emotion, of meeting, and relationship, (…)
>
> (Holbrook 1996:23)

So central to this commission to foster a life flame lies a 'poetic humanism' (Abbs 1995: 113) which is first of all "understood negatively" (id.), as distinguished from "all that is prosaic, liberal, mechanical, factual, all that remains untouched and unredeemed by the transformative powers of individual sensibility and transpersonal imagination." (id.). Positively, in *English for the Rejected* Holbrook defined the 'poetic function' as: "the capacity to explore and perceive by the exercise of the whole mind and all kinds of apprehensions, not only intellectual." (Holbrook 1968: 10). It should be noted that this function, like all variations of literary intelligence analysed previously, is epistemic.

This epistemic dimension becomes more clear in *English for Meaning*: "English is a discipline of <u>thought</u>: and it has to do with language as the expression of 'whole' experience, that is: all our existential reality." (Holbrook 1967: 115) As such, English cannot but be concerned with the ultimate questions, the questions of our ultimate concerns. The Leavisian choice of words ('discipline', 'experience') makes it perfectly clear he builds upon those foundations. English, in so far as it deals with literature, is and must also be a moral, even a *religious* discipline as well for it is essentially preoccupied with "the pursuit of meaning through symbolism" (Holbrook 1967: 116)

The pursuit of meaning is itself a creative act. It is impossible to passively imbibe existential meanings from a corpus of texts or by didactic exposition: the pursuit of existential meaning is essentially an exercise in creative self-fashioning.

English as a 'creative subject' involves encouraging "the individual to explore his own authenticity, and to enrich and foster his effective relationship with others and the world" (Holbrook 1967: 117) . Glancing back at virtue theory we are reminded that *phronesis,* the faculty of practical judgement that is the hallmark of the mature mind, cannot be anything but authentic. Virtues, being deep qualities of the individual psyche, must be lived through, experienced and acquired through existential self-fashioning or they are not virtues. Holbrook, too, uses a notion of intelligence much broader than that used by the 'rationalists', the imagination is central to the exercise of this intelligence. And honing one's imagination is to be considered vital for our epistemic development. These ideas, too may be considered in an Aristotelian fashion: Nussbaum states:

> All though, for Aristotle, is of necessity (in finite creatures) accompanied by an imagining that is concrete, even where the thought itself is abstract. This is just a fact of human psychology. But whereas the mathematician can safely disregard the concrete features of his or her imagined triangle when she is proving a theorem about triangles, the person of practical wisdom will not neglect the concrete deliverances of imagination when thinking about virtue and goodness. Instead of ascending from particular to general, deliberative imagination links particulars without dispensing with their particularity.
>
> It would involve, for example, the ability to recall past experience as one with, as relevant to, the case at hand, while still conceiving of both with rich and vivid concreteness. We are now prepared to understand that the Aristotelian will hold this concrete focusing to be not dangerously irrational, but an essential ingredient of responsible rationality, to be cultivated by educators.
>
> (Nussbaum 1990: 77-78)

Without the powers of the imagination we cannot come to an understanding of the particulars of existence, in their richness and fullness. An education worth the name should foster these powers. And this is Holbrook's goal in his educational writings as well. If only to explore those 'subjective' realities that contemporary ideologies such as Freudianism, Nihilism and Marxism are unable to touch. They offer: "too little recognition of the dynamics of consciousness and of symbolism: op metaphor and the subjective truths it explores." (Holbrook 1975: 83)

Not only is the virtue of *phronesis* open to the workings of the imagination, it is also intimately entwined with our selfhood; virtues are part of our selfhood. Virtues are existential traits. If a person is deeply inauthentic, then that is a very strong indicator of that person not having acquired a noticeable measure of practical judgement. This insight takes us further to an understanding of how literary intelligence or the poetical function becomes an educational kernel for what is essentially an *existential* project.

It is through a sustained exposure to literature, both through extensive reading and creative, imaginative writing that we engage in a personal relationship with in "the sharing of meanings in words":

> This sharing of a great artist's disturbing investigation of 'life', and his capacity to hold complexities in unresolved suspension.
>
> (Holbrook 1968: 118)

This sharing of another person's search for life's meanings becomes then, in education, a necessary condition for our own search for a meaningful existence.

It cannot be otherwise: no person can acquire existential meaning for him- or herself in a state of existential isolation. Once again, in Holbrook as in Harding the theme of a literary education as a preservative against solipsism and mere subjectivity is taken up.

§3.2 Existentialism and Virtue Ethics

But what are we to make of Holbrook's own theoretical positions. Described by Roger Poole (Poole 1995: 211) as "England's only native Existentialist philosopher"? It is pertinent to ask oneself whether Holbrook's work can fit in a virtue-ethical model of literary intelligence as the one I proffer. I would argue that Holbrook's existentialism is not incommensurable with virtue ethics – that in fact it shares a common outlook.

First, it should be realised that, as Poole points out, Holbrook's existentialism has little in common with the better-known atheistic existentialism of Sartre. Holbrook in fact entertained a considerable antipathy against Sartrean existentialism, as he reported in his "Reading and Discrimination":

> I was appalled by [*Huis Clos*], because of its hatred of human beings, and its nihilistic picture of the inevitable frustration of inter-human relationship and love. I have loathed Sartre ever since, and I still find it hard to understand his love-denying nihilism became the main focus of avant-garde culture, and of the Left.
>
> (Holbrook 1975: 84)

Holbrook's 'existentialism' is then to be understood in positive distinction against Sartre's 'negative' existentialism. Indeed, a 'positive existentialism' (Poole 1995: 216) and existentialism which draws its water from the wells of a humanist and idealist tradition: "which descends from Kierkegaard through Jaspers, Marcel and Maritain and includes his own favourites Buber and Tillich" (ibid.).

The reference to Maritain will gain particular salience when I will analyze Maritain's *Art et Scolastique* as a primal text treating the artist as a subject of virtue theory.

Central to Holbrook's existentialist tradition is the individual's search for a *telos,* a transcendent goal towards which to order one's life. Holbrook's disgust of un-telistic ('nihilistic') visions of the human condition are relevant in this regard. A life ordered towards some good cannot but be a rich, and interesting life.

Holbrook considers himself an existentialist – and we may follow him in his conception of existentialism for it is not contradictory to a virtue-ethical interpretation of literary education. As I have stated before: a virtue is an existential trait or it is not. It is a deep quality of the self or it is not. It is and must be oriented towards a *telos,* say the goodness of the Good Life, a state of *eudaimonia* transcending the immediately contingent here and now. To be a virtue theorist is then not unlike being an existentialist for the true aim of an existentialist, or virtue-ethical educator is then "not to convert others, but to encourage them to embark on a quest for their own self-realization" (Holbrook 1967: 121) – in other words: to aid others on their way to the Good Life by helping them search for what the Good Life means *for them.* So too Bantock, who in his "The Education of the Less Able Child quotes L.H. Myers' saying that "Every action is personal at its roots" (Bantock 1963). For the Good Life to *be* a Good Life means that it is a Good Life *for me,* and as such it will have to be recognized as such *by me.* Holbrook points out that such an outlook has profound and radical educational implications: he recognizes that it is a basic question whether or not we live in a society which fosters this kind of moral and existential development.

If it does not, we may argue that society has been found wanting. A society that pressures people into accepting inauthentic alternatives to our personal existential development undermines the very possibility of authentic – and thereby moral – living. As such Holbrook's existentialism is an existentialism which allows for deep subjectivity – and at the same time avoids the vagaries of a negative existentialist solipsism.

On the contrary: coming into oneself, fostering one's own being, is a social task, a common task, a project which can only be pursued in a community and in a given culture, through the medium of the arts:

> Holbrook shows us how our culture and the arts can go on nurturing us toward full-hearted living. We can do this for each other on a large scale when we establish a community (…).
>
> (Ulanov & Ulanov 1995)

Indeed, this is not far off from Nussbaum's promotion of the imagination and emotions to being of prime importance in education:

> [Aristotelians] will promote an education that cultivates fancy and feeling through works of literature and history, teaching appropriate occasions for and degrees of response. They will consider it childish and immature *not* to cry or be angry or otherwise to experience and display passion where the situation calls for it. In looking for private models and public leaders, we should desire to be assured of their sensitivity and emotional depth, as well as of their intellectual competence.
>
> (Nussbaum 1990: 82)

So, we have come full circle to Book VII of Aristotle's *Politics*: we need to organize ourselves in a community in order to foster or nurture our own selves to fulfil their potential. The Good Life can be pursued only in a cultural community and through cultural development, through civilisation, and this civilisation has to be rebuilt every generation anew. As Bantock puts it: "The right ordering of the social life depends on the right ordering of the personal life" (Bantock 1963: 203)

The recipients of 'tradition' which includes the very way we transact our bodily existence and exercise our emotions are everybody, every child. It is then no coincidence that Holbrook found the questions concerning the education of the intellectually less able to be of the greatest possible concern. If literary intelligence is a virtue, a universal trait, it should be at least a *relevant* trait to everyone, including those who face intellectual challenges.

§3.3 Holbrook on the education of intellectually less able.

Toute vertu étant ainsi determine à l'ultimum don't la puissance et capable.
(Maritain 1965: 22)

It is striking that Holbrook's definition of the poetic function: "the capacity to explore and perceive by the exercise of the whole mind and all kinds of apprehensions, not only intellectual." (Holbrook 1968: 10) leads to a similar critique of the centrality of (formal) intelligence as is to be found in *Scrutiny*. In his *English for the Rejected* we can glean a criticism of formal intelligence very similar to that crafted by Leavis and Harding. Holbrook like Harding identifies that problems concerning 'less intelligent' pupils may have their foundations not in the students themselves but rather in the structures of society defining and privileging certain forms of intelligence over others.

> Are [lower-stream pupils] 'inferior beings'? This question I hope will be in the reader's mind throughout the book – ***because our society and its system of education at the moment imply inevitably and often mercilessly that children who do badly in intelligence tests are inferior creatures.*** Such mere organisational changes as the comprehensive school do not amend this fundamental wrong. [In this book I will] reveal the capacities for fineness and vivid perception of an average class of such children. They are not capable of certain intellectual uses of the intelligence. But they *have* intelligence, and they are human.
>
> (Holbrook 1968: 7)

Holbrook on the contrary focuses on what 'lower-stream' pupils *can* do and is outspoken in identifying the intelligent traits that these pupils *do* have:

> I think there is no child who is not capable of fine feelings, of sorrow, of sympathy, love and delight. There are some who are coarse, limited, obtuse, maddening – and some in whose company one would not choose to spend more of one's time then one was forced to. But all – except for some very sick or disturbed, subnormal or damaged children, - all 'bottom stream' secondary school children are capable of much more finer things than are usually put before them, or expected of them.
>
> (ibid: 11)

It should be noted that it is exactly the possession of 'fine feelings' is what is at makes one – essentially – 'intelligent' in a Leavisian sense of the word. And the interpretation of Holbrook's notions Leavisian is also borne out by the following passage, explaining that 'finer feelings' are brought about and fostered by the arts – both literary and otherwise:

> True art disturbs our awareness, and the reward is that it fosters our sympathy. Through it we may grow to understand others, and understand both the common elements in human experience, and the uniqueness of each human experience of life. We may, through art, grow more reverent, more full of awe at the mystery of human life, more aware of its reality, including the reality of human nature – and more tolerant and compassionate. We may become more able to be positive and creative in our attitudes to our own living and in our actions and choices – less afraid of the exceptional, the challenging, the mysterious. The arts may bring us through these stages, not only by informing us about these aspects of human life, but by affecting our spirits, by stirring our deepest nature, and changing it, enlarging perceptions and potentialities. Many of our potentialities from childhood to maturity depend upon our souls being nourished from imaginative sources by the creative power of metaphor. Our unconscious phantasy, which art nourishes and helps towards order, is the source and basis of many of our capacities, including our intellectual ones. The nourishment and exercise of the imagination is the root of true literacy in all, from low stream children to the genius.
>
> (ibid: 18)

Holbrook's "true literacy" hence takes the same form as Leavis and Bantock's 'literary intelligence' and should not be approached in theoretical isolation from them, but rather recognized as drawing from the same intellectual well. What is particularly interesting is that Holbrook does take Leavis' and Bantock's notions further – and states that the training of 'true literacy' not only affects the reader – and expands his or her sensitivity and intellectual potential, but also, and this is important, that the teacher may come to a greater understanding of the child through the results of their creative efforts:

> We will not only know 'about' difficult children – we shall enter their very natures, and find, perhaps, how sad, how brave, how beautiful their inward creature can be.
>
> (Ibid: 21)

And:

> I think that there was no child among those I taught, with I.Q.s from 70 (say) to 100, who could not produce an imaginative piece, *understanding what he was doing and what good it did him.*
>
> (Ibid, 31)

Allowing children to express themselves by means of the arts is then also an educational means of countering disruptive societal influences[18], fostering those "human attributes and powers that [society] values too little – the intuitive, the creative, the creatureness – the simply *being* and living, and relishing that. 'Being' brings no 'results', of the kind that our society expects. (ibid: 37)

Holbrook also uses a notion of common culture, but what he means by it is obviously much broader as the fairly limited and exclusive notions as 'the great tradition' (ibid: 192) of 'high' culture. In fact- Bantock too renounces concepts of narrow and limited common culture, stating that "A common culture is a mirage which, if pursued, will not benefit the majority and runs a considerable danger of ruining the minority as well." Indeed, a real common culture will be, according to Bantock plural, open to all:

[18] Which includes, as in Leavis and Denys Thompson, the mass media: "[As] we find in children's writing, only a small part of their outlook is ever wholly subject to television, the cheap novelette, or the popular song and magazine. Human nature continues to strive for a better truth, even when the mass media seek to head off and debase the striving. There would be no point in objecting to the lowest common denominator of the content of mass media if it were not far below the potentialities of each reader." (Holbrook 1968: 157)

> My aim is not to imply an isolated minority remote from the concerns of the folk majority. As a matter of social reality there will be enormous variety of levels of achievement; and a new folk culture will inevitable encompass a substantial number of levels.
>
> (Bantock 1963: 201)

It is very fascinating to consider that Bantock, in his *Education in an Industrial Society* , describes an educational programme for lower-ability pupils in which he seems to be of one mind with Holbrook – in fact going so far as to refer to David Holbrook's educational work as being 'magnificent' (ibid: 222).

He takes Holbrook up in his contention that we should move towards an idea of educational attainment and psychological potential transcending the merely intellectual; an example is for instance this passage in which Bantock advocates dance education for the less able:

> There is [in the less able child a] desire for movement, one branch of which leads to dance with its association with music, the other to mime and drama – role playing, in effect, with its possibilities of empathy. There is the desire to shape and make – partly technical, let it not be forgotten – and partly a matter of initiative, yet trainable delight in shape and contour. In all these matters there is a folk tradition to reawaken.
>
> (Bantock 1963: 216)

Bantock, too agrees with Holbrook that it is more important for children to read than that linguistic niceties such as correct spelling and grammar be inflicted on them (ibid.)

So too, for Bantock, the mental efforts of the 'backward' may well be 'sparks from a different element but that does not mean they are of any less value, in a passage that could have been lifted from one of Holbrook's works he writes:

> Intellectually, these children are inferior (...) but simply to dismiss them in this way – to lump them together (...) as 'the stupid' – is to ignore possibilities of growth, sensitivities and awareness which our 'rational' education leaves untouched. What I want is a schooling that will enable these children to realize their natures as much as in their own way our able children realize theirs through intellectual accomplishment.
>
> (Bantock 1963: 221)

Where Leavis was mostly preoccupied with conceptualizing a notion of literary intelligence of service to small fully-sensitive minority we see Holbrook taking this notion to its logical conclusion: in so far as there is anything intrinsically human to this development of intelligence, everyone is capable of acquiring it to some extent.
It is never a small minority who are 'the most virtuous', as a virtue – as Maritain points out – is a relative maximum development of our inborn powers. A virtue is a success concept – but what constitutes a success is dependent on our natural capacities.
If literary intelligence is a virtue, then a 'dull' child who manages to develop its limited capacities to its relative maximum is more virtuous, or at least certainly more admirable, than an intelligent man who chooses to let his talents go to waste. In their case it is especially the training of the imagination that takes precedence:

> First, that so called 'backward' children are not inferior beings, but are in fact sensitive, perceptive, and full of deep feelings, ambitions and capacities for making contributions to human life and culture. Second, that the best way to make them literate, in the fullest sense, is by imaginative work; that this is well within the capacities of any teacher.
>
> (Holbrook 1968: 44)

Holbrook than strongly emphasizes both the practice of creative writing and the reading of literature. Central to him is the moral dimension of the praxis of literary education. To study a work like Dickens' *Great Expectations* is for Holbrook: "an existential act" (Holbrook 1967: 125), for it is: "concerned with true and false self, and true and false solutions to the problems of life."

If literary intelligence is a virtue, it is a goodness which can only be acquired and used with integrity. It can serve no ill purpose, it must be received in integrity and out of love, for we must choose to pursue it. A virtue is that which cannot be imposed, or drilled but must be received in Newman's words "in love and faith". Holbrook and Abbs (Abbs 1978)[19] chose to describe their position as 'existentialist' – but I believe their position may just as well be described in virtue theoretical terms. Abbs' words are particularly relevant in this regard:

> We need, desperately, a concept of wholeness, of an education committed to the simultaneous development of the emotional, sensory, intellectual and imaginative faculties. (...) We need (...) to develop the whole person, to make him passionately intelligent and intelligently passionate. It is vital that we impregnate scientific studies with aesthetic feeling and with moral concern, that we do not remove them from the philosophical question "How do I know?" and the existential and moral question "How can I be responsible for that which I know"?
>
> (Abbs 1978)

Abbs, like Holbrook, Bantock, and Leavis recognizes that certain kinds of intelligence are moral, are good in themselves. Because certain forms of knowledge and intelligence are good in themselves we may (and are) responsible for what we know and how we come to know it.

---

[19] Abbs, P. (1978). "An existentialist approach to education." Times Educational Supplement. 19 May 1978

But what is it, specifically, in the nature of the literary work of art which makes a literary intelligence a morally good intellectual trait to have? That question shall be treated in the following chapter.

Chapter 4: Literary Intelligence as a form of Practical Wisdom

§4.1 The Unity of Art and Life in Maritain, Macintyre, Leavis, and Murdoch

If we are to approach literary intelligence as an intellectual virtue, the question *why* it is that literary works of art are of such a nature that reading them has this effect raises itself. In order to explain the moral dimension of literary intelligence, of the philosophical dimensions of being able to read qualitative texts with intelligence and sensitivity, we first need to explain what it is in the literary text which renders it an object of moral worth. In this chapter a number of perspectives on the relationship of art and life are considered. It will be argued that Leavis' union of art and life, and his concomitant, vigorous defence of the humanizing power of art, is not an isolated theoretical stance but may be defended by drawing on the work of such diverse thinkers as Jacques Maritain and Iris Murdoch.

Leavis himself, of course, does not separate 'art' from 'life' (Bilan 1979: 116). For him there is no such thing as an 'aesthetic judgement' which can be separated from other value judgements. In fact, he apodictically states:

> Art is a manifestation of life or it is nothing. The creative writer's concern to render life *is* a concern for significance, a preoccupation with expressing his sense of what most matters. The creative drive in his art *is* a drive to clarify and convey his perception of relative importance. The work that commands the reader's most deeply engaged, the critic's most serious attention, asks at a deep level: 'What, at bottom, do men live for?' And in work that strikes us as great art we are aware of a potent normative suggestion: '*These* are the possibilities and inevitablenesses, and in the face of them, *this* is the valid or wise (or the sane) attitude.'
>
> (Leavis 1965: xvii)

And it is no coincidence that Leavis is here found to be writing about Henry James. Nussbaum, in her essay on James, puts the matter in a surprisingly similar manner. To focus on the moral value of the literary work of art is, according to her, not 'an aestheticization of the moral', rather, she recognizes that:

> the creative artist's task is, for James, above all moral, "the expression, the literal squeezing out of value" Second, to call conduct a creation in no way points toward a rootless relativism. For James' idea of creation (like Aristotle's idea of improvisation) is that it is thoroughly committed to the real. "Art deals with what we see ... it plucks its material in the garden of life." The Jamesian artist does not feel free to create anything at all: he imagines himself as straining to get it right, not to miss anything, to be keen rather than obtuse.
>
> (Nussbaum 1990: 163)

Style is about reality, not about ornament, and in its involvement with a living, human, social, and cultural reality it is necessarily moral. It represents something of value in value-laden and valuable ways. A novel never *presents* reality neutrally and unproblematically, rather: Life in a novel is "always *represented* as something.(ibid: 5). In Leavis's terms, life is *manifested* in the literary work of art. But what does this mean?

How does life come to be manifested? An obvious but erroneous explanation would be that the work of art is an outpouring of the artist's selfhood, arguably 'a life', but this is not what Leavis has in mind. For a great work of art to *be* a great work of art there must be at least a *potent normative suggestion.* But is it merely the normative suggestions that make art *great*?

Obviously not, because otherwise each exercise in propaganda would be the highest art: art's normative suggestion needs to be of a certain *kind* as is borne out by Leavis' critique of Johnson's moralism:

> For Johnson then, literature is moral by being didactic – it enforces values that exist prior to the work; but Leavis does not hold a didactic view at all, for he thinks the creative use of language as involved in the exploration and creation of values – not their enforcement. We should recall that his recent harsh criticism of *Lady Chatterley's Lover* is based on the view that it is a didactic novel, one where Lawrence writes with a willed purpose to enforce his moral. In a successful work, Leavis insists, values are not stated but *enacted* by the whole work; the concept of 'enactment' is at the centre of Leavis thinking about morality and the novel. He praises, for instance, *Women in Love* because 'an experimental process of exploring, testing and defining does seem really to be enacted, dramatically, in the "tale"; so little are we affected as by any doctrine formulated in advance, and coming directly from Lawrence' (F.R. Leavis, *D.H. Lawrence, Novelist,* p.387). The morality of the novel is inseparable from its integrity as art."
>
> (Bilan 1979: 124)

The morality of the novel is inseparable from its integrity as a work of art. It enacts itself and is itself the bearer of its normative suggestions. It is for its moral content independent on its enactment of propositional values existing outside the work.
A literary work of art *qua* work of art can never be propaganda and to think otherwise would be to be mistaken about the nature of moral communication. This is not just a position taken by Leavis but also one defended by Martha Nussbaum:

> Moral communication too, (...) is not simply a matter of the uttering and receiving of general propositional judgements. Nor is it any sort of purely intellectual activity. It partakes both of the specificity and of the emotional and imaginative richness of their individual moral effort.
>
> (Nussbaum 1990: 153)

In so far as art is life, it enacts its own values. It explores, tests, defines, makes normative appeals, and opens vistas of experience. In reading a literary work of art we are then of necessity bound up with the experiences of the artist. But this experience too, must be of a certain kind:

> The potentialities of human experience in any age are realized only by a tiny minority, and the important poet is important because he belongs to this (and has also, of course, the power of communication). Indeed, his capacity for experiencing and his power of communicating are indistinguishable; not merely because we should not know of one without the other, but because his power of making words express what he feels is indistinguishable from his awareness of what he feels. He is unusually sensitive, unusually aware, more sincere and more himself than the ordinary man can be. He knows what he feels and knows what he is interested in. He is a poet because his interest in his experience is not separable from his interest in words; because, that is, of his habit of seeking by the evocative use of words to sharpen has awareness of his ways of feeling, so making these communicable."
>
> (Leavis 1982: 19)

The poet then has a range of experience of reality to an uncommon degree. What makes the poet *relevant* is that he has the unique power to *communicate* these experiences. The experience of the poet is not solipsistic but is rather communicated in such a way that we can partake in it. What is communicated by the poet is *not* his selfhood, but rather his experiences which are by their communication rendered 'impersonal' – and are hence open to the world. A remark Leavis makes about George Eliot further illuminates his concept of impersonality:

> 'No life would have been possible for her that was not filled with emotion: her sensibility is directed outward, and she responds from deep within. At this level, emotion is a disinterested response defined by its object, and hardly distinguishable from the play of intelligence and self-knowledge that give it impersonality
>
> (Leavis 1948: 94)

The author's creative activity is fuelled by an emotion that is not self-regarding, is not egotistical, is not obsessed with the selfhood - but is *defined by its object* – it is focused on something outside the self – and is hence impersonal. Moreover an emotion is 'impersonalized' when it is understood by intelligence, or rather: an impersonal response is a response that includes emotion, intelligence, and self-knowledge (Bilan 1979: 173) and is as such accessible through the use of intelligence and self-knowledge.

Impersonal art, by communicating the intensely subtle experiences of the artist, thus offers not an escape from reality, but must necessarily be an involvement in a disinterested *grasp* of reality. What the artist experiences is *real*. But his perception of reality, as it exists in his consciousness, is not open to us save in the form of a (literary) work of art. And just as we use a 'universal', a 'literary' intelligence that cannot be compartmentalized but pervades our entire being to interpret a work of art, the impersonality of the artist in its own way cannot be compartmentalized either:

> Impersonality (...) results from the creativity of the whole being or whole psyche (...). The artist does not create with any special faculty – the imagination or fancy – but from the depths of the whole psyche.
>
> (Bilan 1979: 175)

This at the very least seems to imply there is some level of structural similarity between the artist's creative intelligence and the reader's literary intelligence. Leavis does not go into great detail to discuss the cognitive nature of the artist's creativity as he does to describe his notions of literary intelligence. At the same time there are a number of reasons to assume that literary intelligence and poetic creativity are linked – they are both cognitive processes which have reality as their object and they are both uncompartmentalized – integrating 'the whole psyche' rather than being the activity of a single mental faculty. Before further consideration of the artist's creative power, literary intelligence ought to be interpreted in its own right.

Literary intelligence, as understood by Leavis, can at any rate be interpreted as a form of 'phronesis' or practical wisdom. A few of the qualifications Leavis uses to critically approach literary effort leave some hints how such a relationship between *phronesis* and literary intelligence may be perceived. In particular it is his insistence on 'maturity' in an author which is especially interesting. R.P. Bilan is at pains to explain "[the] moral assumptions [that] are involved with praising maturity in literature and condemning immaturity." (Bilan 1979: 176) but upon close reading, and keeping the notion of *phronesis* as an experiential, affective, contextualized and virtuous knowledge in mind, it is possible to see in Leavis' insistence on maturity a gesture towards *phronesis.* Maturity according to Bilan, "involves understanding" (ibid: 177) and he consequently describes it as involving "control of the emotions by the intelligence, or, at least, a proper balance of emotion and intellect. To be mature [then] is, in effect, to be intelligent." (ibid: 178)

Now it is no coincidence that Aristotle describes moral maturity as a necessary condition of *phronesis.* One can have technical knowledge and be young, one can be a young mathematician, but Aristotle explicitly denies one can be a young *phronimos.* The reason for this is exactly *because* phronesis requires experiential knowledge; children are incapable of realizing this state of experiential wisdom:

> There is also confirmation of what we have said in the fact that although the young develop ability in geometry and mathematics and become wise in such matters, that are not thought to develop prudence. The reason for this is that prudence also involves knowledge of particular facts, which become known from experience; and a young man is not experienced, because experience takes time to acquire.
>
> (Aristotle 1976: 214-215)

Bilan could not explain the moral salience of Leavisian 'maturity', because he did not, perhaps, think of analysing this notion of maturity in terms of an Aristotelian virtue-theory.[20] The 'maturity' of the artist seems to be related to him or her having practical wisdom. And though being in the possession of a literary intelligence does not seem to be enough to be a competent author, the two competences seem to have some affinity.

To create a literary work of art would then be to use one's practical intelligence to discern and communicate given experiences in the form of a literary work of art which itself enacts both experiences and judgements. A reader who engages this literary work of art is then engaging this condensed evaluative experience and partakes of the author's experiences.

By becoming a party to these experiences the reader may come to experience what he could not have outwith the literary work of art. A literary work of art is open to *phronesis* because the work of art itself is an effort to *communicate* experiences.

If it is *practical wisdom* which is involved in producing a work of art, then the capacity to produce a work of art is itself also a virtue. And this view, that the capacity to produce a work of art is a virtue of the intellect closely related to *phronesis* – is proffered also by Jacques Maritain, in his *Art et Scolastique*.

---

[20] This is of course not to impute any failure of scholarship on the part of Professor Bilan whose "The Literary Criticism of F.R. Leavis" (Bilan 1979) remains one of the groundbreaking studies in Leavis scholarship.

§4.2 Art and Life in Maritain's *Art et Scolastique*

Art et Scolastique, though perhaps best understood as an exercise in theological aesthetics, draws heavily on a virtue-ethical tradition which has found new expression in the late twentieth century. As such there are elements to it which are relevant to approaching the work of an artist – literary or otherwise – from the viewpoint of intellectual virtue.

To begin with, it is clear for Maritain, drawing on the work of Cajetan[21] and Aquinas – approaches Art, as the product of the well-formed intelligence of the artist, or *artifex.*

> L'art est avant tout d'ordre intellectual, son action consiste à imprimer une idée dans une matière: c'est donc dans l'intelligence de l'*artifex* qu'il reside, ou, comme on dit, qu'il est subjecté. Il (Art, JJvP) est une certaine qualité de cette intelligence.[22]
>
> (Maritain 1965: 19)

This 'quality' of the intelligence must be of the nature of a *habit* or *habitus* which is the neo-scholastic correlate of the Aristotelian *arête,* that is, an excellence of character or a virtue. The *habitus* is described in much the same terms as one would a virtue:

> Les habitus sont des surélévations intrinsiques de la spontanéité vivante, des développements vitaux qui rendent l'âme meilleure dans un ordre donné.[23]
>
> (ibid: 20)

[21] The reference is to Thomas, Cardinal Cajetan (1469-1534). He ought not to be confused with his contemporary Cajetan of Thiene (1480 – 1547), founder of the Theatine Order.

[22] Art, first of all, is of the intellectual order, its actions consists in imprinting and idea in some matter: it is therefore in the intelligence of the *artifex* that it resides, or, as is said, this intelligence is the subject in which it inheres. It is a certain quality of this intelligence.

[23] Habitus are intrinsic superelevations of living spontaneity, [they are] vital developments which render the soul better in a given order.

They are indeed:

> comme des titres de noblesse métaphysiques, et autant que les dons innés ils font l'inégalité parmi les hommes. L'homme qui possède une habitus a en lui une qualité que rien ne peut payer ni remplacer[24]
>
> ibid: 21)

In other words, a virtue is a trait of an individual's character which is both admirable and desirable. A virtue is both a metaphysical 'title of nobility', indeed rendering one noble, and is yet a deeply personal inalienable 'possession'. This does much to explain the plurality of different forms in which a habitus may be said to be exercised. It may even explain why different, even conflicting readings of the same text may yet be proffered by intelligent readers: it is in our individual acts of judgement that our cognitive individuality expresses itself. Now, what kind of a habitus is art, or the artistic competence of the artist?

Maritain boldly states that: "L'Art est un habitus de l'intellect pratique"(ibid: 22): "Art is a habitus of the practical intellect." This habitus, because it is a habit of the practical intellect, is a virtue. Which, insightfully and poetically described by Maritain is a trait which is:

[24] Habitus are, as it were, like metaphysical titles of nobility, and as much as innate gifts they make for inequality among men. The man who possesses a habitus has within him a quality which nothing can pay for or replace.

> [Une] qualité qui triomphant de l'indétermination originalle de la faculté intellective, aiguisant et trempant à la fois la pointe de son activité, la porte à l'égard d'un objet défini *à un certain maximum de perfection, donc d'efficacité operative.* Toute vertu étant ainsi determine à l'ultimum don't la puissance et capable (...) et tout mal étant un manqué et une infirmité, la vertu ne peut porter qu'au bien: impossible d'user une vertu pur mail fair; elle est essentiellement *habitus operatives boni* (*Summa theol.,* I-II, 55, 3)[25]
>
> (Ibid: 22)

A virtue is *a triumph* over our natural faculties' 'original indetermination' – and is at the same time a certain maximum of perfection tied to the original status of our faculties. My maximum, though as virtuous as any others – because of being *my* certain maximum – may not be equal to yours, or anyone else's.

Now what makes the virtue of Art – as an intellectual virtue of the practical intelligence - distinctive? The difference is one of *telos.* All virtues aim towards some good and cannot be used for evil. The virtue of Art as an intellectual virtue of the practical intelligence is *related* to *phronesis* (ibid: 26) but cannot be said to be entirely co-extensive with it. For prudence essentially differs from art in so far as its goal is concerned :

---

[25] This habitus is a virtue, that is to say, a quality which, triumphing over the original indetermination of the intellectual faculty, at once, sharpening and tempering the point of its activity, draws it, with reference to a definite object, to a certain maximum of perfection and thus of operative efficiency. Every virtue being thus determined to the ultimate of which the power is capable, and every evil being a lack and an infirmity, virtue can only tend to the good: it is impossible to use a virtue to do evil; it is essentially a habitus, operative of good (habitus operatives boni, cf. Aquinas S.Th.I-II q.55, a.3)

> [Phronesis] opère pour le bien de celui qui agit, *ad bonum operantis,* L'Art opère pour le bien de l'œuvre faite, *ad bonum operis*, et tout ce qui le détourne de ce but l'adultère et le diminue lui-même. (…) L'Art ne tend nullement à ce que l'artiste soit bon dans son proper agir d'homme, il tendrait plutôt à ce que l'œvre produite.[26]
>
> (ibid: 27)

Art is a virtue, it an intellectual excellence of the mind of the artist and oriented squarely to some good, for as a virtue, it must have a *telos* or a goal. But the goal's goodness is the goodness of a work, it is not self-directed. It is the work that eventually is good, not the artist. Maritain concludes that though the work is good, the artist may be, when considered formally in himself entirely amoral[27]. This conclusion is however problematic, as Murdoch points out in her *Metaphysics as a Guide to Morals.*

At any rate, art, though related to *phronesis* is not *phronesis* because the *telos* of the two faculties differ. There is an amazing parallel here between Leavis' and Maritain's description of the *telos* of the artist's efforts. They are directed outwards, not inwards.

It is the *impersonality* of the literary artist which divorces the activities of the virtue of art (to use Maritain's phrasing) from the self. In order for an activity to become art, it must become divorced from the self: it must become impersonal to the extent where experiences may become communicable.

---

[26] Prudence works for the good of the one acting, *ad bonum operantis*; Art works for the good of the work made, *ad bonum operis*, and all that turns it from this end perverts it and diminishes it. (…) Art in no way tends to the artist's being good in his own action as a man; it would tend rather to the work produced.

[27] "Il reste néanmoins que le pur artiste abstraitement pris comme tel, *reduplicative ut sic,* est quelque chose d'entièrement amoral." – "The fact remains that the pure artist abstractly taken as such considered formally in itself, is something entirely amoral."

Because, according to Maritain, the beautiful, is a Good rather than a Truth[28], it follows that an aesthetic sense, the intelligence needed to recognize beauty, is closer to *phronesis* than it is to *theoria,* allowing for differences of opinion, taste and indeed wildly varying judgements concerning the aesthetic worth of a given work. This is not to say beauty is *relative* but that our capacities to recognize it may differ. (ibid: 51)

> A great work of art explores and evokes the grounds and sanctions of our most important choices, valuations and decisions – those decisions which are not acts of will, but are so important that they seem to make themselves rather than be made by us.
>
> (Leavis 1965, xix)

---

28 Murdoch, on the contrary, does not make the orthodox Aristotelian distinction between Truth and Goodness. It is rather the transcendent and unitary concept of the Good which is considered by her to make Truth possible.

§4.3 Alasdair Macintyre's model of the relationship between Art and Life

Leavis's contention that Art and Life are intrinsically related finds expression in the work of another philosopher as well. Alasdair Macintyre's *After Virtue* is a seminal text in the development of contemporary virtue ethics and one of the most striking aspects of *After Virtue* is the centrality of the concept of narrative. By considering the narrative form as the basic carrier of moral knowledge and self-realisation, Macintyre contends that:

> [Narrative] is not the work of poets, dramatists and novelists reflecting upon events which had no narrative order before one was imposed by the singer or the writer: narrative form is neither disguise nor decoration.
>
> (Macintyre 1984: 211)

This means that life, for Macintyre is a kind of enacted narrative and can only be *understood* in narrative terms, by means of stories. Its necessary corollary is that for fiction to be successful must be enacted *life*. This is not far off from Leavis's views. Fiction is then understood to be a category of narrative, with certainly not all narrative being fiction: "Stories are lived before they are told – except in the case of fiction" (ibid. p.212). Macintyre's union of narrative and social reality is another reason to assume Harding was essentially right in considering *spectatorship* to be the primary psychological mode in both discerning our social realities and approaching fictional, narrative texts.

The fact that our lives may be understood in narrative form does not imply that individuals thereby become authors of their own stories, but neither are they merely 'actors' (had they been solely actors, conventionalism holds).

On the contrary, Macintyre considers individuals are both author and actor in their own and in other people's stories:

> Only in fantasy do we live what story we please. In life, as both Aristotle and Engels noted, we are always under certain constraints. We enter upon a stage which we did not design and we find ourselves part of an action that was not of our making. Each of us being a main character in his own drama constrains the others. In my drama, perhaps, I am Hamlet or Iago or at least the swineherd who may yet become a prince, but to you I am only A Gentleman, or at best Second Murderer, while you are my Polonius, or my Gravedigger, but your own hero. Each of our dramas exerts constraints on each other's, making the whole different from the parts, but still dramatic.
>
> (ibid: 213 – 214)

And not only life is 'enacted dramatic narrative', but so is history:

> What I have called a history is an enacted dramatic narrative in which the characters are also the authors. The characters of course never start literally *ab initio;* they plunge *in medias res*, the beginnings of their story already made for them by what and who has gone before. But when Julian Grenfell or Edward Thomas went to France in the 1914-18 war they no less enacted a narrative than did Menelaus or Odysseus when *they* went off.
>
> (ibid: 214)

And this insight has important consequences for how we understand ourselves. Macintyre holds that narrative takes a central place in human self-understanding – and as a consequence learning how to read both fictional and existential narratives intelligently is highly pertinent to us both being able to understand our own human condition as well as that of others. Man is 'essentially a story-telling animal' (ibid. 216) and:

> He is not essentially, but becomes through his history, a teller of stories *that aspire to truth*. But the key question for men is not about their own authorship; I can only answer the question 'What am I to do?' if I can answer the prior question 'Of what story or stories do I find myself a part?' We enter human society, that is, with one or more imputed characters – roles into which we have been drafted – and we have to learn what they are in order to be able to understand how others respond to us and how our responses to them are apt to be construed. It is through hearing stories about wicked stepmothers, lost children, good but misguided kings, wolves that suckle twin boys, youngest sons who receive no inheritance but must make their own way in the world and eldest sons who waste their inheritance on riotous living and go into exile to live with the swine, that children can learn or mislearn both what a child is and what a parent is, what the cast of characters may be in drama into which they have been born and what the ways of the world are. (id.)

Therefore:

> The telling of stories has a key part in educating us into the virtues.
>
> (id.)

For Macintyre, the very notion of the unity of the self cannot be founded on mere Lockean 'psychological continuity'. On the contrary the unity of the self is a narrative unity: we are selves only in so far as we are characters, and being a character means being existentially wound up in a narrative:

> I am forever whatever I have been at any time for others – and I may at any time be called upon to answer for it – no matter how changed I may be now. There is no way of *founding* my identity - or lack of it - on the psychological continuity or discontinuity of the self. The self inhabits a character whose unity is given as the unity of character (...)[Personal] identity is just that identity presupposed by the unity of the character which the unity of a narrative requires. Without such unity there would not be subjects of whom stories could be told.
>
> (ibid: 217 - 218)

As a consequence, we cannot approach the narrative arts as a trivial aesthetic parlour game. They have a high moral pertinence. Indeed especially Macintyre's contention that "I can only answer the question 'What am I to do?' if I can answer the prior question 'Of what story or stories do I find myself a part?'" (ibid: 216) is very closely related to Leavis' stricture that "In coming to terms with great literature we discover what at bottom we really believe. What for – what ultimately for? What do men live by?". (Leavis 1972: 56) The question is unanswerable without recourse to the narrative arts, to great works of literature, to iconic stories that resonate our very being.

The question "what ultimately for" is consequently then a moral question, to ask it is not to indulge in vain curiosities but is the question surpassing all others, indeed the question we *need* to answer for ourselves if we are to pursue a good life. To ask it is to be involved in one's own moral growth, to learn about our final goals, our *telos,* is to acquire a virtue of the intellect. The ability to 'read' ourselves as we read great narratives is a mental trait of moral relevance: literary intelligence is a virtue, and it is the virtue of practical wisdom.

§4.4 Literary Intelligence as a form of Practical Wisdom: Martha Nussbaum.

Maritain and Macintyre leave us with tentative suggestions concerning a virtue-theoretical analysis of literary intelligence. However, Maritain's emphasis is on the artist, not the audience and Macintyre though interested in narrative and the narrative structure of social life, does not dwell on the capacity to read well, or the status of the literary work of art. However, of late, other philosophers have linked a notion of literary intelligence with a theory of the virtues. Martha Nussbaum's work on the interrelationship between literature and philosophy; and especially on the importance of literary texts for moral development, will prove to be particularly relevant:

> [Certain] truths about human life can only be fittingly and accurately stated in the language and forms characteristic of the narrative artist
>
> (Nussbaum 1990: 5)

These truths can, according to Nussbaum, only be discerned by someone who has a specific sensibility. Nussbaum explicitly states that this sensibility can be trained and this view also entails a specific *kind* of reading of literary texts, a kind of ethical criticism she associates with F.R. Leavis, Lionel Trilling, and Wayne Booth. (ibid: 22) [29] She also states that ethical criticism is by definition unmoralistic (but not amoral), at least in the sense it "subvert[s] simple moralisms" (id.)

> [T]he best ethical criticism, ancient and modern, has insisted on the complexity and variety revealed to us in literature, appealing to that complexity to cast doubt on reductive theories.
>
> (id.)

[29]Leavis's interest in both criticism and education is arguably not a coincidence; his form of ethical criticism implies an interest in moral formation and vice versa. On page 190 Nussbaum speaks of the "major figures of past theory with whom I implicitly link my proposal – FR. Leavis, say, and Lionel Trilling".

This approach comes very close to Leavis's denunciation of didactic literature, which also explains his distaste for *Lady Chatterley's Lover,* and his deep respect for works such as *The Secret Sharer* which enact individual and existential moral choices in exactly such a fashion as Nussbaum describes. So, if it is possible that a sustained ethical reading of the works of prominent narrative artists increases moral sensitivity and 'offers ethical education and stimulates the ethical imagination' (ibid: 38), it follows that literary education has a special role to play in the moral cultivation of the reading public:

> The Aristotelian conception [of rationality, JJvP] contains a view of learning well suited to support the claims of literature. For teaching and learning, here, do not simply involve the learning of rules and principles. A large part of learning takes place in the experience of the concrete. This experiential learning, in turn, requires the cultivation of perception and responsiveness: the ability to read a situation, singling out what is relevant for thought and action. This active task is not a technique; one learns it by guidance rather than by a formula.
>
> (ibid: 44)

Here, Nussbaum explicitly associates literary with moral perception, and literary experience with the kind of experience needed to acquire *phronesis* , or 'practical wisdom'[30]. The insistence on *guidance,* rather than *teaching* has, as we shall see, interesting implications for reading and literary education. At least she, like Harding, does not dissociate with regards to moral relevance the experience of the concrete in empirical reality, and the experience of the enacted moral qualities expressed by a novel, or other work of literary art.

She goes further, though, than merely associate the two perceptions: like Leavis she claims that both the aesthetic nature of the literary work of art and its preoccupation with form and style, make moral claims:

---

[30] Cf. Aristotle, *Ethica Nicomachea,* Bk. VI, § v

> Literary form is not separable from philosophical content, but is, itself, part of content – an integral part, then, of the search for and the statement of truth.
>
> (Nussbaum 1990: 3)

Style is relevant, not for its own sake, but because of its epistemic consequences; every writing style and genre makes its own cognitive claims:

> My first claim insists that any style makes, itself, a statement: that an abstract theoretical style makes, like any other style, a statement about what is important and what is not, about what faculties are important for knowing and what are not.
>
> (ibid: 7)

The genre of philosophical writing with its distinct style therefore appeals to different modes of knowing than poetry or the novel. This does not mean that the novel is in itself a superior or inferior means of knowing certain truths compared to the philosophical tractate. Rather:

> [The] very choice to write a tragic drama – or, as we can now say, a novel – expresses already certain evaluative commitments. Among these, seem to be commitments to the ethical significance of uncontrolled events, to the epistemological value of emotion, to the variety and non-commensurability of the important things. Literary works (…) are not neutral instruments for the investigation of all conceptions. Built into the very structure of a novel is certain conception of what matters.
>
> (ibid: 26)

What is, then, the epistemic dimension of the novel? Nussbaum claims that the kind of rationality exhibited by the novel as a genre is "a richly qualitative kind of seeing, (ibid: 36) which she calls 'perception' but which for all practical purposes is structurally isomorphic to what Leavis' calls 'sensitivity'.

It is the epistemic element, the element of discernment, in the mental faculty of judgement that is to say, of practical wisdom. Nussbaum makes abundantly clear that this epistemic notion is to be understood in a thoroughly Aristotelian manner:

> "The Aristotelian conception argues that this ability is at the core of what practical wisdom is, and that it is not only a tool toward achieving the correct action or statement, but an ethically valuable activity in its own right. [The commitment to 'perception'] seems to be built into the very form in the novel as a genre."
>
> (ibid: 37)

Because the novel as a genre has this specific epistemic element, which cannot be exemplified as such in, say, technical or philosophical writings, Nussbaum argues that it must follow that: "certain truths about human life can only be fittingly and accurately stated in the language and forms characteristic of the narrative artist." (ibid: 5)

Also, like Leavis, Nussbaum considers the practical goal of ethical inquiry to involve both self-understanding and a degree of communal attunement. For our capacities of judgement to function, to be able to judge, there must be something concrete *for* them to pass judgement on. Consequently for both Nussbaum and Leavis, the faculty of judgement needs a literary tradition in which to operate. In her essay "*The Princess Casamassima* and the Political Imagination" (Nussbaum 1990: 195-219) Nussbaum describes her position in the form of an analysis of Henry James's *Princess Casamassima.* She claims that: "any viable conception of progress must insist upon the continuity of culture, and on a careful, patient conservatism toward the social traditions and the works of art through which human beings express and identify themselves." (ibid: 196) This 'conservatism' is not, however, to be understood as an excluding conservatism but rather as a kind of social ecology, a *caring* for what is culturally valuable and a recognition of its socially and morally empowering qualities:

> (This view) insists that not all human lives are equally complete, equally flourishing even where moral development itself is concerned – and that this is so, in great part, because the central human capabilities have, for their development, material and educational necessary conditions that are not, as things are in most actual societies, available to all. The latter (Aristotelian) view is not a conservative view. If we combine it, as Aristotle does, with the claim that it is the essential task of politics to make people, everyone in the city, capable of living well in the most important human ways it generates a radical demand for social and educational change, with the aim of bringing to all human beings the conditions of *eudaimonia* and practical wisdom.
>
> (ibid: 201)

To recapitulate the argument so far: Virtue ethics leaves room for a conception of literature which is amenable to the development of a moral sensitivity needed for the development of *phronesis,* or practical wisdom; a deeply contextual and situational rationality serving as a necessary precondition for human flourishing. The context and situation in which *phronesis* operates, also consists of a concrete cultural tradition that we find ourselves embedded in.

§4.5 Iris Murdoch, the concept of "attention", and its relevance to a theory of literary intelligence.

Another thinker whose thoughts on the matter are pertinent is Iris Murdoch who also argues that the arts in general, including the literary arts, offer a privileged cognitive path to discern both the world and the realm of moral goodness, which in Murdoch's Platonic fashion is termed "the Good".

Although we can never come to a full comprehension of the Good, it is not completely outwith our reach: it can be *apprehended* but only so with *infinite difficulty*. Art plays an important role in discerning the Good, and as a consequence, everything else. This also makes for a powerful argument for the cognitive dimension of the literary arts.

How do we apprehend the Good? The apprehension of the Good is the apprehension of "the individual and the real" (Murdoch 2001: 41) and we do not always, or even manage to do so. Goodness, when we seek it out, is: "both rare and hard to picture" (ibid: 51).

Discerning the Good is quite difficult but Murdoch offers a possible avenue for achieving the kind of subtle 'attention' we need to identify the Good. We need to expel the self, achieve a level of impersonality in order for the Good to emerge.

Murdoch considers both the literary and the visual arts, and indeed a capacity to appreciate artistic and natural beauty as deeply relevant to this notion of impersonal attention:

> To silence and expel self, to contemplate and delineate nature with a clear eye, is not easy and demands a moral discipline. A great artist is, in respect of his work, a good man, and, in the true sense, a free man. The consumer of art has an analogous task to its producer: to be disciplined enough to see as much reality in the work as the artist has succeeded in putting into it, and not to 'use it as magic'.
>
> (ibid: 63)

Indeed, a failure to see the reality the artist succeeded into putting in the work may well be described in Kierkegaardian terms as being in the aesthetic phase of existence. The aesthete in *Either/Or* practices deliberate *inattention* in order *not* to be confronted with the Good. There is therefore *more* than mere enjoyment going on when we contemplate a superior work of art, something far outstripping either personal wants and desires or that of the artist:

> Of course great artists are 'personalities' and have special styles; even Shakespeare occasionally, though very occasionally, reveals a personal obsession. But the greatest art is 'impersonal' because it shows us the world, our world and not another one, with a clarity that startles and delights us simply because we are not used to looking at the real world at all. (...) Consider what we learn from contemplating the characters of Shakespeare or Tolstoy or the paintings of Velasquez or Titian. What is learnt here is something about the real quality of human nature, when it is envisaged, in the artist's just and compassionate vision, with a clarity that does not belong to the self-centred rush of ordinary life.
>
> (ibid: 63-64)

What 'attention' makes possible in the mind of the 'consumer' of art is that level of impersonality which allows one to approach a work of art - be it literary or visual - as something which somehow defies the grasping self, something which somehow *confronts* us with something quite radically other. Indeed at some level it is difficult to argue that to be confronted by a great work of art is to 'consume' it:

> Great art teaches us how real things can be looked at and loved without being seized and used, without being appropriated into the greedy organism of the self. This exercise of *detachment* is difficult and valuable whether the thing contemplated is a human being or the root of a tree or a vibration of a colour of a sound.
>
> (ibid: 64)

Attention, in Murdoch's reading is then: "unsentimental, detached, unselfish, objective" (id.) – it is also existentially tied to the idea of the Good because the objectivity, and the detachment of self, is necessary to see reality. Realism implies goodness because we cannot be realists, cannot recognize the real as it presents itself beyond the fog of the ego without some relation to the *good*. Or, as Murdoch puts it: "The necessity of the good is then an aspect of the kind of necessity involved in any technique for exhibiting fact". (ibid: 66) Of course, whether that fact be natural or cultural is immaterial, as the exhibition of that fact must always be mediated through human action.

A great artist must therefore be *good* in view of his unique relationship to the real. In so far as a great artist shows forth the realness of the real, the own-ness of the real, he suppresses his self, which he cannot do without being good. The direction of attention is: "contrary to nature, outward, away from the self (...) toward the great surprising variety of the world, and the ability to so direct attention is love" (ibid: 65) This *love* shows itself in being able to see the objects of one's attention "whether they are sad, absurd, repulsive or even evil (...) in a light of justice and mercy" (id.)

It is not difficult to see how Murdoch's observations relate to some of the educational ideas considered earlier: especially in the work of David Holbrook do we find such an attentive *love* in the way he treats and looks compassionately for what is unique and worthy of attention in the narrative products and drawings of often severely challenged and challenging children.

It is *love* for Iris Murdoch which transcends the self and so doing, frees the self from what she refers to as 'fantasy'. Fantasy is "the proliferation of blinding self-centred aims and images". (id.) It is the mental disposition existentially opposite to attention, and therefore opposite to love. Murdoch associates fantasy with the will. It might be possible to consider her notion of fantasy in *The Sovereignty of Good* in terms of daydreaming.

A daydream is by definition indulgent, self-centred, possibly sentimental, if not downright self-pitying. It may well be harmless but is necessarily a-moral. Attention on the contrary is never indulgent, and cannot be. Even so, attention is its own reward: "in the case of art and nature (...) attention is immediately rewarded by the enjoyment of beauty". (id.)

Attention is also essentially linked to freedom, Murdoch separates the notion of freedom from the mere exercise of the will. She defines freedom as "the experience of accurate vision which, when this becomes appropriate, occasions action." (id.)
The importance of this statement is not to be underestimated. Contrary to some views which hold aesthetic enjoyment to be passive and in opposition to the active life, a tepid luxury even, Murdoch holds that freedom is dependent on attention. We cannot be free if we are not attentive to the unicity of the Real, and cannot be free if we are obsessed with self-directed action or interests. Indeed, we cannot even achieve a modicum of self-knowledge if we are self-obsessed:

> "Self is as hard to see justly as other things and when clear vision has been achieved, self is a correspondingly smaller and less interesting object"
>
> (ibid: 66)

Now, what can be said of the Good? Unsurprisingly little, for the Good is transcendent. Murdoch illustrates the relation between goodness and attention by drawing attention to the Platonic metaphor of comparing the Good to the Sun. We cannot look into it, but we can see clearly because of it. This makes: "all just vision, even in the strictest problems of the intellect, *a fortiori* when suffering or wickedness have to be perceived, (...) a moral matter." (ibid: 68) Because we cannot know what is right without such a level of moral insight, the concept of right action is derivative of the concept of goodness.
The concept of 'utility' is consequently considered to be of little use. Indeed the Good entirely "excludes the idea of purpose". The Good is good in itself; it is not good because it works towards something else that is good.
But what points at the Good if it is transcendent? Can we come to knowledge of the Good in any way if we follow this reading? It seems to be possible. But our access to the Good is necessarily limited:

> There is (…) something in the serious attempt to look compassionately at human things which automatically suggests that 'there must be more than this'. If it is not to be corrupted by some sort of quasi-theological finality, must remain a very tiny spark of insight, something with, as it were, a metaphysical position but no metaphysical form. But it seems to me that the spark is real, and that great art is evidence of its reality. Art indeed, so far from being a playful diversion of the human race, is the place of its most fundamental insight, and the centre to which the most uncertain steps of metaphysics must constantly return.
>
> (ibid: 71-72)

This insight, though of an epistemic nature is not, however, *intellectual* in the restricted sense. Like Leavis and Nussbaum mere manipulation of abstract concepts is not considered to equate to intelligence in the broad sense of the world. The kind of insight described here might then well be found among those with no schooling or little intellectual development. A peasant may know this attention, have this kind of attention even, though 'what he knows he might be at a loss to say'. By the very fact that the attention is directed towards a spark of goodness suggesting a *Good* which is itself transcendent, the communicability of that goodness – by definition non-representable and indefinable –is limited.

Without wanting to tie Murdoch to the procrustean bed of virtue ethics, she does assume a 'unity of virtue' – or at least a 'unity of the Good' – the unity of which depends on an epistemic awareness of the reality of things, artworks and people. This kind of awareness is the pivot on which the unity of Good turns, for all practical purposes it plays a structurally similar role. Both 'attention' in Murdoch and 'phronesis' for Zagzebski occupy the same locus in their respective philosophies of mind. Also, it should be noted that *phronesis* and *attention* both point at some Good which cannot be exhaustively defined: it can be illustrated, pointed at, suggested, but never completely acquired.

The Good in Macintyre as in Murdoch, is *implied,* it is sought after and in our search for it we partake in it to some extent: the good life is spent searching for the good life. There is a telos, a goal to the journey, but the journey is never ended.

Human life is characterized by non-finality and can only end as an *Unvollendetes*. Frank Kermode, in his *The Sense of an Ending* (Kermode 2000) states that:

> Men, like poets, 'rush into the middest', *in medias res,* when they are born; they also die *in mediis rebus,* and to make sense of their span they need fictive conchords with origins and ends, such as give meanings to lives and poems
>
> (Kermode 2000: 7)

And so it must be – we are drawn to the good throughout our lives – but the Good remains transcendent, not a kind of Gnostic metanarrative which can somehow be deciphered by the philosophical elect. Yet we may find it suggested in great works of art and great works of literature, and these suggestions both give meanings 'to lives and poems'.

Therefore it is only in concrete human existence, the concrete human cultural products, and the relationships we forge with other people that a shimmering of the Good seeps through ever so subtly. Great art in general, and great literature in particular, is one of the possible ways in which we may come to catch a glimpse of the Good.

This implies that where Nussbaum speaks of the 'richly qualitative kind of seeing' (Nussbaum 1990: 36) Murdoch agrees, and calls this 'seeing' 'attention'. In Murdoch's *Metaphysics as a Guide to Morals* she offers a few more pointers as to what the role of art is in discerning the Good.

For one it is not merely so that art tells us something about a transcendent Good, it also informs us about the dispositions of the artist: "Bad art displays the base aspects of human nature more clearly than anything else, though of course not so harmfully. One might even say the *exemplification* of human frailty in bad art is a clearer warning to us than its *representation* in good art." (Murdoch 2003: 85) The kind of goodness (or lack of it) that art communicates to us is then a *human* goodness, and in discerning art we may come to discern moral goodness:

> Truth is always a proper touchstone in art, and a training in art is a training in how to use the touchstone. This is perhaps the most difficult thing of all, requiring that *courage* which the good artist must possess. Artists indicate or *invent,* in the invention of their work, their own relevant tests of truth. A study of good literature, or of any good art, enlarges and refines our understanding of truth, our methods of verification.
>
> (ibid: 86)

The imagination plays, in Murdoch as in Nussbaum, a pedagogic role in this process of truth-finding. Murdoch would also agree with Maritain that the artist's discipline "includes the *exercise* of virtue: patience, courage, truthfulness, justice." (id.) Like Maritain she recognizes that the good artist, 'may sin as a man, but not as an artist' but would reject the idea that the good artist is something – considered in itself – to be *amoral.* The artist cannot be immoral if what he produces "expands our present consciousness and teaches us to live inside it" (ibid: 88) She is also more persuasive than Maritain in arguing that the perceived 'amorality' of artists may better be understood as an (arguably radical) form of moral specialization. (ibid: 87) And what they specialize in, is first and foremost an epistemic affair. A good artist may then be good *as an artist* but fail as a father and a husband. An artist may not possibly a good artist if he is not good at some level.

The goodness of the artist must however be seen as a goodness mostly preoccupied with the activities of the imagination. There are for Murdoch predominantly of a cognitive nature, but are also necessarily evaluative. The good and the true can never be fully isolated from each other:

> Imagination, if the concept is in question at all, can scarcely be thought of as morally neutral. When we settle down to be 'thoroughly rational' about a situation, we have already, reflectively or unreflectively, imagined it in a certain way. Our deepest imaginings which structure the world in which 'moral judgements' occur are already evaluations. Perception itself is a mode of evaluation. Any account of morality must set up a problem here.
>
> (Murdoch 2003: 317-318)

More concisely, the True and the Good are not two distinct ontological entities, it is rather the Good which – like the simile of the Sun in Plato – makes knowledge possible *at all.*

There cannot properly be, then, epistemic judgements which are not in some sense moral. Nor can there be moral judgements made independently of the imagination, or independently of moral perception. The kind of perception that is a condition for making sound moral judgements is the evaluative perception which also operates at an aesthetic level. There is no substantial difference between Murdoch's imaginative *perception,* Leavis' *sensitivity,* Harding's *spectatorship* and, finally, Aristotelian *phronesis.*

Every act of perception, well-understood, is in itself an act of judgement, and no worth can be ascribed to an evaluative judgement which is not grounded in a proper perception, in a well-trained sensibility. This imagination is necessarily both truth-seeking and creative – it cannot be subsumed under previously thought-out schemes. It is not a matter of rule-following. Creativity then necessarily moves toward "the expression and elucidation (and in art, celebration) of what is true and deep" (ibid: 321)

Art is thus a form of truthful communication about the world:

> 'Truth' is something we recognise in good art when we are led to a juster, clearer, more detailed, more refined understanding. Good art 'explains' truth itself, by *manifesting* deep conceptual connections. Truth is clarification, justice, compassion. This manifestation of internal relations is an image of metaphysics."
>
> (id.)

To teach art then is necessarily to teach both metaphysics and morals (ibid: 322), for having knowledge of (metaphysical) Truth comes close to having knowledge of the (moral) Good. (ibid: 325)

Murdoch's 'artistic' and creative sensibility is a form of intelligence which is also an intellectual virtue, that is to say, it is a form of intelligence which is good in itself. Admittedly, this is an unconventional way to speak of intelligence, as we are more used to treat intelligence, of whatever sort, as a morally neutral trait. This dissertation argues that intelligence should first and foremost be approached as a virtue. The cognitive capacities involved in reading well are in no way and cannot possibly be rightly considered to be morally neutral.

§4.6 In what sense is a book both good and moral?

What is particularly interesting about Leavis's moral perspective on literature is that he nonetheless does not make many explicitly moral qualifications. John Casey has gone into this matter in some detail and his conclusions are quite interesting. Casey quotes Leavis's remarks on Jane Austen in *The Great Tradition* and consequently comments:

> It is important to notice what Leavis does *not* say. He does not say that Jane Austen arrives at the right moral *conclusions* about life... Nor does he suggest that the moral code which emerges in Jane Austen's novels is one which, if we admire her as a writer, we should be prepared to adopt, or at least to approve. Indeed the question arises whether the word 'moral' is being used with anything like the force it traditionally has... The moral significance of her work, then, lies in its dealing seriously, or intensely, or maturely, with experience.
>
> (Casey 1966: 181)

As a description of what Leavis generally does, this seems accurate enough. Casey's point is that Leavis assesses morality in terms of the emotional qualities it displays, and he raises a question about the limitations of this kind of judgement: "But the assessment of the quality of the emotional or mental states is not the whole of morality. We do, after all, also judge a man's actions and we often judge them in terms of their consequences."
(Bilan 1979: 84-185) This is certainly true, but for the purposes of moral evaluation, to think consequences more fundamental than mental states, and virtues are mental states, or more fundamental than motivations, and motivations are emotions, is to miss the point of what moral evaluation is, or should be. It is understandable that Casey would seek a 'moral code' to approve or disapprove of, but to think of morality in these terms is to miss the point. Also it does not recognize that the goodness of the work of the art is the goodness of the entire *work of art.*

The goodness of the work of art is *not* determined by how successful it is in converting us to a set moral code. On the contrary the moral importance does not lie in its propagandic value, rather what is truly of value is the acquisition of the intellectual virtue of *phronesis* and this virtue may be part-acquired through intensive reading because "literary intelligence", as described by Leavis and his circle, is isomorphic to the virtue of *phronesis.* This is turn is so because art in general and literary art in particular isomorphic to life itself.

This insight limits the worth of theories that seek to understand moral behaviour in terms of rule-following. On the contrary, virtue theory points at an idea of the moral which transcends moral rule-following. Indeed *phronesis* the capacity of moral judgement, by its very nature cannot be subsumed under a rule. The good life is underdetermined by any moral code. This follows from the very concept of *phronesis.* If there were an exhaustive moral code which could resolve every possible moral problem, then the application of such a code (say, the smooth operation of a Benthamite moral calculus) would itself be a morally neutral, impersonal technique. It would be a skill. It could not be a virtue: it could never be *phronesis* because to judge well is itself virtuous. There could not exist a trait like phronesis in a situation where we had an exhaustive moral calculus, or an exhaustive moral code. This is not to say moral codes are unimportant – but they only go so far and to conflate morality with conformity with any code, no matter how well-drafted is to inhibit unthought-of of possibilities of moral action.

In the following chapter, the notion of an 'intellectual virtue' and some of the implications of considering intelligence to be morally salient will be analyzed. Murdoch already offers some pointers as to what kind of implications such ideas have for education: becoming better is a "process involving an exercise and refinement of moral vocabulary and sensibility" (Murdoch 2003: 324). The growth of the moral life itself is then dependent on "deep areas of sensibility and creative imagination (…) upon shifts of attachments, upon love and respect for the contingent details of the world." (ibid: 337).

What it means, philosophically, to speak of intelligence as a virtue will be treated at some length in the following chapter. It will be argued that treating intelligence as an essentially moral trait is both philosophically tenable and allows us to come to a proper moral evaluation of the cognitive aspects of discerning moral goodness.

Chapter 5: Towards a Theory of Intellectual Virtue

§5.1 Introduction: Virtue Ethics and Narrative

We may gain knowledge of the human condition by meeting characters who only exist in fictional narratives. As we can only learn what virtues are through experience, the literary experience then takes on an isomorphic role. This is also recognized by the noted American virtue-epistemologist Linda Trinkaus Zagzebski:

> One way of (determining what makes a motivation a good one and what makes a trait a virtue) , is to appeal to experience. Many of us have known persons whose goodness shines forth from the depths of their being, and if we have not met them in person, we may have met them in literature, such as Dorothea Brooke in *Middlemarch*.
>
> (Zagzebski 1996: 83)

For Zagzebski, as for, Denys Harding, Nussbaum, and Alasdair Macintyre, the literary experience is one that is structurally similar to the 'real-life' experience. If it is possible that a sustained, ethical, reading of high-quality works of literary artists increases moral sensitivity and 'offers ethical education and stimulates the ethical imagination' (ibid: 38) it follows that literary education has a special role to play in the moral cultivation of the reading public. Literary education may consequently offer a special pedagogic route towards human flourishing. To recapitulate the argument proffered in the previous chapter: literary intelligence in Leavis's understanding is a universal[31], evaluative and teleological, "perceptive wisdom about ends", and in so far as it is co-extensive with a 'sensibility' preoccupied with the concrete rather than the abstract its evaluative reflection on the concrete is not merely 'aesthetic'.

[31] "[Intelligence is also] an exercise of the sense of value, [and] is controlled by an implicit concern for a total value-judgement." (Leavis 1964: 71)

Leavis explicitly equates the "finer discriminative feeling for life and personality" in a literary text with "our finer moral sense" (Leavis 1948: 159) and states that the exercise of the value judgement is 'total' – it cannot be compartmentalized. This contention, it will be argued, has radical consequences for how we look at literature and its pertinence in the fostering of practical wisdom. It subsumes even what could be perceived as purely literary 'form':

> Is there any great novelist whose preoccupation with 'form' is not a matter of his responsibility towards a rich human interest, or complexity of interest, profoundly realized? – a responsibility involving, of its very nature, imaginative sympathy, moral discrimination and judgement of relative human value?
>
> (Leavis 1948: 41)

Literary intelligence being – at least theoretically- acquirable through education makes it a *disposition,* an acquired character trait and as such we can approach it as a virtue rather than as an inborn faculty. Had it been an inborn faculty, we would not have been praise- or blameworthy for either having or lacking it. The fact that it is an acquired excellence renders one praiseworthy by acquiring it:

> "[It is] obvious that none of the moral virtues is engendered in us by nature, since nothing that is what it is by nature can be made to behave differently by habituation. For instance a stone, which has a natural tendency downwards, cannot be habituated to rise, however often you try to train it by throwing it into the air; nor can you train fire to burn downwards; nor can anything else that has any other natural tendency be trained to depart from it. The moral virtues, then, are engendered in us neither *by* nor *contrary to* nature; we are constituted by nature to receive them, but their full development in us is due to habit."
>
> (Aristotle 1995: 91)

Also, literary intelligence is not a skill. Had it been a skill it would not have had the structural similarities it has to practical wisdom. Also skills are generally defined as traits not essentially connected to anything valuable whereas virtues *are* intrinsically valuable. Being a skilful typist is a good thing to be when I'm motivated to pursue a good end; but not so when I use those skills to pursue a bad end. There is nothing *intrinsically* good or bad about being a skilful typist as all it does is facilitate the actualization of my motivations. The relationship between virtues and skills is therefore a *pragmatic* one: "Skills serve virtues by allowing a person who is virtuously motivated to be effective in action." (Zagzebski 1996: 103). Even though one needs skills in order to be effective in the exercise of our virtues, virtues are ontologically prior to skills. We need to be *motivated* to pursue certain ends before being able to acquire the skills which will allow us to actualize these motivations. An example: if I am to pursue the virtue of honesty as a teacher, I will have to acquire grading skills which will allow me to grade both fairly and efficiently; however *merely* possessing those skills is not enough to grade fairly. I must also have a disposition towards honesty and it is this disposition which is virtuous, and it is because of this disposition towards honesty that I am motivated to acquire and maintain said grading skills.

If literary intelligence were a skill, it would be ontologically secondary to another virtue; however as literary intelligence is itself understood as a universal, evaluative and teleological "perceptive wisdom about ends" it does not seem sensible to approach it as a skill, as skills do not have these features. As it cannot be a natural faculty, it must be of necessity a virtue of the mind. The actualization of literary intelligence does, however, demand the acquisition and application of certain reading skills, and it can only be acquired on the basis of faculties that we already have. Literary training then both encompasses the 'habituation into sensibility' as the acquisition of technical reading skills.

Also, the exercise of literary intelligence must lead to personal judgements, as virtue is not achieved by merely mimicking social conventions. Virtue can only be acquired as a "deep quality of a person, closely identified with her selfhood" (ibid: 104).

Even though virtues must be acquired socially, habituation into received social practices, this does not make it an exercise in passive social reproduction. This is borne out by Macintyre's insistence that we can only understand virtues as excellences which are relative to a given 'practice', particularly to its internal good.
Literary training in the Leavisian sense is –in this reading - a possible way in which one can acquire practical wisdom but it cannot reasonably be held to be the *only* way in which one can acquire practical wisdom and this follows not only from Aristotle.
Leavis emphasizes communal habituation into moral and aesthetic sensibility and it would therefore be disingenuous to argue that he conflated literary intelligence and practical wisdom to the extent that one cannot be a *phronimos* without being literate.
It is possible to be a *phronimos* without having an inkling of 'high culture' or without being able to read literary works with intelligence and ease. The sphere of the literary is one locus where practical wisdom can be exercised. The uniqueness of literature with regards to *phronesis* consists therein that it vastly enlarges our scope of possible experiences. It is therefore a rich field for moral inquiry.
Literary intelligence is then the *proper exercise of practical wisdom in the sphere of literary interpretation.* Literary education is therefore a morally pertinent activity because we can only acquire a virtue by being experientially habituated into it. If we can exercise practical wisdom through being inducted into literary reading practices, we can acquire practical wisdom through literary education. In the same way as one can only become courageous by perpetrating courageous acts it is by engaging in literary interpretation, by immersing oneself in sustained reflection on the human condition as enacted by literary works, that we come upon this unique way of acquiring practical wisdom.

> Practical wisdom is a kind of intelligence which can therefore be trained – among other ways – by reflecting upon the interaction of characters in a literary work, after all: [the study of literature] is, or should be, an intimate study of the complexities, potentialities and essential conditions of human nature.
>
> (Leavis 1943a: 4)

Reading Harding we may also argue that literary experience does not differ essentially from everyday experience, and if everyday experiences are salient for the development of practical wisdom, then there is no reason to assume literary experience isn't.

In this chapter I will further analyze the notion of an intellectual virtue. It may be argued that literary intelligence is a virtue of the mind, but what does this mean? How can we speak of intelligence as being morally good? Can we have a moral duty to be intelligent? And what are the philosophical and educational implications of such a notion?

§5.2 An Introduction to the Theory of Intellectual Virtue

In my analysis of the concept of intellectual virtue, with Virtue Epistemology being the remit of a subsection of contemporary epistemologists and ethicists, I focus mostly on the work of Linda Zagzebski. I focus on her work because it is more distinctly ethical in scope than other virtue-epistemological work, which tends to be more strictly epistemologically oriented and as such more preoccupied with technical debates concerning the justification of knowledge.

This dissertation is preoccupied with researching the ethical claims made for 'literary intelligence', in short: the argument that the intelligent and sensitive reception of quality literature has a beneficial moral effect. This argument has a cognitive and epistemological dimension, therefore this dissertation will restrict itself to the theoretical study of the intellectual foundations of moral behaviour. The interest in 'intellectual foundations' is to be understood in the broadest sense of the word. 'Intelligence' in this sense is not reducible to 'formal' or purely rationalistic and disembodied intelligence: with Nussbaum, Zagzebski and Leavis and Bantock this dissertation defends the proposition that well ordered emotional states are beneficial, if not downright a precondition, of epistemic and ethical success.

Linda Trinkaus Zagzebski, in her seminal *Virtues of the Mind,* (Zagzebski 1996) sketches a theory of virtue which does not recognise distinctions between moral virtues and what she terms 'intellectual virtues'. Stating, in fact, that "Intellectual virtues are, in fact, a form of moral virtue" (Zagzebski 1996: xiv) her aim is to "extend the range of moral concepts to include the normative dimensions of cognitive activity" (ibid, xv). Justifiedness of belief, in her understanding, corresponds to virtue in the same way that moral activity corresponds to moral virtue. Epistemological problems than are argued to have an ethical dimension, indeed may be essentially *ethical* problems. Looking at epistemological questions in terms of intellectual virtue rather than individual belief states is parallel to looking at ethical questions in terms of moral virtues and character developments rather than the analysis of acts.

This approach has a number of advantages, receding from a classical rule-oriented ethics to an approach more amenable to particular circumstances. The most pressing particular circumstance is, of course, the makeup of the individual person perpetrating certain acts. It is not, according to virtue-theorists, possible to approach the dense richness of the moral life from an impersonal perspective, as act-based theories are prone to do. (ibid: 21)

Virtues are not *reducible* to specific acts, or even dispositions; or at least cannot be satisfactorily *reduced* to concrete and observable acts and dispositions. Virtues are more fundamental than acts for the purposes of moral appraisal.

It is also, at least on the surface, similar in to what Leavis and Bantock described as 'literary intelligence'. The likeness seems to be more than that when Zagzebski asserts that fictional portrayals can help us "obtain a better sense of the morality of acts" and "it is also likely that we can obtain a better sense of the goodness or badness of ways of thinking and believing from fictional portrayals as well". (ibid: 22) If there is no essential difference between moral and intellectual virtues, than certain forms of cognition may be endowed with moral worth and stimulated for their moral contents. Literary intelligence as Leavis describes it, seems to be such an intellectual virtue.

Literature seems to be at least connected at *some* level with the fostering of intellectual virtue in general and cognitive integration in particular. Zagzebski herself also argue that knowledge is only possible within a holistic social, cultural and epistemic framework.

Understanding is not only holistic in relation to external reality but it is also the case that 'belief' in – say – an isolated proposition *p* can itself only be understood in terms of cognitive integration. Integration here understood as a balanced cooperation between the different mental faculties, including desires and emotions. Leavis refers to the same characteristic of intelligence when he describes literary intelligence as a mental trait that is both affective and universal and hence, necessarily, integrating the personality.

Zagzebski also makes a strong case for the role of emotions in the wider cognitive process. Readers of Leavis, Harding and Bantock will hardly be surprised by the salience of a well-ordered emotional life for our cognitive functioning. Zagzebski also argues that desires can be argued to be epistemically beneficial, drawing on recognizable examples:

> "A person enthusiastic about the subject of a lecture (or even the lecturer himself) will hear more and learn more than a bored distracted person listening to the same talk"
>
> (Zagzebski 1996: 57)

This suggests that, in the very least, emotional states are epistemically *relevant*.

§5.3 A possible counterargument to the ethical approach to epistemology

If beliefs and belief states are open to *moral* evaluation, than we must bear some kind of responsibility for our beliefs. But how can this be as patently we do not generally consider ourselves free to hold or discard deeply held beliefs.

Our holding true beliefs seems to stem from their truthfulness rather than our voluntary choice to hold them. We cannot simply 'will' ourselves to believe something we do not believe. Epistemic voluntarism seems to be counterintuitive. So too with regards to any form of literary intelligence. At some level it does not sit well that we seem to be morally responsible for our own (lack of) intelligence.

If we are not responsible for our mental states and beliefs, we could not seriously consider the existence of intellectual virtues. A mental trait which does not allow for a degree of voluntariness in holding it, cannot properly be a subject of moral evaluation.

A mental trait which cannot be morally evaluated cannot be a virtue, hence if we have no freedom, and consequently no responsibility to develop certain mental traits, there cannot be intellectual virtues, and by extension it would follow that literary intelligence cannot be good in itself, or even morally good at all. It would just be another a-moral psychological phenomenon.

Quite a few philosophers have held positions implying or affirming epistemic involuntarism. David Hume, for one, holds that belief states are 'straightforwardly involuntary':

> "Belief consists … in something that depends not on the will, but must arise from certain determinate causes and principles, of which we are not masters"
>
> (Hume 1967: 624)

On the other hand, Descartes argued that it is not the intellect that affirms or denies a proposition, but rather the will. This position was later robustly defended by John Henry Newman in his *Grammar of Assent* and finds an even earlier defender in Thomas Aquinas, who himself believed that the epistemic voluntarism was foundational to his theory of intellectual virtue. Epistemic voluntarism may, however, be defended cogently if we dissociate the voluntary from the chosen, and allow for gradations of voluntariness:

First, a virtue, that is: an excellence of character, being good by definition, must be subject to evaluative analysis. This is impossible without there being some element of voluntariness in the cognitive process. An action *φ* cannot be evaluated if one has not, at some level, been at liberty not to *φ*. In so far as 'to believe *x*' is an action *φ*, than we can only evaluate *φ*, and the belief in *x*, if the belief is at some level voluntary. But even though it does not seem we have complete control over our beliefs, it is also the case that, in order to be found responsible for a certain action, we do not generally presuppose *total* control over our circumstances. Our lives are not totally manageable and we are bound both to extrinsic situations as we are to our own personal psychological make-up. Our acts are never *completely* under the control of our will. And yet no one would seriously suggest we are not free, or rather, this does not mean we do not have gradations of freedom, the use of which we are responsible for.

The case is even more pertinent when considering the relationship between the will and the intellect. If the intellect functions in a state of complete independence of the will epistemic responsibility is a contradictory notion. If the intellect were to be utterly subjugated to the will, there could be no rational thought, for every utterance of the intellect would be conditioned by the will.

It seems then that 'the voluntary' must then be separated, as a category, from 'the chosen'. Aristotle identifies, for instance, the mental state of *akrasia,* that is, a lack of self-command. Akratic individuals, people characterised by a weakness of the will, are responsible for the results of their *akrasia* even though the responsibility is not caused by any act of the will. On the contrary: *akrasia* is one notion that renders the category of the voluntary much wider than the category of the chosen. Though we do not choose our beliefs, as such, we may be responsible for holding them.

Given that there are few philosophers who would hold a convincing case for absolute epistemic (or doxastic) voluntarism it would seem that we would have to consider epistemic voluntarism as being 'arranged on a continuum of degrees of voluntariness'.

This is also the position held by Lorraine Code:

> "[The] midposition is illustrated by examples of things people can choose to do: to stop being overweight, to be an informed opponent of Apartheid, to stop being an alcoholic, to be a good driver. The results are reasonably described as voluntary outcomes of voluntarily embarked upon courses of action
>
> (Code 1987: 84)

The use of empirical examples is helpful: in fact, empirical examples of blame or praise for epistemic states or doxastic conclusions may be witnessed all the time, whether one is aware of it or not. Holding or advertising certain beliefs may lead one to be confronted by negative ethical judgement. Holocaust negationism, Young Earth Creationism and, to a lesser extent, holding and advertising a variety of conspiracy theories are examples of doxastic conclusions which are either generally derided, are subjected vehement moral judgement or even criminalized.[32] The persecution of those who communicate their views is controversial, but coherent ethical defences for the persecution of, say, Holocaust negationists, have been offered. As German historian Hans Ulrich Wehler, argued:

---

[32] A case in point would be the sentencing of David Irving, a notorious Holocaust denier, under article 3h of the *Verbotsgesetz (1947)* of the Federal Republic of Austria. Article 3h makes it a criminal offence in the Federal Republic of Austria to 'deny, trivialize, be an apologist for, or offer an attempted legitimization for National Socialist genocide or other National Socialist crimes against humanity' when these 'are published in any way, are public in some way that they are accessible to a plurality of people." He had previously been sentenced by a German court in 1992 for *Volksverhetzung* (incitement to hatred) and had also been sentenced in 1997 by a Mannheim court for 'defaming the dead'.
The *werdegang* of David Irving, once a respected military historian, to a convicted criminal would be an interesting case for any student of intellectual virtue – or intellectual vice.

> Die Leugnung eines so unvorstellbaren Mordes an Millionen - ein Drittel aller Ermordeten waren Kinder unter 14 Jahren - kann man nicht so einfach hinnehmen als etwas, was durch die freie Meinungsäußerung gedeckt ist. Es sollte schon eine Rechtszone geben, in der diese Lüge verfolgt wird. Bei einer Güterabwägung finde ich - so sehr ich für das Recht auf Meinungsfreiheit bin -, kann man die Leugnung des Holocausts nicht mit einem Übermaß an Generösität hinter freier Meinungsäußerung verstecken.
>
> (Der Spiegel, 21.02.2006) [33]

Also, Zagzebski argues, it takes a bad will to entertain certain beliefs – and holding certain beliefs than implies having a bad will: Also, beliefs do not exist in a mental vacuum, but influence our behaviour. If someone's beliefs "are his justification for being dishonest, then he is blameable for holding a belief that, as he believes, justifies him in being dishonest." (Pincoffs 1986: 147)[34]

In the very least, our mental states have consequences for our actions and, since we must want to hold certain beliefs they are to an extent voluntary. They are therefore minimally of a derivative evaluative nature. But can we say that certain mental states are *in themselves* virtuous or vicious?

Zagzebski has argued that some mental states – but not individual beliefs -are virtuous *in themselves.* Being cognitively well-integrated is a virtuous state regardless of any acts one could commit as a result of being morally integrated.

---

[33] "The denial of such an unimaginable murder of millions, and a third of the murdered were children under the age of 14 – cannot simply be taken as something covered by freedom of speech. There ought be a legal sphere in which this lie may be prosecuted. All things being equal I find, no matter how strongly I support freedom of expression – that Holocaust denial cannot be generously covered up with an appeal to freedom of speech."

[34] Pincoffs, E. L. (1986). *Quandaries and Virtues.* Lawrence, University Press of Kansas.

It would be possible to conceptualize a vicious mental state which would be vicious regardless of any ensuing actions – say a state of hatred which would consume us even though we were incapable of acting upon these feelings. That person would be in a state of intellectual vice.[35]

Because acts are derivative of mental states we cannot judge an act without an analysis of the mental state. This is so because, as Zagzebski states, "persons are ontologically more fundamental than acts. (…) It is reasonable, then, that the moral properties of persons are ontologically more fundamental than the moral properties of acts (….)." (Zagzebski 1996: 79) Because one's personality structure is ontologically prior to any personal act we are quite right to focus on the agent, rather than the act. But if the goodness of the act is predicated on the goodness of the actor, why should we consider the actor to ontologically fundamental? Actors too, move towards some Good and this Good may well be (as Murdoch answers) again more fundamental than the actor. Rosalind Hursthouse argues for a variant of the good-based virtue theory. A virtue is, according to her, "character trait a human being needs to flourish or live well". (Hursthouse 1991: 226) In this dissertation it is this eudaimonic perspective on the agent which will be followed.

Living well, living in a state of *Eudaimonia,* is at any rate conditional upon having virtuous traits. One cannot lead a 'flourishing' life without being in possession of those traits. *Eudaimonia* is then conceptually foundational to a virtue, and a virtue is foundational to the rightness of an actions. Acts of goodness never exist in isolation but need morally admirable mental traits to bring them about. If this is so than possible ways in which to bring about admirable mental traits ('virtues') should be stimulated. Literary intelligence is argued to be not so much one admirable trait among many but rather intimately related to the universal capacity of practical wisdom. If this is so, the fostering of literary intelligence is of vast moral importance.

---

[35] That hatred proper (*odium inimicitiæ*) – as distinguished from anger (*ira*) or loathing (*odium abominationis*) – is an intrinsically evil mental state is argued, among others, by Thomas Aquinas and the wider Catholic tradition of moral philosophy.

§5.4 Virtues, goodness, and experience

As noted before, what makes a trait a virtue may de discovered by appealing to experience. Zagzebski explicitly states that this appeal need not be to *factual* experience: knowing persons 'whose goodness shines forth from the depths of their being' is not a knowledge restricted to the strictly empirical realm. We may come to know such persons through literature as well. (Zagzebski 1996: 83) *Middlemarch*'s Dorothea Brooks is a case in point.

Here once more we find a continuum between empirical and literary experience which is morally salient. In Zagzebski as in Harding, there is an isomorphic relationship between literary and real-life experience. Arguing that virtues may be experienced directly, goodness in the human realm recognized as such, has interesting consequences. It suggests that virtues can be described as good in themselves, and not merely in reference to a transcendental Good. What *is* a virtue and in what sense a virtue can be said to be *good?*

If we say that a characteristic *y* is 'good' with regards to a person *a* we may mean to say that *y* makes *a* good, or that *y* is good for *a*. These two uses of the term 'good' are not equivalent. Learning, for instance, can be said to be good *for* a person, but few who have dwelled in academia for any extended period of time can argue that learning makes a person good *per se.* While having – say – a marketable knowledge of chemical processes may be *desirable* it is far from *admirable* if used to supply a totalitarian regime with weapons of mass destruction. What is good *for* us – at least in an economic sense – does not entail it makes us good. Is a virtue *always good* for its possessor? It would seem that it would be good in the sense that it makes a person *admirable.* It makes us good. But is this position not very vulnerable to counterexample? It seems to be the case that it is.

This position is vulnerable to the objection that – say - courage in a Nazi soldier makes that soldier worse *overall.* Zagzebski's answer to such attempts to argue that individual virtues may not make a person good is rather ingenious: she argues that 'the good-making properties of [individual] virtues and vices do not always add up arithmetically to yield a rating of the agent's overall goodness" (ibid: 92).

Virtues are good for its possessor in the sense that virtues are related to good "by invariably making its possessor closer to a high level of admirability" (ibid: 100). It would be true to say that a courageous Nazi is more admirable (or, perhaps, somewhat less odious) than a cowardly Nazi. A case in point would be the character of the teacher Kantorek in Remarque's *Im Westen Nichts Neues.* A pompous militarist, he cajoles and bullies his charges into enlisting in the German Imperial Army after the outbreak of the First World War. Years later Kantorek finds himself enlisted and the painful truth is laid bare: Confronted by his former charges Kantorek proves a worthless soldier and a coward to boot.

Had Kantorek been courageous it might not have been a redeeming feature as such and might have even resulted in worse consequences, but he would have been a less despicable person. At the same time, this answer is at some level problematic. If we are to believe in a coherent unity of the self, we would need to assume that there is some level of *moral* unity to the self as well. If individual virtues are good, regardless of an effect they might have on the *overall* goodness of a person, a radical thesis of *plurality of the virtues* , what vouches for the moral unity of the self? Zagzebski would argue that the sole virtue 'tying together' all other virtues is *phronesis.*

§5.5 How do virtues relate to skills?

In what way does a skill differ from a virtue? They differ in a variety of ways. Skills are seen as *capacities* that people have, to be used whenever the possessor likes. A virtue, if it is truly an acquired and excellent state of character, would be exercised whenever appropriate. To, once again, analyse the virtue of courage: a person *a* cannot said to be courageous if only now and then she were to exercise this virtue. One is either *consistently* courageous or one isn't courageous at all. A skill, on the other hand, may be exercised at will. Skills and virtues are, however, *linked.* Although the virtue is ontologically more fundamental than the skill, virtues cannot operate without skills.

Thoroughness may be a skill, rather than a virtue, and it is not a skill that is difficult to acquire either. However, people who lack a love of truth may not have the patience to be consistently thorough. Thoroughness *itself* is a skill and as such morally neutral and susceptible therefore to uses both for good and ill. Thoroughness in, say, persecuting innocent people is not morally justified, whereas thoroughness in searching for a cancer vaccine is.

Wallace (1978: 46), referring to Aristotle's *Nicomachean Ethics,* argues that another major difference between a skill and a virtue is that a skill can be forgotten in time, whereas a virtue cannot be forgotten without a change of personality. One may lose typing skills over time, or find it more difficult to *concentrate* on a certain task. But one cannot lose the virtue of truthfulness, at least not without a change in character taking place at the same time. Zagzebski consequently argues that a virtue is 'a deep seated quality of a person, closely identified with her selfhood'. (Zagzebski 1996: 104) If this is so, one cannot 'forget' a virtue without undergoing a radical change in one's personhood as well. Moral formation must then always be personal formation.

Perhaps it would be safer to say that virtues cannot be forgotten in the same way as skills can be forgotten and that the forgetting – or acquisition - of skills does not lead to personality changes in the way that the acquisition – or decay – of our virtues changes our personality. That virtues, being excellences of character, have a degree of permanence not shared by skills is also borne out by Aristotle:

> No other human operation has the same permanence as virtuous activities (they are considered to be more persistent even than the several kinds of scientific knowledge); and of these themselves the most highly esteemed are more persistent [than the rest], because it is in them that the truly happy most fully and continuously spend their lives: this seems to be the reason why we do not forget them.
>
> (Aristotle 1995:83)

Not only are virtues desirable to have, and conducive to the realization of a state of *eudaimonia,* but it would be illogical to presuppose a possessor of a virtue would ever voluntarily let go of it as one could voluntarily let go of a skill. The virtues are both admirable in a person and desirable to have because they are a condition of the good life. This would also imply that a possession of a virtue *presupposes* a motivational – and intellectual – component. If we are not motivated to have a virtue, or remain in a virtuous state, it is questionable to state that we *have had* that virtue in the first place.

The essential difference between a skill and a virtue is that the exercise of a skill is not essentially connected to anything valuable, whereas it *is* in the case of a virtue. A virtue, then, is intrinsically valuable. Skills *serve* virtues by allowing a person who is virtuously motivated to be effective in action. Intellectual virtues are ontologically prior to intellectual skills. Skills can be associated with certain virtues, but there is no specific tie between one specific virtue and another specific virtue (von Wright 1963: 139) but a virtuous person is motivated 'to produce external consequences desirable to the point of view of virtue' (Zagzebski 1996: 115). With regards to literary intelligence, the underlying motivation could be one of curiosity, a desire to expand one's range of experiences and emotions. The external consequence desirable to the point of view of literary intelligence would then be the act of reading intelligently. One cannot have literary intelligence and yet permanently refrain from acquiring and maintaining a reading praxis.

If a virtue did not have a motivational component, one would not be motivated to acquire the skills needed for actualization of said virtues. It is illogical to talk about the virtue of Fairness if one is, at the same time, not motivated to acquire 'fairness skills'. Let us postulate two persons, *a* and *b* who are both deemed to have the virtue of Fairness. *A* is motivated to acquire fairness skills whereas *b* isn't. *A* will be generally more successful in achieving fairness than *b* and a necessary consequence, given that *a* and *b* share the same essential capacity for fairness, is that *a* is more virtuous than *b*. Hence skills are necessary related to virtues and by their underlying motivations – even if we cannot connect specific skills to specific virtues.

A motivation to acquire relevant skills is therefore an essential precondition for a virtue. It is in this sense the deontic, so to say, is presupposed by the aretaic. One cannot have a virtue without being – and remaining - motivated towards virtue.

How are these observations relevant for this dissertation ? They have far-reaching consequences: if skills are unlike virtues and my thesis that literary intelligence is *good,* holds, than literary intelligence cannot be a skill, but must be considered and analysed as one would a virtue. We may have to acquire skills to allow us to develop our literary intelligence – but the acquisition of such a set of skills must not be confused with the fostering of the virtue itself. This has radical implications for our thinking about literary education, which then becomes the fostering of a virtue, rather than the instruction in a skill. If we consider literary intelligence a virtue, and hold that it is good for people to acquire it. We must first consider how it is possible *at all* for a person to acquire a virtue.

§5.6 Can Virtues be Acquired through Artificial Experiences?

Assuming one is benevolent and motivated to acquire virtues. How does one acquire a virtue? As a virtue is not a natural capacity it is not simply 'there' to begin with and as it is not a skill it cannot be acquired as one would a skill. Aristotle, in Book II of his *Ethica Nicomachea,* argues that we cannot acquire the virtues, which are excellences of action, without committing the acts that are related to the virtue in question. We can only become virtuous through exercising acts of virtue, courageous through acting with courage, temperate by attempting to – say – keep within a budget – friendly through making friends and investing in our relationships with them.

"[The] virtues we (...) acquire by first exercising them (...) Anything that we have to learn", says Aristotle, "we learn by the actual doing of it" (Aristotle 1995: 91) We therefore need an active experience of doing things in order to become just and virtuous. But what is the nature of the morally salient experience? It could be argued that only 'real-life' experiences are morally salient. Indeed, a strong argument against the isomorphic structure of literary experience and 'real' experience would be that although we may 'experience' events in novels, these experiences are unreal and consequently are deprived of moral salience. If this claim can be shown to be convincing, than the praxis of reading cannot have any specific moral worth. In order to defend the moral importance of a literary education, the moral salience of artificial experiences must be proven. The argument that this is the case will be based on a thought experiment framed by Robert Nozick in his *Anarchy, State and Utopia.* (Nozick 1974)

Among a number of other thought experiments he posits in this book a hypothetical 'transformation machine' which would be able to *transform* us into whatever sort of person we would want to be. Could being plugged in to a 'transformation machine' render us virtuous? Nozick describes the philosophical situation engendered by such a machine as follows:

> Imagine a transformation machine which transforms us into whatever sort of person we'd like to be (compatible with our staying us) (...) Some wouldn't use the transformation machine at all, it seems like cheating. But the one-time use of the transformation machine wouldn't remove all challenges; there would still be obstacles for the new us to overcome, a new plateau from which to strive even higher. And is this plateau any less earned or deserved than that provided by genetic endowment and early childhood environment? But if the transformation machine could be used indefinitely often, so that we could accomplish anything by pushing a button to transform ourselves into someone who could do it easily, there would remain no limits we *need* to strain against or try to ascend. Would there be anything left for us to *do?*
>
> (Nozick 1974: 44)

'The most disturbing thing', Nozick concludes, 'is that they [the machines JJvP] are living our lives for is.' (id.). Zagzebski agrees with Nozick that it is impossible for anyone to acquire a virtue, let alone *phronesis,* in this way. This is so because *phronesis* is itself central to the good life:

> The virtuous person has a superior form of moral knowledge. She is able to know the right thing to do in a way that cannot be predicted in advance. Aristotle claims that moral virtue is logically connected with *phronesis* and phronesis involves an insight into particulars (...). This means that *phronesis* is logically connected with experience (...) so it is logically impossible to obtain virtue without experience
>
> (Zagzebski 1996: 119-120)

It is clear that a 'transformation machine' cannot 'make' us virtuous. Zagzebski rightly says that such a machine could make a person 'less susceptible to fear' (Zagzebski 1996: 120) but it cannot infuse a person with an instant 'moral identity'. Such an identity is forged through experiences, not through the waving of a magic wand, or the whirr of a Nozickian 'transformation machine'.

Experience and virtue are necessarily entwined. Experience cannot be avoided: we cannot be injected with virtue. We might be prescribed certain drugs to help us cope with irrational fears, but we can never be medicated into being courageous. Experiences are unavoidable, but what about artificial experiences?

Nozick also framed a second and related thought experiment involving another hypothetical 'machine': the 'experience machine'. This machine would allow us to 'experience' whatever we desire. He then asks himself whether it would be reasonable for one to be plugged into this machine. Nozick argues that one would not. His argument raises a number is significant philosophical issues. Firstly, he argues that we would not want to spend our lives being plugged into an 'experience machine' because of three distinct reasons:

> First, we want to *do* certain things, and not just have the experience of doing them. (Nozick 2007: 146)

> A second reason for not plugging in is that we want to *be* a certain way, to be a certain sort of person. Someone floating in a tank is an indeterminate blob. There is no answer to the question of what a person is like who has long been in the tank....Plugging into the machine is a kind of suicide. (id.)

> Thirdly, plugging into an experience machine limits us to a man-made reality, to a world no deeper or more important than that which people can construct. There is no *actual* contact with any deeper reality, though the experience of it can be simulated. (id.)

These are powerful arguments against hedonism, but can these arguments be used as a critique of seeking too much 'unworldly' experience? Could they, by extension, be used to undermine arguments for the moral salience of literary experiences?

Essentially, Nozick would argue that it is not the case that we will be happier if we surround ourselves with unreal, but pleasurable, experiences and as such they are an argument against pure hedonism. However, Nozick's argument *cannot be used to argue against the moral salience of artificial experiences* .

It is possible to offer a counterexample to Nozick's though experiment with regards to the moral salience of artificial experiences:

Imagine that a person is unwittingly placed in an experience machine which is calibrated to the extent that it will generate a set of experiences indistinguishable from the ones the person can reasonably be expected to have in his daily life. For all he knows, the person is still living where he lives, working where he does, and maintaining the same relationships with the same people he has known over the past years. These experiences are perfectly simulated and hence ontologically unreal: the experienced phenomena do not correspond with a common reality.

If he were to be released from the machine and once again go about his business – he would be found to have matured in the meantime, as one matures over time. He will have had morally salient experiences as one has in daily life. The mere fact that the *experiences* of doing things do not correspond with a common empirical reality does not therefore detract from their moral salience.

Indeed, it cannot be otherwise: to have experiences means to learn, to be altered as an individual, to mature: often in imperceptibly small steps, but still so. Therefore, the most unrealistic aspect of a children's book such as *The Lion the Witch and the Wardrobe* is then not so much the prevalence of talking animals, but rather that we are led to believe that after the Pevensie children spend more than fifteen years in Narnia after treading through the Wardrobe, but upon returning to their own world find that only seconds have elapsed, and that they are children again.

Now it would not, I suppose, be logically impossible for them to return to a state of *physical* childhood. However, they are also portrayed as returning to the *psychological* state of childhood as well, and yet somehow we are supposed to believe they do not lose their memories of their experiences of the past fifteen years. This is philosophically impossible.

The 'children' after such a breadth and depth of experience, could not have been anything else than adults in children's bodies. Salient moral experiences leave their trace on the personality – they are truly indelible marks on the soul which cannot be undone without severely disrupting the structure of personhood itself.

So too, then, with regard to *literary experiences*. These, as Harding argued, are fictive and objectively unreal but are yet isomorophic to the experiences of witnessing some scene. It is this isomorphism which guarantees the moral salience of literary experiences. It could be argued that in the example of the unwitting enclosure in the experience machine, the person in question is not *aware* of the fact that his experiences are unreal.

How can artificial experiences, which one *knows* to be artificial, have moral salience? It is important to remember that a virtue is ontologically more fundamental than correlate acts and that it is through salient experiences of action that we acquire virtues. Now to limit ourselves to the virtue of *phronesis,* or right judgement, how can it possibly be acquired through the aid of artificial experiences?

A literary experience can facilitate moral development because a virtue does not necessarily need to lead to actions in the 'real world'. Some virtues, like wisdom and integrity, have no correlative world-oriented actions; so too *phronesis* or practical intelligence. The object of the virtue of phronesis does not lie *in* the world but rather in our own mind. It is this orientation on the actor's selfhood that distinguishes the *phronimos* from the artist. To restate the words of Maritain:

> La Prudence opère pour le bien de celui qui agit, *ad bonum operantis,* L'Art opère pour le bien de l'œuvre faite, *ad bonum operis*, et tout ce qui le détourne de ce but l'adultère et le diminue lui-même. (...) L'Art ne tend nullement à ce que l'artiste soit bon dans son propre agir d'homme, il tendrait plutôt à ce que l'œvre produite.[36]
>
> (Maritain 1965: 27)

When we read, we act. We witness what is going on in the scene the author presents to us, we sense approval or disapproval, or even an interest - which is itself a value judgement - in what is going on. Also, hopefully, we come to sensitive and sensible judgements about the presentation of the scene and the characters involved in it.

---

[36] Prudence works for the good of the one acting, *ad bonum operantis*. Art works for the good of the work made, *ad bonum operis*, and all that turns it from this end perverts it and diminishes it. (...) Art in no way tends to the artist's being good in his own action as a man; it would tend rather to the work produced.

These acts of judgement have the reader's individual mind as its object. We judge a certain situation to be so-and-so, but our judgement in itself is not directed outwards but inwards. We do, therefore, *act* when we undergo literary experiences. And it is these acts which will eventually make us more virtuous.

The literary experience, as Denys Harding has pointed out, is isomorphic to the real-life experience of witnessing a certain situation. The *mere* fact that what we witness has no correspondence to a common empirical reality is irrelevant to whether or not it has moral salience. The responsive act (the judgement), which follows the literary experience, is directed inwardly towards the self.

We do not have the illusion of having 'real-life' experiences when we read, we do not have the experience of acting as we might have when plugged into an 'experience machine'. We cannot, therefore, say, become brave by reading *His Dark Materials* and witnessing the very real bravery of the trilogy's protagonist Lyra Belacqua. We can however come to an appropriate understanding of what bravery is, and why we should admire it throughout the trilogy. In doing so we become more capable of recognizing the virtues where they may be found: and this is the hallmark of the virtue of *phronesis*. We cannot become brave by reading about bravery or cowardice; we cannot become patient by reading about rashness or sloth. This is so because the acts related to the virtues of courage and patience are, unlike the judgements related to the virtue of *phronesis,* directed outwardly into the world.

We can, however, come to a justified judgement concerning these character traits. We can come to admire what ought to be admired and may be brought to experience rightful indignation against manifest injustice. All of these are virtuous traits; all of these are actualizations of the virtue of *phronesis*. Through extensive reading of quality literature I can train myself in passing justified judgements on real or imagined situations and hence train myself in the virtue of *phronesis* for it is only through attempting to exercise a virtue that may I come to acquire it.

So is a literary education a School for Virtue? Yes and no. Literary experiences aid us in our acquisition of the virtue of *phronesis* but, at the same time, as Aquinas has argued, we cannot acquire *phronesis* in isolation from the other virtues. Because these, in turn, *cannot* be acquired through a literary education we can say that though a literary education has pride of place in a moral education, it can only go so far.

It is philosophically impossible that a literary education may offer a complete moral training in lieu of activities undertaken in our common world of human action.

There is therefore an element of merit in the charge that the unworldliness of a fanatical reader may somehow inhibit his or her moral development. A literary education is an important element of, but never a complete, programme of moral training.

A literary education should be, first and foremost based on the fostering of a motivation to read extensively. If literary intelligence is a virtue, it must have a motivational content. Literary intelligence is consequently something that can be acquired without the assent of the person aiming to inquire it. The role of motivation for the acquisition and maintenance of the virtues will be elaborated on in the next paragraph.

§5.7 Motivation is an emotion

According to Zagzebski, we cannot be in the possession of virtues without having a well-ordered emotional life. This is so because "a motive is an action-initiating and directing emotion" (Zagzebski 1996: 134) Obviously, we cannot *intend* to commit any act φ without, at some level having a motivation to φ.

If virtuous acts are intentional, they necessarily have a motivational component. Now motives, according to Zagzebski's theory of virtues, have an emotional content. It is impossible therefore to act well without being capable of affect, and we cannot draft a theory of intellectual virtue without an idea of an 'intelligence of the emotions'.

Zagzebski states that having a well-ordered emotional life is central to being able to be properly motivated which in turn is central to becoming virtuous:

> A "motive" in the sense relevant to an inquiry into virtue is an **emotion or feeling that initiates and directs action towards an end.** Motives are connected with virtues in that virtuous persons tend to have certain emotion that then lead them to want to change the world or themselves in certain ways. Virtuous persons have motives associated with the particular virtue. A [virtuous] person is motivated out of emotions characteristic of the virtue (...). An open minded person is motivated out of delight in discovering new truths, a delight that is strong enough to outweigh the attachment to old beliefs and to lead to the investigation of previously neglected possibilities. In doing so, she is drawn by the desire to form more true beliefs or, at least, to get closer to the truth than she was previously.
>
> (ibid: 131, emphasis in original text)

What is the state of this emotion or feeling? Zagzebski argues that there are emotions characteristic to each virtue, such as feeling delight in discovering new truths. Such a delight, tied to the intent or the desire to form more true beliefs is essential as the motivational component of the virtue of open-mindedness.

Emotions are consequently fundamental to us becoming competent knowers and a well-ordered emotional life is therefore a necessary condition of our cognitive life.
We cannot be considered 'motivated' to pursue an action without emotions, but not every emotion is equally relevant or appropriate given our aretaic state. Zagzebski makes it clear that the *kind* of emotions she is talking about is 'persistent low-level emotion' (Ibid: 132). These emotions are not of a particularly intense nature and we may not even be very conscious of them. Examples of such low-level emotions are:

> Pride in one's work, delight in one's family, aesthetic enjoyment, or the dull sense of anxiety that drives people daily to get done what has to be done are among the more important motives because they drive most of our behavior.
>
> (id.)

Motivations, then, are defined by Zagzebski as 'a persistent tendency to be moved by a motive of a certain kind'. (id.) Motives are attached to particular virtues. Virtues themselves are defined by Zagzebski as: 'a deep and enduring acquired excellence of a person, involving a characteristic motivation to produce a certain desired end and reliable success in bringing about that end.' (ibid: 137). A motivation is then also a persistent tendency to be moved by a motive of a certain kind. The motivation being the efficient cause of an action, the motive may be seen as the final cause of the motivation and, by extension, the final cause of the act.
Having a virtue, being virtuous, does not in itself guarantee that one will be successful in the pursuit of virtuous acts: being compassionate does not guarantee one will *always be* compassionate when one ought to be. However, as Zagzebski argues, a virtue *does* 'reliably lead the agent to do as much as in her power to be successful'. (ibid: 133) This is an important insight, for if we are to presume that there are such things as 'intellectual virtues' these may be postulated even in a situation where the agent is factually wrong, or mistaken about a state of affairs. Intellectual virtue is not incompatible with 'any false beliefs' (ibid: 134) about a situation, but: "a virtuous person [in general, JJvP] cannot be systematically wrong in her judgments about the about the world as they apply to her feelings and choices.".

At the same time, a virtue is a *success* concept: even though having the virtue of honesty does not necessarily entail that we are *always* honest, it *does* seem to imply that the possession of this virtue must result in more honesty.

This may be illustrated as follows: Let us postulate two agents, *A* and *B,* of whom *A* possesses the virtue of honesty to a greater extent than *B.* It is possible that there will be specific contexts in which *B* speaks fewer untruths than *A,* say in a situation where *A* is sorely tried whereas *B*'s comfort or principles are not challenged in any way.

Nonetheless if *A* and *B* live in identical – or even roughly comparable – moral and social contexts it follows from *A*'s greater possession of the virtue of honesty that *A* will speak fewer – or less serious - untruths than *B.* If a virtue is a success concept we cannot claim to possess a virtue *X* without, all things being equal, such a possession resulting in an increase of actions associated with virtue *X.*

Analyzing motivation as an emotion is helpful and relevant as it points out to the moral fact that we cannot act well unless we have the right feelings towards the right things, people, and acts. Emotions are not only pertinent in discerning the right response to the right motivation; but we cannot even conceptualize moral action without them.

Also, it should be borne in mind that this entails that we cannot act virtuously if we do not feel for the things we are aiming for. Emotionally and morally there is no comparison between act ψ done out of a *motivation* to ψ and the same act ψ perpetrated because of an expectation of a pay-off. The act may still be *good,* to an extent. But it certainly is not virtuous.

In the context of a literary education this means that literary intelligence as such can only be fostered if the student in question develops positive feelings towards the activity. Every schooling into a virtue must have an emotional dimension – to bypass this dimension by, say, making an appeal to extrinsic 'pay-offs' to bribe students into exhibiting desired behaviour cannot be expected to bring about changes in the personality structure of the student. After all, the student won't have been taught to value some processes and traits for their own sake. This insight will be found to be important when thinking about ways in which to promote reading and hence foster literary intelligence.

A well–ordered emotional life is then found to be a necessary condition for the acquisition of both intellectual and moral virtues. Though both undoubtedly virtues it may be asked how moral and intellectual virtues relate. It will be argued in the next paragraph that we cannot have moral virtues if we are not in the possession of the requisite intellectual virtues. In so far as a literary education trains the literary intelligence and this intelligence is in turn an intellectual virtue structurally similar to the virtue of *phronesis* or practical judgement, then a literary education may be said to foster the moral virtues.

§5.8 The relationship between moral and intellectual virtues.

There are strong arguments why intellectual traits such as patience and open-mindedness can be described as virtues and not as skills. The first argument is that from the distinct position of the virtue of judgement, *phronesis.*

Phronesis seems to be an architectonic intellectual virtue underlying all others; one *cannot* logically find oneself in a situation where one is inhibited from exercising *phronesis* and yet be capable of exercising the other virtues. Zagzebski, then, considers the virtue of *phronesis* to be the architectonic virtue *per se,* connecting the intellectual and moral virtues. In positing the centrality of the virtue of prudence, she assumes that this specific virtue is the one uniting moral and intellectual virtues.

In doing so, she follows the example of Thomas Aquinas who, in his *Summa Theologica* (Pt. I-II Q.58 arts. 4 & 5), argues that intellectual and moral virtues cannot exist without each other. No moral virtues can exist without the (intellectual) virtue of prudence (Pt. I-II Q.58, art 4):

> Moral virtue cannot be without prudence, because it is a habit of choosing, i.e. making us choose well

And prudence, in turn, cannot, in turn, exist without the moral virtues (Pt. I-II Q.58 , art. 5):

> [Prudence] cannot be without moral virtue; the reason for this is that prudence is the right reason about things to be done (and this not merely in general, but also in particular); about which things actions are. (…) [When] reason argues about particular cases it needs not only universal but also particular principles. (…) [In] order that he be rightly disposed with regard to the particular principles of action viz. the ends, he needs to be perfected by certain [particular] habits (…). This is done by moral virtue: for the virtuous man judges aright of the end of virtue (…). Consequently, the right reason about things to be done, viz. prudence, requires man to have moral virtue.

Putting it simply: we cannot be courageous if we have not learned to recognize courage; and vice versa cannot come to a full understanding of how and when to be courageous if we are not disposed towards acting courageously. Knowledge of self and honesty to ourselves must be had in order for one to be virtuous.

Another powerful argument why intellectual traits can be considered virtues is that some intellectual traits are, like virtues, incapable of being *taught and learned.* Zagzebski writes about this distinction:

> What can be taught are skills (…). What cannot be taught, or, at least, cannot be taught so easily, are intellectual virtues such as open-mindedness, the ability to think up an explanation for a complex set of data or the ability to recognize reliable authority. These qualities are no more teachable than generosity or courage.
>
> (Zagzebski 1996: 150)

So if moral and intellectual qualities can both be described as virtues, how are *intellectual* virtues acquired? Can we speak of a literary education at all if we cannot teach or learn the intellectual virtue of literary intelligence? It would seem that intellectual virtues are acquired in much the same way as moral virtues are: by exposure to and imitation of those who already possess them being the starting point. Zagzebski states that the stages of learning the intellectual virtues are the same as the stages of learning the moral virtues in Aristotle. These, she writes,:

> begin with the imitation of virtuous persons, require practice which develops certain habits of feeling and acting, and usually include an in-between stage of intellectual self-control (overcoming intellectual *akrasia*) parallel to the stage of moral self control in the acquisition of the moral virtue. In both cases the imitation is of a person who has *phronesis.*
>
> (ibid: 150)

If *phronesis,* or 'prudence', is the architectonic virtue underlying all others we also have a strong case for the, albeit derivative, unity of virtues. The virtuous person is then, necessarily, the person who has *phronesis. Phronesis* is an intellectual virtue with moral effects, hence the fostering of intellectual virtue (as a virtue it cannot be *taught*) is of prime importance.

The principle of the unity of the virtues has long standing credentials and in fact it is quite questionable if we can isolate the virtues *as virtues* and still be able to speak in terms of well-formed characters. It is difficult to ascribe admirability to a person who is *only* honest and does not possess any other distinct virtues, or someone who is *only* courageous, excluding the other virtues. Well-formed characters, characters that are *admirable* are characters that are – if not uniformly or universally – at least broadly developed.

§5.9 The Two Components of Intellectual Virtue

The two components of intellectual virtue are defined by Zagzebski to be a *motivation for knowledge* and *reliable success*. Now the second condition is unremarkably in the sense that a virtue has already been identified as a success concept. An intellectual trait cannot be a bona fide virtue if it lacks the component of reliable success. It is, hence, unsurprising we find reliable success among the two components of intellectual virtue. But what are the 'reliable successes' of an intellectual virtue? And how can we understand the 'reliable success' of literary intelligence if we approach it as an intellectual virtue? How can we understand these components in their relationship to literary intelligence?

Firstly: for a virtue to be distinctly an *intellectual* virtue there must be an *intellectual* motivation, that is to say there must be a motivation for knowledge. The motivation for knowledge is the foundational motivational element of all intellectual virtues (Zagzebski 1996: 166) and it is 'the only theoretically relevant difference between intellectual virtues and the other moral virtues'. (id.) The motivation for knowledge is central, primary, and hence *foundational* to a virtue. The success component, though real, is ontologically derived from the motivation. It is the motivation for knowledge that leads to the development of reliable, truth-conducive, cognitive procedures. Considering that skills are more applied than virtues or qualities we can come to a basic distinction between the two: learning how to operate a statistical package is a useful skill to have, but isn't of much use outside relatively restricted scopes such as quantitative research in the social or economical sciences.

In contrast, cognitive qualities such as acquiring a fine sense for detail or recognizing reliable authorities are much more akin to a virtue and could even be defined as virtuous intellectual qualities to have.

So too with regards to reading literature: having a broad knowledge of literary history is a helpful 'skill' to have in reading literature, but it is not in itself valuable. On the contrary, the capacity to intelligently read a text, recording the complex psychological structures and interactions of characters however isn't. For what is demanded *there* is more a matter of insight, sympathy and curiosity than a matter of technical training.

This reading capacity should consequently be approached as a virtue. This means that it, too, has a motivational component. But what is the motivational component of literary intelligence?

To begin with, the above suggests that the motivation for knowledge should not be misunderstood as a motivation for propositional knowledge exclusively (ibid: 179) and the aim of many practices for which we need intellectual virtues is something other than the pursuit of propositional truth.

Phronesis seems to demand a kind of insight into the human condition which, although non-propositional, should not be denied the status of knowledge, or the final motivation of an exercise of intellectual virtue may even be something else than knowledge. Zagzebski argues that:

> 'many intellectual virtues (…) not only arise from and serve the motivation to know the truth, but are also crucial in such activities as the arts, crafts, and games. The ultimate aim of these activities is not knowledge, but something practical: creating an artistically superior sonnet, making a fine violin, winning a chess game."
>
> (ibid: 179)

We might add that the aim of reading a novel may well be a motivation for knowledge, but also the enjoyment that reading brings about for its own sake is a delectable intellectual pleasure – which may also result in a greater understanding of the human condition. Motivation is a much broader concept intention. We may intend to read for pleasure – and yet share in the motivation for knowledge about the human condition which reading brings.

One does not generally read fictional books for explicit cognitive purposes: we read them for pleasure, but the pleasure in turn is brought out – apart from the pleasure conferred by reliving pleasant memories by revisiting of old literary haunts, we also find pleasure in discovering new aspects of the narrative that remained undiscovered before.

For instance, in rereading *The Lord of the Rings,* we are of course already aware that the Quest will be successful and Sauron defeated. However, in rereading I may discover that the doomed Denethor, Steward of Gondor, is not so much evil – as a superficial reading would suggest - but rather a desperate and tragic character. By reappraising one's previous literary judgements one allows for a growth of sensitivity in discerning the moral complexities of the human condition in general.

The question as to what kind of knowledge is acquired by reading works of literature will be treated in the next paragraph.

§5.10 Truth Conduciveness and the Motive to Know

The motive to know has already been identified by Aristotle in his *Metaphysics* as one of the distinctive traits of humanity as a whole. The motive to know is not circumscribed to any one distinct group, sex, ethnicity or social stratum. This makes intellectual virtue in principle attainable by everyone, as everyone naturally desires knowledge to some extent. But if the motivation for knowledge is universal, how does this motive translate itself to the reliable success in attaining knowledge? How does, in other words, the motivation to know translate itself into traits which are *truth-conducive*?[37]

Now the truth-conduciveness, or reliability, of a certain trait may not be known *a priori*. In fact we cannot know *in advance* whether or not a certain trait is reliable. If it were, it would not be virtuous, but rather a skill or a technical method.

As Zagzebski puts it:

> I suggest we may legitimately call a trait or procedure truth-conducive if it is a necessary condition for advancing knowledge in some area even though it generates very few true beliefs and even if a high percentage if the beliefs formed as the result of this trait or procedure are false. (...) As long as these traits are self-correcting, they will eventually advance human knowledge, but many false beliefs have to be discarded along the way.
>
> (Zagzebski 1996: 184)

An essential component of a truth-conducive trait or procedure is then its being able to self-correct itself this itself presupposes other things as well.

First, a truth-conducive trait or procedure can only exist in a temporal continuum; it must have a past, a present and a future. Second, because by definition a truth-conducive trait or procedure must be self-correcting, any truth-conducive trait or procedure must be of a provisional nature.

---

[37] Zagzebski adopts a traditional 'correspondence' theory of truth, which assumes the existence of an empirical objective reality which is intelligible to the extent that the intellectually virtuous subject may, eventually, come to achieve reliable knowledge about it.

Therefore, no truth-conducive trait or procedure can be identified with knowledge itself. *An intellectual virtue is itself not knowledge.*
Literary intelligence is consequently not knowledge as such, but the *fruits* of literary intelligence are. Knowledge is therefore underdetermined by the truth-conducive traits or procedures supplying that knowledge. If a truth-conducive trait or procedure is by definition self-correcting it is easy to see why open-mindedness is an important cognitive trait:

> [Even] in those cases in which [a] closed-minded person is lucky enough to have the truth, his closed-mindedness generally prevents him from having knowledge, even if he has true beliefs.
>
> (ibid: 188)

This would also lead us to assume that the *good* of knowing is not reducible to the good of having true beliefs: therefore having knowledge is also not reducible to having true beliefs and the motivation for knowledge differs from the motivation for having true beliefs.
Indeed, Zagzebski states that the motivation for knowledge differs from the motivation for having true beliefs in the sense that the motivation for knowledge also includes a 'motivation to possess the components of knowledge' (ibid: 188) which are understood to be the *justification* of the person's knowledge, i.e. the going through the process that justifies one's belief. It is this process of justification that gives 'a high quality grasp of the truth'.
In other words, we may chance upon true propositions but having a *justified* true belief in x is a higher quality grasp of x than merely having a true belief about it. Open-mindedness is hence essential to having justified true beliefs and hence to having high quality grasps of truth.
Zagzebski further analyses the epistemic consequences of varieties of closed-mindedness and comes to an interesting conclusion with regards to dogmatism, a trait not unlike closed-mindedness:

> [Even] if the dogmatic individual loves truth, he does not love knowledge because his dogmatism does not permit him to penetrate the grounds for justifying or warranting his beliefs, and his love does not embrace the value of understanding.
>
> (ibid: 193)

Considering that dogmatism generally inhibits the process of warranting beliefs – even if it may, by chance, be truth-conducive in a limited epistemic area – dogmatism is not generally truth-conducive, is hence generally inhibitive of the success component of an intellectual virtue and hence is not an intellectually virtuous trait.

If knowledge is that which results from the contact of the virtuous mind with our common empirical reality than we should realize that literary artefacts are part of that reality and also that in so far we can only come to understand a number of aspects of the human condition in narrative terms – a capacity for literature is truth conducive. As Dylan Thomas famously said:

> A good poem is a contribution to reality. The world is never the same again once a good poem has been added to it. A good poem helps to change the shape and significance of the universe, helps to extend everyone's knowledge of himself and the world around him.
>
> (Dylan Thomas 1992: 61)

As humans we inhabit a world of human culture, and it is this human world that we cognize. To have literary intelligence is to have the capacity to come to an understanding of this world. The cognitive object of literary intelligence is to the world of literary artefacts which in turn contain great insight in the human condition. Literary intelligence is therefore a truth conducive trait.

But intellectual virtues are not virtues solely for the sake of their truth-conduciveness. The goodness of the virtue is that they are necessary components of the good life.

Knowledge is necessary for the acquisition of such a life: not only knowledge of our material world, but indeed knowledge of our cultural world as well, of our history, and of the great perspectives on humanity as sketched by the greatest authors of our age.

How virtues are to be understood as being conducive to a state of happiness will be treated in the next paragraph.

§5.11 Intellectual Virtue and the Flourishing Life

'Each of the virtues', says Zagzebski: 'is a constituent of the flourishing life.' (Zagzebski 1996: 197) The relations of individual virtues to a flourishing life is a matter for debate, with some having argued that a flourishing life is dependent on being virtuous, rather than that 'the possession of virtues is an intrinsic part of [leading a flourishing life]' (ibid: 98)

This is not to say that virtues are good *because* they are constituents of a flourishing life: teleology does not necessarily entail consequentialism. The Good Life and the life in which we can exercise the virtues are not ontologically distinct.

This, in fact, is Aristotle's position. The Good Life is the life in which we can flourish – and to flourish is to have actualized our potential to a degree of excellence – in other words: to be virtuous. The Greeks in general and Aristotle in particular consequently refused to make fundamental distinctions between goodness and happiness. Indeed the virtues being by definition so entwined in the very essence of one's personality, indeed being the foundation-stones of a well-formed character, it does not seem necessary to restrict the virtues to being little more than the 'causes' of the good life. The good life is lived in and through the virtues.

Now Zagzebski's theory of intellectual virtue places the locus of moral evaluation in the motivational component of the virtue. Whereas the success-component is necessary to every virtue it is the *motivational* component which forms the virtue's evaluative core. The success-component is universal for all virtues. Not, perhaps, in equal measure, but certainly in *kind.* This follows from the fact that all virtues aim towards bringing about some good.

The motivational component of a virtue is, however, individual to each virtue: The good of the motivation for knowledge is therefore an individual, intrinsic and separate good which is not derivative of any other good. The good of the motivation for knowledge must then be, if intellectual virtues be true virtues, non-derivative, even from the good of knowledge itself (ibid: 203). This follows from the fact that if the good of the motivation for knowledge would be derivative from, or identical to, the good of knowledge; consequentialism ensues.

If the good of the motivation is the same as the good of the ensuing result there is no way in which we can approach an individual virtue as being good in its own right. Now, intellectual virtues are linked to the acquisition of knowledge. In order to analyse the good of an intellectual virtue and its role in the flourishing life, we have to analyse the evaluative aspects of knowledge and the motivation for knowledge.
Zagzebski points out that the 'desire for knowledge is a widespread and important motive of human persons' (ibid: 206). She does not go as far as Aristotle who starts the *Metaphysics* with the statement that the desire for knowledge is universal, but she does assert that the desire for knowledge is not 'restricted to certain culture, nor to certain era of history, nor is it restricted to certain social classes.' She does, even if she doesn't entirely assert universality, make a strong case for the desire for knowledge being *nearly* universal:

> And in fact, the extent to which [the desire for knowledge] is *not* precisely universal only serves to demonstrate its value because if it were possessed by everyone and to an equal degree, we probably would not give it much notice.
>
> (ibid: 206)

This is a fascinating argument. It is rather like saying that even though people generally desire what is good this does not rule out that there are people who, for whatever reason, have become utterly apathetic with regards to the good without this disproving the premise.
The fact that the desire for what is good is not – in the strictest sense – universal, does not detract from it having a very high *degree* of universality. The desire for knowledge can safely be said to be part of the human condition and it seems this desire must in some sense be satisfied; in fact the good is, for Aristotle, the fulfilment of rightful desires. Because the desire for knowledge, being (near) universal is a natural desire, it must necessarily be a right desire. It may therefore be assumed we can be neither truly happy, nor truly good, without the acquisition of knowledge and in turn having a motivation to acquire knowledge.

Even so, it must be remembered that the acquisition of knowledge, in fulfilling the rightful desire for knowledge, is therefore a good, but the good of the motivation for knowledge is distinct from the good of having acquired knowledge and this is brought out by Zagzebski as well:

> It is also bad to fail to have knowledge, but the badness of a bad motivation is not derivative from the badness of the failure to have knowledge.
>
> (ibid: 208)

It is only a central coordinating intelligence, *phronesis,* which vouchsafes a certain measure of unity of the virtues, not an ontological unity, but a unity of function. This functional unity of the virtues is distinctively Aristotelian:

> [One might meet] the dialectical arguments by which it could be contended that the virtues exist independently of each other, on the ground that the same man is not equally endowed by nature in respect of them all, so that he will be already the possessor of one, but not yet the possessor of another. As far as the natural virtues are concerned, this is possible; but it is not possible when the virtues are those that entitle a person to be called good without qualification; for the possession of a single virtue of prudence will carry with it the possession of them all. .
>
> (Aristotle 1995: 225)

Phronesis is an indispensable virtue for any attempt to lead a good life, to achieve a state of eudaimonia. As a literary education may be considered a powerful aid in the acquisition of this virtue, literary education consequently can be said to be of great moral importance. For it is not just *any* virtue which may be acquired through a literary education: *phronesis* is pre-eminent among the virtues as it vouchsafes the unity of the virtues. To analyse this functional unity of the virtues we need to analyse the concept of a central coordinating intelligence: *phronesis*; 'practical wisdom' or 'good judgement'.

Because *phronesis* is a virtue, it is unlike a skill in the sense that it does not take the form of a decision-making procedure which can determine the right decision to be taken in advance. If there is such a procedure as a utilitarian calculus it is, in so far as it is a procedure, not a virtue.

The indeterminability of the outcome of *phronesis* is linked to its primary theoretical need, which is 'to determine the mean between extremes in those cases in which the virtue is the mean (Zagzebski 1996: 221). The doctrine of the mean is an essential element of the Aristotelian understanding of what a virtue is.

Aristotle, in his *Ethica Nicomacheia,* illustrates the doctrine of the mean as follows:

> By virtue I mean moral virtue since it is this that is concerned with feelings and actions, and these involve excess, deficiency and a mean. It is possible, for example, to feel fear, confidence, desire, anger, pity, and pleasure and pain generally, too much or too little; and both of these are wrong. But to have these feelings at the right times on the right grounds towards the right people for the right motive and in the right way is to feel then to an intermediate, that is to best, degree; and this is the mark of virtue. Similarly there are excess and deficiency and a mean in the case of actions. But it is in the field of actions and feelings that virtue operates; and in them excess and deficiency are failings, whereas the mean is praised, and recognized as a success: and these are both marks of virtue.
>
> (Aristotle 1995: 101)

Because the mean is not a compromise between excess and deficiency, the mean is formally indeterminable. My means are particular to me and it is only my well-developed *phronesis* which can determine where they lie. Determining a mean is a difficult affair because there are a theoretically infinite number of ways to be wrong, ways in which to fall in either some excess or some deficiency. This basic insight shows how easy it is to be bad, and how difficult to nurture someone into finding one's unique, personal, mean. In fact, aiming for the mean could well be thought of as a task which will last a lifetime, and will never be quite finished.

This essential incompleteness of the good life is recognized by Macintyre as well, when he says that the good life is spent searching for the good life:

> The good life for man is the life spent in seeking the good life for man, and the virtues necessary for the seeking are those which will enable us to understand what more and what else the good life for man is
>
> (Macintyre 1984: 219)

The mean is not a compromise between evils. On the contrary: virtue is *not* the path of tepid mediocrity. A virtue is an *excellence,* and it therefore *transcends* all deficiencies and excesses. All virtues are relative to individual persons, that is to say they are inextricably bound up with both my own personal make-up and my contextual relations to all around me. We cannot, however, assume virtues to be 'relative' in a 'relativistic' fashion, which would go so far as to state that since *my* good is particular to *me,* it is *incomparable* to *your good* and ontologically utterly distinct from it.

If the word 'good' is to mean anything, it must mean more than 'good for me'. Were we to assume an *incomparability* of virtue we would not be able to speak of virtues at all, since we cannot but speak of virtues in terms of admirability and desirability but if *your* good is incomparable to mine, I cannot admire nor desire your good, hence it would not be a virtue, hence it would not be good. To state that a virtue is relative to the point of incomparability is therefore absurd. Individual differences are differences in measure, not in kind. That does not detract from the fact that the goodness of my virtue may be quite distinct from the goodness of your virtue – in the sense that my virtues are good independently of the fact whether or not anyone else is in the possession of like virtues.

Because it is the faculty of practical wisdom, *phronesis* is central to the exercise of all moral virtues. Hence, practical wisdom in its coordinating role assures the *unity of the virtues,* making it possible for us to speak of people in terms of *good* or *virtuous* in general rather than merely having to describe them as *honest,* or *courageous.*

How is practical wisdom acquired? It is acquired in the same way as all virtues are acquired, through exposure to those who have already acquired them.

Acquisition of the virtues presupposed virtuous people. It does not seem we can pull ourselves up by our boot-straps: indeed, the acquisition of any virtue has a necessarily *social* basis:

> Aristotle makes it clear that a virtue is learned by imitation and depends upon the presence of people with *phronesis* in the community, and *phronesis* itself is never found among the young (NE VI.8.1142a12-21). If I am right that the intellectual virtues have the same relation to *phronesis* as do the moral virtues, it follows that good thinking is socially based as well. (…) We learn from others how to believe rationally, just as we learn how to act morally. The social basis of belief formation is in some ways even more striking than the social basis of acting since we are probably even more dependent upon other people for the rationality or justifiability of our beliefs than for the rightness of our acts. *This means that the intellectual healthiness of the whole community is vitally important for the justifiability of our own beliefs.*
>
> (Zagzebski 1996: 228)

The stunning conclusion that good thinking is socially based would give us reason to explain how entire nations may be said to be –say – in denial about unsavoury elements of their national history, or even explain how societies in given times may collectively show symptoms of what might almost be termed a psychosis.

Phronesis is underdetermined by decision-making procedures, and this leads to the interesting conclusion that rationality itself is underdetermined by rational procedures (ibid: 224). Cognitive procedures are epistemic aids and are, as such, no substitute for knowledge itself. This is so because knowledge, in so far as it is a consequence of having practical wisdom (and practical wisdom is, it must be recalled, at least a necessary condition for having knowledge: "a truth-attaining intellectual quality concerned with doing and with the things that are good for human beings" (ibid: 230), is itself underdetermined by practical wisdom. Two people, both endowed with practical wisdom, may come to epistemic conclusions that are both justified and yet propositionally different.

If the necessary condition for having knowledge (at least knowledge about certain things) is itself underdetermined by procedures, then knowledge is underdetermined by procedures. In fact, with practical wisdom having been recognized as a truth-attaining intellectual quality, the attractive theoretical distinction between thinking and acting becomes problematic: Zagzebski, indeed, denies any theoretically relevant distinction between thinking and acting, between normative epistemology and ethics:

> I intentionally watch a film or read a novel but unintentionally think of a way in which it is related to my theory on intellectual virtue. There is no special order between thinking and acting. We do both most of the time. It takes tremendous philosophical ingenuity to devise a theory that separates these activities to permit a division in normative theory between ethics and normative epistemology. It is my position that this ingenuity is misplaced.
>
> (ibid: 231)

We cannot act without thinking, nor is thought as such insulated from our acting in and upon the world. We cannot act virtuously, and hence cannot act *well,* without the truth-attaining intellectual quality of practical wisdom. Neither is it possible to come to acquire the virtue of *phronesis* without salient life experiences. Literary experiences are to be considered salient and are therefore important factors in the acquisition of phronesis and consequently a good and moral life.

We may admit there are many degrees of thinking and acting, but we cannot escape the conclusion that everyone must to develop his intellectual as well as his moral virtues, and these cannot be separated from each other. This insight has far-reaching implications for our thinking about education and moral development, as this dissertation will argue.

§5.12 The Formal Definition of Deontic Concepts

If virtues are more fundamental than acts, acts are than morally derivative from virtues. Zagzebski comes to the following formal definitions. I include these definitions to show how the notions of right and wrong acts, moral duty, justified act, justified belief and unjustified belief might be derived from the aretaic concepts introduced earlier. These moral definition will be found to be useful when we are to determine whether or not a literary education can be morally defended.

1: A *right act* is what a person who is virtuously motivated, and who has the understanding of the particular situation that a virtuous person would have, might do in like circumstances. (Zagzebski 1996: 235)

2: A *wrong act* is what a person who is virtuously motivated, and who has the understanding of the particular situation would have, would not do in like circumstances (id.)

3: A *moral duty* is what a person who is virtuously motivated and who has the understanding of the particular situation that a virtuous person would have, would do in like circumstances. (id.)

4: A person *A* is praiseworthy (justified) for doing an act (having a belief) *S* (...) in case *A* does what a virtuous person would (probably) do (believes what a virtuous person would [probably] believe) in the same circumstances and is motivated by virtuous motives. (ibid: 236)

Now the role of the virtue of *phronesis* is such that we cannot have *phronesis* without being both virtuously motivated and having an understanding of the particular situation. This allows us to rephrase the above definitions, allowing for a convergence of virtuous motivation and understanding of the particular situation:

5: A right act, all things considered, is what a person with *phronesis* might do in like circumstances. A *wrong act, all things considered,* is what a person with *phronesis* would not do in like circumstances. (ibid: 239 -240)

6: A *moral duty, all things considered,* is what a person with *phronesis would* do in like circumstances. (ibid: 241)

Interpreting epistemic concepts as moral also allows us to regard justified beliefs as being theoretically related to right acts, and even allows us to think in terms of epistemic duties:

7: A *justified belief* is what a person who is motivated by intellectual virtue, and who has the understanding of his cognitive situation a virtous person would have, might believe in like circumstances. (id.)

8: An *unjustified belief* is what a person who is motivated by intellectual virtue, and who has the understanding of his cognitive situation a virtuous person would have, would not believe in like circumstances. (id.)

9: A belief of *epistemic duty* is what a person who is motivated by intellectual virtue, and who has the understanding of his cognitive situation a virtuous person would have, would believe in like circumstances.

Now the notion of epistemic duty is particularly interesting. It implies that we would be necessarily wrong in holding certain views in particular circumstances. What would be examples of epistemic duty?

In general it would be an epistemic duty not to entertain false beliefs if it is possible that with the necessary effort we could reach an epistemic state which excluded these false beliefs; for example avoiding epistemic positions such as those held by the Flat Earth Society or the Institution for Creation Research, the latter organization holding that the universe is roughly 6,000 years old. Less amusing, but definitely more sinister examples of epistemic duty would be to avoid giving credence to anyone defending positions such as 'Holocaust Revisionism'. More positive epistemic duties would be to trust reliable epistemic authorities, change one's beliefs in the face of strong evidence, and be willing to investigate possible new solutions to epistemic problems:

10: A belief of *epistemic duty* is what a person who is motivated by intellectual virtue, and who has the understanding of his cognitive situation a virtuous person would have, would believe in like circumstances." A belief is a *duty all things considered*, just in case it is what a person with *phronesis* would believe in like circumstances

11: A belief is an epistemic duty (strong sense) in certain circumstances, if and only if it is unjustified not to believe it. A belief is an epistemic duty (weak sense) in certain circumstances if and only if it is wrong to choose to reject it.

12: An *act* is a moral duty (strong sense) in certain circumstances if and only if is wrong not to do it. An act is a moral duty (weak sense) in certain circumstances if and only if it is wrong to choose to reject it.

13: A *justified belief, all things considered,* is what a person with *phronesis* might believe in like circumstances. An unjustified belief, all things considered, is what a person with phronesis would not believe in like circumstances. A belief is a duty, all things considered, just in case it is what a person with *phronesis* would believe in all circumstances.

And

14: "Let us call *an act of virtue* A if and only if it arises from the motivational component of A, it is something a person with virtue A would (probably) do in like circumstances, and it is successful in bringing about the end (if any) of A because of these features of the act." (ibid: 248)

The fact that virtues are success concepts does not entail we are *necessarily* successful, merely that we cannot be structurally entertain faulty interpretations about ourselves and the world we live in, in so far as these directly influence our moral and epistemic behaviour. The medieval natural philosophers cannot be attributed a lack of epistemic virtue, merely because – say - Buridan's natural philosophy has been proven to be an untrue model of the natural world.

Natural philosophers such as Jean Buridan had, of course, no concept of the scientific method and cannot be blamed for not using these concepts. What counts is that, under the circumstances, one 'makes the best' of the moral and epistemic situation one finds oneself in. As such, even though a medieval natural philosopher's approach – stemming from a motivation for knowledge – was not successful in the strictest sense of the word we could say it was not without success *at all.* Buridan's work, for instance, *is* a reasoned approach to natural phenomena and – looking back – may be considered an advance with regards to previous models.

The question of whether or not Aristotelian natural philosophy is 'knowledge' in the strictest sense of the word is relevant. We know now it is not *truthful,* in the sense that it does not correspond to reality. It was however *believed* to be truthful and therefore *to the best of people's capacities* was considered knowledge about the natural world.

At the same time we cannot easily relegate the status of classical and medieval natural philosophy to non-knowledge. It follows from the principle of correspondence that a belief – or belief system – *X* is true if and only if it corresponds to objective reality. The very fact of cognitive progress, both individually and as a society, makes clear that many of our beliefs or belief systems about one's objective reality are conditional.

Strictly speaking, Newtonian Mechanics isn't *true,* because we know now physical reality to be much more complex than the Newtonian system can vouch for. At the same time Newtonian mechanics *is* a very real cognitive result, a very real cognitive response to our physical reality as it was understood. As such it is perhaps too stringent to speak of 'knowledge', as a correspondence of our mental images with our common empirical reality, being the result of a motivation for knowledge. It might be concluded that the success component of intellectual virtue is not met if and only if the motivation for knowledge does not result in a qualified epistemic response to our experience.

There are good reasons for assuming that the level of correspondence with reality may not be determinable at the moment of epistemic response, and Zagzebski refers to this situation in her analysis of the difference between knowledge and justified belief.

> [A] belief may be [epistemically] justified because it follows epistemic rules, the following of which tends to lead to the truth or because it is an instance of a reliable belief-forming process (reliabilism) or, on my account, because it is a belief an intellectually virtuous person might have in the circumstances. That is to say, it is a member of a class of beliefs that a person who has virtuous motivations and is reliable in bringing about the end of those motivations (...) In the case of each theory of justified belief , success in reaching the truth is likely, or as likely as one can get under the circumstances, but it is not guaranteed.
>
> (ibid: 268-9)

Knowledge, then is a much more multi-faceted concept then 'truth'. If knowledge is the result of the exercise of virtue, then knowledge is commendable, admirable and desirable not merely because of it corresponding with objective truths but also because the agent's activity results in knowledge "*through* the operation of her virtuous motives and activities" (ibid: 270). A subject *A* acquiring knowledge *not* through the operation of virtuous motives and activities is less admirable than a subject *B* who *has* acquired knowledge through such motives and activities. Hence Zagzebski adds the following moral definitions of intellectual virtue and knowledge:

15: An act of intellectual virtue *A*, is an act that arises from the motivational component of *A*, is something a person with virtue *A* would (probably) do in the circumstances, is successful in achieving the end of the *A* motivation, and is such that the agent acquires a true belief (cognitive contact with reality) through these features of the act. (ibid: 270)

Knowledge, then, is defined as follows:

16: Knowledge is a state of cognitive contact with reality arising out of acts of intellectual virtue. (id.)

It follows that this knowledge must necessarily be personal, contextual, and culturally-laden. Medieval natural philosophy is knowledge, in the context of the Middle Ages. Also, it is the case that what we learn from exercising literary intelligence upon a fictional text is knowledge as well – and epistemically highly relevant. Also, if knowledge is a 'state of cognitive contact with reality arising out of acts of intellectual virtue' – then literary intelligence, as an intellectual virtue, brings about states of cognitive contact with reality and it this state which we would call knowledge. A greater awareness of the human condition, recognizing subtle social nuances, and knowing how to recognize laudable or deplorable character traits, are all forms of knowledge a literary education may bring about. Of course the 'knowledge' which is the result of an application of literary intelligence need not be necessary knowledge about the 'bare' human condition as it is derived from fictional narratives. Literary artefacts too add to the world, are part of our cultural universe and become legitimate objects of knowledge. Literary intelligence has a specific knowledge of the human condition as its goal.

But what is the relationship between knowledge and truth? Zagzebski curiously states that a belief arising out of acts of intellectual virtue 'entails that is true' (ibid.). It is difficult to understand how, in this sense, she can ascribe truth as correspondence with objective reality to every belief arising out of acts of intellectual virtue. It also seems to contradict her earlier position on the relationship between truth and justified belief. A belief arising out of intellectual virtue may be considered *justified* but there is no guarantee justified beliefs are *true*. If beliefs arising out of acts of intellectual virtue are necessarily *true* than what are we to make of cognitive achievements such as Aristotelian or medieval natural philosophy which were quite possibly justified, but cannot be true? Following Zagzebski's reasoning these beliefs were *not* acts arising out of intellectual virtue which must lead to a questionable conclusion that there are times and places in which people in general cannot be said to have intellectual virtue. This is a difficult conclusion to stomach. However we need not reach this conclusion if we keep in mind that Zagzebski's concept of knowledge is much more encompassing than merely the set of true propositions:

> "Knowledge may include cognitive contact with structures of reality other than the propositional" (ibid: 272)

Most knowledge concerning cultural endeavours and artefacts would fall into this category. It is therefore safe to speak of 'literary knowledge' or 'cultural knowledge' which is the product of the literary intelligence working on literary texts and other cultural objects.

§5.13 Why literary intelligence is an intellectual virtue

It is argued in this dissertation that the notion of Literary Intelligence as conceptualized by F.R. Leavis, Denys Harding and Geoffrey Bantock is conformable to the concept of 'phronesis', with this Aristotelian concept, usually translated as 'good judgement' or 'practical wisdom' being the necessary epistemic precondition for moral action. It follows that if literary intelligence is conformable to *phronesis,* then literary intelligence is also an epistemic factor in moral action.

Concretely, it is argued that reading quality fiction allows the reader to gain experiences that are structurally similar to 'real-life' experiences. These experiences foster practical wisdom, and hence cannot but have a positive effect on the reader's moral development.

Now there are two particularly important questions to be asked: Firstly, whether or not the 'literary intelligence' as conceived by Leavis and Bantock, is a form of intellectual virtue (for *phronesis* is an intellectual virtue) and secondly, what makes a theory of intellectual virtue important from an educational point of view?

Firstly, it must be ascertained whether or not the 'literary intelligence' as conceived by Leavis and Bantock, is a form of intellectual virtue: As stated in Chapter 3, the fundamental argument of this dissertation is that the competence Leavis and his co-contributors to Scrutiny described as *literary intelligence* is a mental disposition structurally similar as the Aristotelian concept of *phronesis*: 'practical wisdom' or 'prudence' which "(is) (...) a higher-order, mediating virtue, operating over the entire range of moral and intellectual virtues." (Zagzebski, 1996: 78)

Literary intelligence is, for Leavis, a universal, evaluative and teleological, "perceptive wisdom about ends". Leavis explicitly states:

> "([Intelligence is also] an exercise of the sense of value, [and] is controlled by an implicit concern for a total value-judgement."
>
> (Leavis 1964: 71)

To the extent that it is co-extensive with a 'sensibility', it is preoccupied with concrete experiences rather than with an abstract object. Leavis' sensibility also reflects on the concrete in an *evaluative* fashion: he explicitly equates the "finer discriminative feeling for life and personality" in a literary text with "our finer moral sense" (Leavis 1948: 159), and the exercise of the value judgement is 'total' and cannot be compartmentalized. It is not, and cannot be, merely 'aesthetic' or detached. It is difficult to argue that one universal, evaluative, teleological mental disposition that we describe as 'literary intelligence' can be structurally different from the architectonic, general, evaluative mental disposition described as *phronesis,* the mental disposition underlying all virtues.

Literary intelligence being – at least theoretically- acquirable through some form of education renders it a *disposition,* an acquired character trait. As such we can approach it as a virtue rather than as an inborn faculty.

The form of acquisition is, however, indirect. It is, as has been argued in §2 of this chapter, acquired as a *virtue,* not as a *skill.* Virtue cannot be taught, therefore literary intelligence as such cannot be taught directly. This has obvious educational implications.

Virtue cannot be taught of a text-book, is not a matter of repeating propositional moral sentences or the acquisition of a 'technique'. This is not to say that skills are entirely irrelevant: the actualization of literary intelligence demands the acquisition and application of certain reading skills. We can only suppose that literary training both encompasses the 'habituation into sensibility' as the acquisition of technical reading skills. These skills are in themselves morally neutral but are needed in order to develop oneself as an efficient, competent and sensitive reader.

The sphere of the literary is – if literary intelligence is a virtue - a possible locus of the exercise of practical wisdom: Literary intelligence is than the *proper exercise of practical wisdom in the sphere of the interpretation of literary texts.* Literary education is consequently a morally pertinent activity because we can only acquire a virtue by being experientially habituated into it. If we can exercise practical wisdom through being inducted into literary reading practices, we can acquire a degree of practical wisdom through literary education.

In the same way one can only become courageous by perpetrating courageous acts it is by engaging in literary interpretation, by immersing oneself in sustained reflection on the human condition, that we come upon a means of acquiring practical wisdom. This leads us to the following question: whether a theory of intellectual virtue is educationally relevant, especially considering that virtues *as such* cannot be directly taught:

Firstly, a virtue is a social concept. A human being growing up in isolation cannot become a virtuous person.[38] Intellectual virtue is consequently and necessarily a social concept. For the exercise of any virtue, moral or intellectual we find ourselves dependent upon others. We are not merely dependent on others for our moral and intellectual formation but also, indeed, for our continued exercise of these excellences of character. We cannot fully possess intellectual virtue outwith of a social structure facilitating it:

> As I would put it, knowledge is transferred from person to person via a network of acts of intellectual virtue. To the extent that a person relies for knowledge on someone else, her resulting state is not knowledge if that someone else does not also have knowledge. This means that to perform an act of the virtue of proper reliance on others, one must get to the truth not only through one's own virtuous motivations and processes but through the virtuous motivations and processes of those others. Knowledge is the result of acts of intellectual virtue by both the agent and others in her epistemic community upon whom she relies in forming a subset of her beliefs. This aspect of knowledge makes it something for which we have social responsibility. And, in fact, it is one of the main reasons knowledge is something for which we are *morally* responsible. Others in our society have the moral right to expect us not to harm them, and passing on to them something that is not knowledge is one way of harming them.
>
> (Zagzebski 1996: 319)

[38] It could be argued that he could not become vicious either, as both are acquired character traits. A radically isolated 'Robinson' would be utterly amoral and – in fact – possibly even barely human in any other than a human in a purely biological sense – if such a thing exists.

Because the practical wisdom guiding our moral existence is to be understood as a particular sensitivity to 'the details of moral living' (ibid: 257), our understanding of moral sensitivity expands as well and may come to include elements which have not generally been recognized as loci of moral evaluation and as elements in moral formation.

Because virtue theory is unremittingly *social* in scope we cannot assume an issue having moral relevance without that issue also being relevant for moral formation. This is so because, in virtue ethical terms, *emulation* is central to moral formation. We can only learn to be good by following examples of goodness. If narrative literature is morally relevant then we cannot escape the conclusion it has a role to play in moral formation.

But *is* narrative literature morally relevant? Zagzebski believes that this is the case, and has an interesting reason for believing it to be so:

> Contemporary virtue theories have broadened their approach to include a sensitivity to the details of moral living as depicted in narrative literature. Literature is less likely to recognize those divisions among the goods of life that leads one group of philosophers to investigate the proper pursuit of knowledge and an entirely different group to investigate the proper pursuit of other goods, such as happiness. Whereas the connections are so often missing in didactic literature, they can be explained in narratives naturally and absorbingly This suggests that the use of literature might be fruitful for philosophers interested in epistemic evaluation as well as for ethicists (id.)

Zagzebski's distinction between the didactical and the narrative hails back to Gallie's identical distinction which he made in his paper "What is a Story?" (Gallie 1964). Gallie also understands narrative in an epistemological sense: a well-crafted story leads to some form of understanding about "the successive actions and thoughts and feelings of certain described characters" (id.):

> The conclusion of any worthwhile story is not something that can be deduced or predicted, not even something that can be seen at a later stage to have been theoretically or ideally predictable on the basis of what had been revealed at an earlier stage. (...)
>
> (Gallie 1964:22)

This is also why didactical stories lose their virtues *as* stories as the conclusion of the homily is, unlike that of a narrative story 'not awaited with eagerness and excitement' (ibid: 23). Didactic narratives cannot have a surprise ending, they are eminently predictable and the 'understanding' of the human condition offered by them - even if valid - is distinctly low-grade. They offer no sense of the world's moral complexity. Narrative literature *is* a means of human understanding exactly because it unifies 'successive actions and thoughts and feelings of certain described characters'. Both moral and epistemic 'actions, thoughts and feelings' allow narrative description in the selfsame characters and this is the reason *why* narrative literature is 'less likely to recognize those divisions among the goods of life', be they epistemic or moral. This after all, is because: "the concept of an act of virtue combines all our moral aims in one concept" (Zagzebski 1996: 270) This is illustrated, for instance, in Lorraine Code's reading of Edmund Gosse's *Father and Son* in the second chapter of her *Epistemic Responsibility*.

Father and Son depicts Gosse's father's struggle to reconcile his fundamentalist Protestant beliefs, in particular Biblical literalism with regards to the Creation narrative in the first two chapters of Genesis, with his scientific work in Marine Zoology into which the findings of evolutionary theory were beginning to creep. His intellectual struggle at last resolves itself in his rejection of Darwinism, fatally undermining both his moral and intellectual virtues.

Father and Son proves to be an excellent illustration of what are primarily intellectual defects, focusing on the elder Gosse's incapacity to suspend his own beliefs – thereby 'locking himself in to a mode of intellectual practice that does not, and perhaps as he conceives it, cannot, allow a self-critical stance' (Code 1987: 21).

Father and Son thus is not merely a description of an otherwise great mind's lack of intellectual virtue: but we can *a contrario* tease out the main characteristics of an intellectually virtuous stance which is, indeed, what Code does in her *Epistemic Responsibility*.

If a lack of intellectual virtue is characterized by closed-mindedness and a lack of self-criticism, a character exhibiting intellectual virtue could be described as a character oriented:

> toward the world, toward one; knowledge-seeking self, and toward other such selves as part of the world. Central to it is a sort of openness to how things are, a respect for the normative force of "realism". This attitude involves a willingness to let things speak for themselves, a kind of humility toward the experienced world that curbs any excessive desire to impose one's cognitive structurings upon it. Intellectual honesty consists in a finely tuned balancing of these two factors, cultivating an appropriate interplay between self and world.
>
> (ibid: 20)

The tragedy of Gosse the elder is of course that, in *Father and Son* he is depicted as having been virtuous in this respect, initially holding this equilibrium between self and world, between faith and scientific enquiry, but not *succeeding* in maintaining this equilibrium, eventually collapsing into a downright rejection of reason in favour of an uncompromising embrace of religious obscurantism.

Although we cannot deny the elder Gosse to have been a man of integrity - and integrity is an intellectual virtue - his integrity was self-enclosed and not moderated by the other intellectual virtue of reflexivity.

Indeed the latter virtue is the closest to the virtue of *phronesis* and hence an integrity unmoderated by reflexivity cannot, in the long run, result in a fully intellectually virtuous stance.

But apart from arguing that there are novels that illustrate problems concerning intellectual character, we can also restate Macintyre's position that human life, as a whole, can only be understood in narrative terms: "virtue can only feasibly be seen as a way of life when life is construed as a whole, a connected history, a structured narrative." (ibid: 27)

As Zagzebski has argued, it is ontologically suspect to approach virtues as if they existed in separation from each other: there is no virtue *as such* that can be theoretically isolated, and studied in such isolation. We can therefore only approach a person's virtues *through the entirety of a person's character.* Descriptions of people's character's, it is argued, demands a temporal unity, coherence and context – and this is what narrative does: it allows us to see virtues as so many parts of "a concept of self whose unity resides in the unity of narrative which links birth to life and death as narrative beginning to middle to end." (Macintyre 1984: 191)

Code points out (Code 1987: 27) that the narrative unity demanded must not necessarily be an exhaustive or totalizing unity. This, indeed, would be impossible. Nor does it demand even that all morally relevant narratives should describe a protagonist's entire life; but the *unity* of that life must be *implied*:

> [The] implied unity is in some sense palpable, drawing together the strands of past, present and future into the set of interlocking events. Something of this unity is evident, for example in Camus *The Outsider* and in Solzhenitsyn's *One Day in the Life of Ivan Denisovitch.*
>
> (id.)

Understanding our – and others – lives is fundamental to our living ethical lives. We cannot be moral when we are ignorant of ourselves, our desires, our capacities, or our relationships. Also, we cannot be ignorant of others. Our lives, both our epistemic and our moral lives are not lived in isolation and literature, according to Code, has consequently a particular moral value in: "its capacity to fill in a textured context where there might otherwise have wrongly seemed to be simply a series of isolated actions." (Code 1987: 28)

Our lives must become an integral whole, not merely because we cannot draw a strict ontological distinction between moral and intellectual virtues, but also because our effectiveness as moral agents is also dependent on us being epistemically responsible, i.e. having intellectual motivations. Our morals need to be connected to our knowing ourselves and others, and there are strong arguments for considering narrative to be a powerful vehicle for understanding the human condition. This makes narrative epistemically relevant and hence morally relevant. The kind of intelligence, literary intelligence, fostered by an intimate acquaintance with narrative art is therefore morally relevant, and this insight has educational consequences. It is possible that it goes too far to say that cognition, virtue, integrity, and selfhood can only be understood through narrative - but at the same time it would be ill-advised to underestimate the epistemic potential of narrative study. It seems difficult to come to a rich evaluative understanding of virtue without the medium of narrative. Narratives are so basic to every culture in every time that we would be hard put to imagine a society without its specific narratives and myths illustrating character traits that are considered valuable.

It *is* probably true that we may come to an (as full as personally possible) "full understanding of virtue, integrity and selfhood" without having recourse to *written* narratives or fictional literature, at least in certain times and places. However, once we find ourselves in a temporal and situational context in which written narrative and fictional literature abounds, which has in fact been the case since the Gilgamesh epos was committed to writing 4,000 years ago, it seems difficult to assume that we can come to a far-reaching characterization of virtue without taking recourse to narrated histories.

Even so, though Code would rather describe "narrative history of a certain kind"(Macintyre 1984: 194) to be *a* rather than *the* "basic and essential genre for the characterisation of human action" (id.), this still makes narrative description of human character, the description of character fundamental to the elucidation of virtue, "basic and essential". We therefore ignore the narrative arts to our peril and, indeed, it does not seem to be the case that someone is a morally worse person for not taking to realist literature. This, however, does not mean that literature is not, as a medium, a powerful vehicle which offers us a unique perspective which mass-media influences may hope to supplant. Because literature is a privileged avenue into the human condition, tells us something about humans, it follows that no-one who claims to be interested in people can wholly escape being interested in literature. To paraphrase Jacques Barzun: literature being about people, and people by definition being interested in themselves, literature cannot avoid being interesting.

So to this extent, literary education has a certain influence on the fostering of practical wisdom. Its influence is by definition limited, and is no surrogate for other forms of fostering practical wisdom, nor is it a necessary condition for the development of practical wisdom. Nonetheless, the position of the virtue of practical wisdom as an *architectonic* epistemic and moral virtue makes that an educational effort having even the slightest positive influence on the acquisition of practical wisdom, is itself of great value. The value of a literary education is then not to be found in a cynical notion of 'cultural capital acquisition' but is inherently grounded in the value of the virtue upon which all other virtues depend. Therefore, the distinction between 'real-world' concerns and the study of literature, as recently made by the QCA as an attempted legitimization for introducing an English GCSE which does not involve any literary reading (Lipsett, A. 2008), is a wholly artificial one.

If education is a normative praxis, then it follows that the educational system should take account of the insights of virtue theory, both in general and in particular where it comes to discerning the proper role of literary education in the wider educational system. This question will be treated in the next chapter.

§5.14 Conclusion: some implications of Virtue Theory for Literary Education

Literary education offers a special pedagogic route towards human flourishing and should be promoted by the state for two reasons: (a) the good life is not achievable without good government; the state should therefore support the good life's *internal goods* with its own *external goods.* (b) good government is itself impossible without virtuous, active citizens.[39] Literary education should be based on affective outcomes and the relation between teacher and pupil is one primarily of guidance. According to this model, teachers of literature have a greater social and cultural responsibility than others. Literary education should then be an indispensable component of public education. Also, according to Macintyre, we cannot postulate the acquisition of virtues without support of institutions:

> Institutions are characteristically and necessarily concerned with what I have called external goods. They are involved in acquiring money and other material goods, they are structured in terms of power and status, and they distribute money, power and status as rewards. Nor could they do otherwise of they are to sustain not only themselves, but also the practices of which they are the bearers. For no practices can survive for any length of time unsustained by institutions (...).
>
> (Macintyre 1985: 194)

Social institutions are necessary for the flourishing of practices but must at the same time be *sustained* by the practices they nurture. An institute, lacking such support, becomes nothing more than a manipulative tool. Macintyre states: "In this context the essential function of the virtues is clear.

[39] Cf. Aristotle *Politics,* book III. "He who has the power to take part in the deliberative or judicial administration of any state is said by us to be a citizen of that state; and, speaking generally, a state is a body of citizens sufficing for the purposes of life."

Without them, without justice, courage and truthfulness, practices could not resist the corrupting power of institutions." (id.)[40]

An educational institution cannot therefore come into being or even be sustained while radically lacking a *real* moral content. The fact that one cannot untie habituation into the virtues from an institutional setting makes that it is necessary to analyze some of the educational implications that a virtue theoretical analysis of the concept of literary intelligence may be said to have. The following chapter will offer such an analysis.

[40] Ibid. The dialectical relationship between *eudaimonia,* the good consisting of the exercise of acquired excellences, and *good government* sustaining *eudaimonia* with the provision of external goods and itself only being kept from corruption if not checked by the public exercise of the virtues citizenry is a theme already expounded on by Aristotle in his *Politics* (bks. III & VII)

Chapter 6: Applying Virtue Theory to Reading Education

Virtue Theory is eminently practical. It is essentially concerned with the moral evaluation of habituated behaviour, describing achieved behavioural excellence as 'virtue'. A virtue, in the sense of an excellent level of acquired behaviour – a character trait, a quality or disposition, is consequently not as such a theoretical, but rather a *success concept*, or, in the very least, has a success-component. A virtue – if we follow Zagzebski's pure virtue theory – cannot be described in terms of a mere *motivation* or *disposition* towards a certain good (as Bailin 2003 argues).

We cannot conceptualize a virtue incapable of instantiating itself at some level. There *must* be a correlation between the disposition and success in achieving the goal of the disposition. A good intention may exist 'merely' in the mind, but a virtue must have a 'real-world' correlate. If I am honest, have the virtue, quality, or disposition of honesty I may, at times, speak an untruth – either because of real or perceived social pressures, a moment of moral weakness (*akrasia*) or simply because I hold mistaken beliefs about the truth.

The fact that my disposition does not *guarantee* success in individual cases does not invalidate the moral importance of my disposition, in fact as long as there is a degree of success to go with the disposition we can say that there *is* a disposition in the first place.

Because a virtue is a 'real world' concept – the theory sketched above leads us to postulate a number of statements which ought to be empirically verifiable – or at least falsifiable. I will draw upon relevant research literature to argue that there are good reasons to assume that literary intelligence has a number of real-world instantiations which may be identified.

First of all, in paragraph one it will be argued that literary intelligence is not merely to be perceived as a theoretical construct but is found to be a verifiably existing moral quality. This verifiably existing moral quality is consequently identified as a virtue on the grounds that it is found to be conducive to the good life (§6.2), does not have the characteristics of a skill (§6.3) or a natural capacity (§6.4). Having identified the art of reading well as an essentially virtuous trait, a number of educational implications may be identified (§6.5).

Because virtues cannot be taught as such it is also the case that literary intelligence cannot be taught as such (§6.6). It may however be acquired in other ways than through direct instruction. At any rate, the acquisition of an intrinsic motivation to read is essential to the acquisition of literary intelligence (§6.7). The reliability component of literary intelligence is treated in §6.8 and in §6.9 it is argued that the *aim* of a literary education is to lay the foundations of a lifelong reading habit with, in turn, literary intelligence being the fruit of such a consistent habit (§6.10).

Concretely, a number of factors influencing the acquisition of literary intelligence are treated in some detail: the teacher (§6.11), the home environment (§6.12), the wider school environment (§6.13) and society as a whole (§6.14). This chapter concludes by stating that the fostering of literary intelligence may well be inimical to the dominant ethos of 'outcome-based education'.

§6.1 Literary Intelligence is a verifiably existing moral quality

If we are to approach literary intelligence in terms of a moral quality – a virtuous trait related to phronesis – than there must be a correlation between the mental disposition and the success. This relationship must be somehow verifiable.

Some of the most interesting research into the psychology of reading has been into the psychology of *reading for pleasure* Krashen (2004) and Clark & Rumbold (2006) define *reading for pleasure* as "reading that we do of our own free will anticipating the satisfaction that we will get from the act of reading" (Clark & Rumbold 2006: 6).
The notion that reading has beneficial empathic effects has been recognized by educational psychologists such as Bruner (1996) and Lahtinen (2003). Cunningham and Stanovich (2001) found that:

> Reading has cognitive consequences that extend beyond its immediate task of lifting meaning from a particular passage. Furthermore, these consequences are reciprocal and exponential in nature.
>
> (Cunningham & Stanovich 2001: 137)

One of the most particular cognitive consequence of extensive reading is the acquisition of vocabulary. It is, according to Cunningham and Stanovich, reading rather than oral exchange which makes for growth of vocabulary. Print exhibits a much larger lexical richness than speech, and a large vocabulary therefore allows for a precise navigation of social particulars unavailable to a non-reader. As Olson (1986) says:

> It is easy to show that sensitivity to the subtleties of language are crucial to some undertakings. A person who does not clearly see the difference between an expression of intention and a promise or between a mistake and an accident, or between a falsehood and a lie, should avoid a legal career or, for that matter, a theological one.
>
> (Ibid: 341)

Verbal intelligence would then seem to be in the very least *relevant* for the fostering of *phronesis* which demands an insight in subtle particulars. If extensive reading fosters the verbal intelligence and verbal intelligence in turn is relevant to us becoming increasingly better at exercising our practical judgement – than that in itself shows extensive reading to be an educational activity of great moral importance.

The reason given as to why extensive reading is so important for the development of verbal intelligence is because print is, lexically speaking, much richer than speech – differences in children's exposure to print offers an easy explanation why children who have been exposed to print from an early age have a much larger vocabulary.

A more defined verbal intelligence in turn translates itself into an increasing volume of print consumption, leading to 'virtuous circle' of verbal intelligence – but at the same time opening an increasingly wide gap between the verbally intelligent and the verbally less intelligent.

In a study involving college students and set up so as to be as conservative as possible with regards to influence of reading volume alone, Cunningham and Stanovich found that "that reading volume made a significant contribution to multiple measures of vocabulary, general knowledge, spelling, and verbal fluency even after reading

comprehension ability and nonverbal ability had been partialed out." (Cunninham and Stanovich 2001: 143) Verbal intelligence – or reading comprehension – and reading volume hence stand in a reciprocal relationship: the more we read, the better we get at it and the more we read. The only way to get better at reading, according to Cunningham and Stanovich, is *to read*:

> We should provide all children, regardless of their achievement levels, with as many reading experiences as possible. Indeed, this becomes doubly imperative for precisely those children whose verbal abilities are most in need of bolstering, for it is the very act of reading that can build those capacities. An encouraging message for teachers of low-achieving students is implicit here. We often despair of changing our students' abilities, but there is at least one partially malleable habit that will itself develop abilities—reading!
>
> (ibid: 147)

Other advantages of extensive reading are mentioned by Benton & Fox who state that:

> Stories provide the possibility of educating the feelings and can offer their readers potential growth points for the development of a more subtle awareness of human behaviour.
>
> (Benton & Fox 1985: 15)

From the first paragraphs of this dissertation it has been argued that the cultivation of the emotions should be an intrinsic part of the intellectual life, without being able to entertain the right feelings about the right things at the right time, we cannot be said to be fully intelligent.

§6.2 Literary intelligence, if it is a virtue, should be conducive to the good life.

One of the problems of moral theory is the relationship between the good and the enjoyable. Many faith traditions, as well as the philosophical influence of deontology – the ethics of duty – have pitted enjoyment *against* morality.

Virtue ethics, however, considers this contradistinction fundamentally inadmissible.

This is not to say that anything which can be considered enjoyable is thereby rendered good: this would demand adoption of the grossest form of hedonism. Rather: what is good, that is to say, what is virtuous is also *conducive to the good life* – and the good life is a happy life.

A life of brutal self-abnegation might please the Kantian, but it cannot be called good as it is not conducive to happiness. It is argued that reading well, if it is to be considered a virtue, must be shown to be conducive to the good life: at least it must be admitted that if there is either evidence to the contrary, or no evidence for the statement, I must consider the thesis to be falsified.

Reading is however widely found to be enjoyable and reading for pleasure is a pastime in which many people partake. Again, the mere fact that reading is enjoyable does not in itself make it *good.* But if reading is good, it cannot be anything but conducive to happiness. Krashen (2004) argues that "there is strong evidence free voluntary reading is very enjoyable", with Krashen (2004), Rane-Szostak & Herth (1995a & b) and others interpret the pleasure associated with free voluntary reading with Csikszentmihalyi's concept of *flow.*

Krashen also refers to a number of studies done in classroom settings, pointing out that where students were given the option between free reading and traditional forms of instruction students overwhelmingly choose free reading and reported it as being an enjoyable activity. Robinson and Godbey (1997) find that even though time spent reading has decreased; it is still a popular leisure activity.

Nell (1988) conceptualizes pleasure reading as 'a form of play'. In this work he has studied 33 'ludic readers' which he defined as those who read at least a book a week for pleasure and relaxation.

As part of his extensive research programme he also researched the physiological effects of ludic reading. Following on Berlyne's (1971) two-factor theory of hedonic value – stating that pleasure "derives from arousal boosts (moderate arousal increments) and arousal jags (relief when an arousal is reversed). (…) One example of such reversal is provided by the bedtime reader: After a long period of pleasurable arousal following the exploits of Magnus Pym, the "perfect spy" of Le Carré's novels, the reader lays the book aside, switches off the light, and at one drifts into a state of delightful relaxation" (Nell 1988: 33-34)

Nell finds that although ludic readers report their ludic reading to be 'effortless' "it is on the contrary physiologically more aroused and more labile than baseline responding". The second striking feature is the predicted deactivation that sets in immediately when the subjects stop reading and close their eyes. The delights of bedtime reading may in part be attributed to this precipitous fall in arousal not only in skeletal muscle but also in skin potential, controlled by the automatic nervous system" (Nell, 36) It would then at least seem that reading in enjoyable, but is it conducive to a deep state of happiness?

There are reasons to assume the happiness resulting from extensive reading is of a different order than that resulting from other forms of enjoyment. Rane-Szostak & Herth (1995b), who both work in the field of geriatric nursing, report that:

> Over and over again, we found that older people who enjoyed reading for pleasure were rarely lonely. For example, an 86-year old woman whose severe heart problems had made it impossible for her to leave her apartment for the past five years had a positive outlook on life. When asked how she felt about being alone and housebound. She pointed at her bookshelves and replied: "I'm not alone, I have the whole world right here with me."
>
> (ibid: 588)

Rane-Szostak & Herth have found that whereas years of education has an influence on choice of reading materials, it is *any* reading for pleasure was associated with lower loneliness scores (Rane-Szostak & Herth 1995a: 104). While accepting that much more research would need to be done to fully substantiate this contention, it does offer in itself powerful evidence that reading is conducive to a deep state of happiness, deep enough to dispel an existential pain as powerful as loneliness.

Of course the mental state of happiness here described may be assumed to be the end-result of a lifetime reading habit. It is the habit I am interested in rather than the mere act. If 'literary intelligence' is a virtue it must be approached as a habit and not as some kind of 'potential' to be instantiated every now and then.

Reading, as such, may not always be pleasurable at each and every moment, but a lifetime habit of extensive reading is arguably one of many ways in which we move towards a state of *eudaimonia.* It is not argued, of course, that it is the *only* way in which a state of *eudaimonia* may come to be achieved – it may be so that reading is particularly beneficial for certain groups of people.

One of the many interesting insights of Nell's psychological research into the characteristics of 'ludic readers'. All 33 'ludic readers' which he studied were found, after application of the Eysenck Personality Inventory and the Cattell Sixteen Personality Factor Questionnaire, to be introverted "with scores strikingly below British norm on the EPI Extraversion scale" (Nell 1988: 45).

It is not entirely surprising that extensive reading is associated with a characteristic personality trait such as introversion. Virtues are deeply personal characteristics of mind and my *phronesis* – though recognizable as *phronesis* – is personal to me. No one else will quite share the specific character traits that I have. *Phronesis* may be acquired in many ways by all kinds of people; extensive reading may arguably be a very good way of acquiring phronesis for people who are dominantly introverted. It could even be argued that introverts may well be both more willing and able to engage in the kind of psychological activity needed for the development of *phronesis.*

As we have seen, where the work of the artist is directed *outwards* into the world, the work of the reader is directed *inwards* to the psyche. As such it is not surprising that we may find more readers among introverts than among extraverts.

However, this contention is no more than tentative and much more research would have to be done on the character traits of extensive ludic readers. At any rate, there is enough psychological evidence to regard a habit of extensive reading to be conducive to happiness.

There is also a large amount of historical evidence to back up this statement. Jonathan Rose, in his *The Intellectual Life of the British Working Classes,* devotes many pages to describing the deep happiness that otherwise culturally deprived people derived from habits of extensive reading. Not only was working-class didacticism an important factor in the emancipation of the working classes – it also provided deep enjoyment and happiness:

> Dorothy Burnham (b.1915) who grew up in an overcrowded home ("circumstances that would have affronted the dignity of a guinea pig") and, after her family disintegrated, in a Catholic hostel, found her private life in Keats, Tennyson, and Arnold: "Communication between these poets and myself was instantaneous. I saw with delighted amazement that all poetry had been written especially for me. Although I spoke – in my back street urchin accents – of La Belly Dame Sans Murky, yet in Keats chill little poem I seemed to sense some essence of the eternal ritual of romantic love. And Tennyson's "Morte D'Arthur" bowled me over. I read it again and again until I lived in a world of "armies that clash by night" and stately weeping Queens. So the poets helped me escape the demands of communal living which now, at thirteen, were beginning to be intolerable to me.
>
> (Rose 2002: 24)

At the same time Rose makes a very strong argument that literature though conducive to a kind of happiness was never a soporific – indeed if it did anything it made people both happy and yet less content with their lot. The thesis that working class literary consumption was a strong factor in working class radicalism is powerfully argued in his work.

The enjoyment of reading cannot act as bromide because reading, apart from being enjoyable simultaneously raises awareness of the human condition. Therefore, a sustained habit of reading may have far- reaching consequences. I consequently argue that evidence suggests that a sustained habit of reading seems to be enjoyable and/or conducive to a good life – at least for a certain group of people.

§6.3 If literary intelligence is a virtue, it ought to have the traits of a virtue, not the traits of a skill

In order to understand the difference between virtues and skills, it is necessary to analyze the relationship between the moral trait and the trait-instantiating skills. Which aspects of literary intelligence are virtuous, and which technical? Which can be taught, and which can be fostered?

This dissertation's thesis would be disproved if 'literary intelligence' could be convincingly conceptualized as a skill. For it to be a skill it would have to have quite different characteristics than a virtue. According to varying virtue-ethicists, from Aristotle to Zagzebski, virtues are fundamentally dissimilar to skills:

A virtue, as distinguished from a skill, is, according to Aquinas something which *cannot be put to bad use.* Skills, however, *can* be put to bad use. A virtue is than a good-making quality of a person that cannot lead to bad use. Furthermore, according to Zagzebski, the behaviour consisting in the exercise of a skill is not essentially connected to anything valuable, whereas it *is* in the case of a virtue.

A virtue is intrinsically valuable. This argument is redolent of Aquinas' observation that a virtue cannot be put to bad use. Skills serve virtues by allowing a person who is virtuously motivated to be effective in action. (Zagzebski 1996: 113) Virtues are then psychologically and ontologically prior to skills and are strongly connected to motivational structure. On the contrary: skills are more connected to effectiveness in action. Virtues are entrenched in a person's character and become a kind of 'second nature' (ibid: 166). This would explain why extensive readers tend to describe their reading process or reading activities as 'effortless' whereas physiological research shows that it is not effortless at all. (Nell 1988a & 1988b)

The question needs to be answered whether or not literary intelligence can be put to bad use: It has sometimes been argued that individual virtues are not conducive to moral goodness. A recurring thought experiment in this regard would be to postulate the existence of a 'courageous Nazi'. Considering his courage arguably made him worse, not better, what consequences does this insight have for conceptualizing courage as a virtue?

Whereas it could be argued that courage in a Nazi makes the Nazi worse *overall* this does not mean that courage is not in itself a trait that is not intrinsically good. As Zagzebski states:

> A (...) response is to say that the traits exhibited by the Nazi (...) is courage and courage is always a virtue and always good to have , but the good – making properties of virtues and the bad-making properties of vices do not always add up arithmetically to yield a rating of the agent's overall goodness.
>
> (Zagzebski 1996: 92)

So we may have to qualify Aquinas' statement that a virtue cannot be put to bad use *at all* and entertain a more fluid notion of how virtues relate to goodness.

Let us now assume the existence of a hypothetical 'evil person endowed with literary intelligence'. Terry Eagleton in his *Introduction to Literary Theory* offers the example of a 'Commandant who wiles away his leisure hours with a volume of Goethe' – but the Commandant's love of Goethe may have more to do with aestheticism or cultural snobbery than with literary intelligence. But let us, for argument's sake, assume the existence of a person who reads voraciously and intelligently and is yet consumed by a cause that is immoral or even downright evil.

This is not an entirely inconceivable hypothesis: indeed quite a number of authors, whom I conceive to be endowed with exactly the kind of intelligence I have been describing as a virtue, have been exceedingly unattractive human beings. Especially in the sphere of politics writers have been attracted to the wilder shores of ideology. Hence it does not seem that literary intelligence is necessarily a 'good-making quality'.

Nonetheless it could be answered that "Virtue is related to good, not by invariably increasing the goodness of its possessor and goodness for the world, but by invariably making its possessor closer to a high level of admirability and the world closer to a high level of desirability." (ibid: 101) and even though having the virtue of literary intelligence may not make its possessor automatically ('invariably') admirable – it renders him more admirable than he would have been had he lacked that form of intelligence.

In much the same way we cannot say that creativity is a bad trait to have, because in specific circumstances it might make the possessor worse, literary intelligence is admirable and desirable. The fact that in individual cases it might make the possessor worse (or perhaps, more effective in evil-doing) does not detract from the admirability and desirability of the specific trait.

Also, a virtue is intrinsically connected to something of value. The question whether literary intelligence is directly connected to something of value should be answered in the affirmative: Literary intelligence, by its very nature a sensibility operating on the subtle and contextualized nuances of the human condition leads fosters an awareness which would seem to be intrinsically valuable. Many other forms of awareness may also be intrinsically valuable – but that does not detract from the individual intrinsic value of literary intelligence. An evil person who has a degree of literary intelligence might be moved more easily to a state of empathy with his fellow man than an evil person who is also closed to moral appeals of literature. In these senses it is more likely literary intelligence is like a virtue than a skill.

§6.4 Is literary intelligence a natural capacity?

A virtue is an *acquired* excellence of character. Were certain traits not acquired, but a natural given – than it could not possibly be a virtue. My contention, that literary intelligence is a virtue would be effectively disproved if it could be shown to be a natural capacity. This is because a natural capacity *qua* natural capacity cannot be morally evaluated: "Again, we have the faculties by nature, but we are not made good or bad by nature" (Aristotle 1995: 99)

If literary intelligence is a natural capacity, than its possession ought to be unrelated to its acquisition, i.e. it ought to be personal to be in possession of a 'literary intelligence' without habituation. This is obviously not the case. Krashen (2004) reports a number of studies on Free Voluntary Reading and concludes that more reading, i.e. more reading experience "results in higher reading comprehension, writing style, vocabulary, spelling, and grammatical development" (Krashen 2004: 17) Literary intelligence, which is fundamental to reading comprehension is therefore unlike a natural capacity – because it is attained through experience. Kraaykamp (2003) points at the importance of literary socialization early in life for the acquisition of a lifelong reading habit:

> Children whose often read literature during their childhood prove to have a 2.9 better chance of also reading literature than children without this parental reading example. (…) Children who were intensively stimulated to read by their parents later prove to have a 2.6 better chance of being literature lovers than those who were not encouraged to read
>
> (Kraaykamp 2003: 249-251)

Kraaykamp (ibid: 251) also finds that cultural instruction at school is significant for the fostering of a lifelong reading habit – regardless of the level of eventual educational attainment. There is no evidence that literary intelligence is a natural capacity.

Of course, our (lack of) natural capacities may be relevant to our acquisition of literary intelligence. Some people will only achieve a limited reading proficiency. Does this mean they are any less admirable people? The fact that certain people never acquire a desirable trait is lamentable but does not detract from any other desirable traits which they might have – and extensive readers might not have.

I myself lack any aptitude for both the musical and visual arts and yet have no doubt that such aptitudes are greatly desirable. Nonetheless, my lacking the aptitude for the acquisition of a desirable trait *a* does not detract from my possible aptitudes for acquiring desirable trait *b*. Literary intelligence is itself particularly valuable because it is one possible way of fostering the architectonic virtue of practical wisdom. I do not state that it is the only way.

And even so, it is extremely unlikely (cf. Holbrook 1968) that people are entirely without literary intelligence, at whatever level. I would say it is a desirable trait to have – even when it can be acquired only to a very limited extent. Reading is one possible way in which we acquire the kind of experience which we need to become successful human beings.

§6.5 Some implications of approaching literary intelligence as a virtue

If literary intelligence is a virtue – or an instance of a virtue – than that has radical implications for both the importance of literary education. For, as Zagzebski argues, we cannot artificially separate moral from intellectual virtues, indeed need to be intellectually virtuous in order to be morally virtuous. It is the virtue of practical wisdom, *phronesis* , which is the 'architectonic' virtue conceptually unifying the different virtues.

To be a good person is to have *phronesis,* but to have *phronesis* is to have "a superior form of moral knowledge" (Zagzebski 1996: 199). The virtuous person is able to:

> (...) know the right thing to do in a way that cannot be predicted in advance. Aristotle claims that moral virtue is logically connected with *phronesis,* and *phronesis* involves an insight into particulars that may not fully be captured by a general rule. This means that *phronesis* is logically connected with experience, at least for humans, so it is logically impossible for humans to obtain virtue without experience.
>
> (ibid: 119-120)

To rephrase: to have *phronesis* is to have a 'superior form of moral knowledge' – which may only be acquired through experience. To be practically wise is not a skill, one cannot be 'taught' to be virtuous as one can be 'taught' to type. To have *phronesis* is to be a mature individual – and to have had a great number of interactions with the world around him. Reading experience is one of the series of experiences which help the individual's mind towards maturity, which aid in the fostering of *phronesis,* which leads to superior moral knowledge.

So what difference does it make if we approach literary intelligence as a virtue? If literary intelligence is a virtue, than it is *good to have*, it renders its possessor more admirable, and the world more desirable. Consequences are even further reaching if we remind ourselves that literary intelligence is a textual instantiation of *phronesis. Phronesis* is not merely any virtue, but the central coordinating virtue without which it is impossible to become a mature moral human being.

More than by any amount of "Personal, Social and Health Education", the moral dimension of any system of schooling may be pursued through intensive attention to literature and extensive reading at any level.

Not only is it possible to defend the practice of extensive reading and literary education in schools by identifying literary intelligence as a virtue: it also has a large number of consequences for schools aiming to foster this quality. Literary intelligence is not a skill, therefore it cannot be taught as one would a skill. What can virtue ethics teach us about the acquisition of *phronesis* that is relevant for an educational fostering of this virtue through the practice of extensive reading?

I identify the following consequences:

(1) Literary Intelligence, not being *essentially* a skill, cannot be *taught,* but only fostered. As a virtue it must be acquired as any other virtue: by practice. This implies that literary intelligence is acquired mostly through extensive reading rather than instruction. This privileges Sustained Silent Reading over assorted forms of classroom instruction.

(2) Literary Intelligence, being a moral trait, has a motivation and success component. The 'motivation' component must be internal rather than external for the trait to be fully moral. Like the example of the Laconian proffered in the *Ethica Nicomacheia* (NE 1248b38-1249a3) it is possible that students may acquire literary intelligence through an appeal to an extrinsic motivation. (Perhaps an appeal to aesthetic prestige in certain social groups.) That being said – if we approach literary intelligence as a moral trait it ought to follow on Virtue-theoretical grounds that the motivational component of literary intelligence is more pronounced if the underlying motivation is intrinsic rather than extrinsic.

(3) The aim of education for literary intelligence ought to be a lifelong reading habit. We may *acquire* literary intelligence for the most part while being subjected to a system of education – but just as we do not cease to be truthful after being habituated into truthfulness so ought we conceptualize habituating literary intelligence as laying the groundwork for a lifelong habit.

(4) Because the aim of education for literary intelligence is the fostering of a lifelong reading habit the focus of reading education should be – unsurprisingly perhaps – on *reading* and the choice of narrative literature to be read should be determined on an individual basis. This follows from the fact that every virtue is a personal character trait and my exercise of literary intelligence is tied into my personhood and individuality. Products of narrative literature too, are unique intellectual products. Whether an item of narrative literature will be to my like or dislike – indeed will strike an individual chord in me is a question that can only be answered *a posteriori.* I need to be acquainted with the text and enter a dialogue with it before that question can be answered. This observation should lead us to question the focus on 'set texts' in education and offers an argument for a level of student autonomy in choosing reading material.

(5) Because the task of the teacher is to foster reading habits, and in literary intelligence, intrinsic motivation is most effective in bringing about success, it follows that the teacher too ought to be actively in interested in reading and have active reading habits. Because a virtue is acquired not only through virtuous action but also by example and emulation, it follows that a reading teacher who is *aliteracy* , being able to read well but not having an interest in it, is not an admirable trait in teachers. (Nathanson, Pruslow & Levitt 2008) and the teacher will be generally less successful than a reading teacher imbued with a love for reading. Dispositions are not only of prime importance for students – we need assume teachers have them before students can acquire them. One could go so far as to argue that someone uninterested in reading should not work in reading education. This might be especially pertinent for primary teachers as secondary teachers are by definition subject specialists. – *dispositions* in teachers and students are of prime importance. Indeed it could be argued that The teacher as *exemplar* means in the first place the teacher as an example in being interested in reading, and hence literature. Also because virtues are acquired through experience, action, and emulation, it would follow that literary intelligence is not only fostered by the school environment but that the home situation is of prime importance in the acquisition of literary intelligence.

(6) Because the goal of reading education is a lifelong reading habit and literary intelligence is a virtue and not basically a skill we may question the wisdom of subjecting reading habits to examinations. Skills can be measured – but virtues cannot as such. An emphasis on testing is an emphasis on external motivation which may well positively inhibit the development of intrinsic reading motivation. Because fostering literary intelligence is primarily a moral exercise it cannot sit well in educational systems which are primarily outcome-based . It is no coincidence that historical advocates of reading education have argued vociferously against (variations on) outcome-based education, from Leavis's 'industrialized education' to Bantock's critiques of 'planned education' and comprehensivization fuelled by external political demands to Holbrook and Cox's critique of neoliberal versions of the same fundamentally utilitarian view on education. The fact that the political decision regarding what is 'useful' changes – does not mean there is a change to the essentially utilitarian ethos of a system of education.

§6.6 Literary intelligence cannot be taught as such, but only fostered.

Reading education may take a number of forms, but Krashen (2004) only identifies two major forms of reading education: *Free Voluntary Reading* and *Direct Instruction.* Free Voluntary Reading is defined by Krashen (2004) as:

> Reading because you want to, no book reports, no questions at the end of the chapter. (…) FVR is the reading most of us do obsessively all the time.
>
> (Krashen 2004: 1)

He states that in-school free reading programmes "provide some of the clearest evidence for the power of reading". Direct instruction as understood by Krashen is 'skill-based' (ibid: 18). If literary intelligence is a virtue than skill-based instruction ought to be less efficient than Voluntary Free Reading in increasing reading comprehension.

As Krashen points out, there is a spate of studies that have found direct instruction to be overwhelmingly less efficient than Free Voluntary Reading. The virtue-theoretical approach to reading education may offer additional reasons as to why this is the case. One of the reasons for this may be is that whereas *phronesis* is preoccupied with training a mental sensitivity towards subtle particulars, direct instruction is focused on rule-following. However, the correct use of natural language is not simply a question of rule-following. And even if a grammatical rule is clear – that does not mean the rule in question will always correspond to the actual use of language. The rule governing the use of the words *less* and *fewer* is particularly clear, nonetheless it is not hard to catch a quality newspapers writing about 'three items or less'.

Through reading we may come across the subtle shades in meaning that words may have , rendering memorisation of vocabulary lists – which restrict the semantic richness of words - less efficient. I, for instance, learned the difference between being 'uninterested' and 'disinterested' from reading a nineteenth-century text speaking of the importance of 'disinterested government' which I found an exceedingly quaint turn of phrase.

Comprehension of complicated texts, including a grasp of the nuances of words is part and parcel of literary intelligence, an instantiation of *phronesis.*
It follows from this observation that a literary education is not and cannot be a subject among others. Raymond Williams argued, when he criticized some of F.R. Leavis's educational proposals in saying that:

> To put on literature, or more accurately upon criticism, the responsibility of controlling the quality of the whole range of personal and social experience, is to expose a vital case to a damaging misunderstanding. English is properly a central matter of all education, but it is not, clearly, a whole education.
>
> (Williams 1958: 255)

However, if literary intelligence, in the form of literary intelligence is structurally similar to *phronesis*, and *phronesis* is the architectonic and central intellectual virtue without which we cannot be said to have any other virtues, we must ask ourselves whether or not Raymond Williams was mistaken, or in what sense, if any, his statements must be qualified.
He may be correct in stating that *English* is not clearly, a whole education, but the particular Leavisian stance to English was such that it prompted Marshall McLuhan to state that Leavis: "ended the idea that English was a subject" (Pradl: 1995). After all, what is central to Leavis's conception of English is the operation of the central coordinating literary intelligence which approaches literature through "an artistic evaluation which is inseparable from the exercise of a delicately poised moral tact". (McLuhan 1944:272)
Marshall McLuhan, who studied with Leavis, exercises the same kind of intelligence in his work in Media Studies and Leavis's influence on McLuhan is well–documented. There seems to be persuasive case that Leavis' concept of literary intelligence has a remit beyond the literary or even the textual.

Although we can speak of *literary* intelligence, it transcends the literary: as Leavis himself put it: "I don`t believe in any "literary values", and you won`t find me talking about them: the judgements the literary critic is concerned with are judgements about life" (Leavis 1972: 97)

English is then clearly not a whole education, but a lifelong training of the literary intelligence is. Any educational system that wished to educate for life rather than merely a living should take an active interest in this notion of intelligence, and the processes that foster its growth. Literary education in so far as it promotes the kind of intelligence concomitant with the virtue of *phronesis* should therefore be a basic emphasis of the wider educational system. Not only because a literary education, fostering Literary intelligence is a *good* thing, but because its basic relationship to the virtue of *phronesis* possibly makes it the *best* educational endeavour from a moral point of view. Taking all of this together, we may say that literary education properly understood cannot be confined to the state of a subject among others, rather we ought to consider it an ethos, pervading the entire educational system.

§6.7 Literary intelligence can only be acquired fully through an appeal to intrinsic motivation

But there is another reason why Free Voluntary Reading is much more successful than its skills-based counterpart. In treating literary intelligence, and thereby comprehensive reading, as a virtuous trait rather than as a skill it is important to pay attention to the motivational component.

Motivation is so particularly important for virtues because the "motivational component of a virtue defines it more than external effectiveness does, whereas it is the reverse in the case of skills." (Zagzebski 1996: 115) For us to have some character trait that is to be considered 'good' – we must at some level be determined to have it. We must want it, or at the very least want its consequences. We cannot be fully mature moral beings if we decide to be something else. If this were not the case, then to be virtuous would not be admirable.

On the contrary, it *is* admirable, so a virtue must be something we want and something we are motivated to be. Again, were we not motivated in some sense towards being good, being courageous, being curious, being thorough, there would be no merit in our being good, being courageous, being curious, or being thorough.

So what, in literary intelligence, is the motivational component, and what is the concomitant reliability component? The motivation component would be a quest for knowledge, a certain kind of knowledge which would exhibit itself even in the question we put ourselves when we turn the pages: "I wonder what happens next", or any kind of curiosity which leads us to pick up a book – being curious, wanting to be part of the narratives contained in it.

The motivation towards virtue is not a matter of a great and existential commitment made under dramatic circumstances: being motivated towards some good is a very deep-seated, work-a-day, unspectacular but nonetheless driving force to keep continuing to do what we do well – whether it is being truthful or being an intelligent reader.

After all, once we have acquired a virtue – and we may not even be very much aware of its being there – we simply go on with what we do naturally. It will have become a second nature to us – and if we were continuously aware of the commitment we make when orienting us towards some good that in itself would be an indication that we would not be in possession of the virtue concomitant to that good, for it would not have become, for us, a second nature.

Our motivation shows itself in the *freedom* of *free reading*. For a virtue to be a virtue proper, we need to be intrinsically motivated to pursue those activities of which the virtues are its excellences. Literary intelligence being the virtue of reading excellently, then has as its motivation component the being motivated to read, the loving to read, the wanting to read without being told to.

This is not to say that actions pursued out of an *extrinsic* motivation are entirely without merit, indeed, Aristotle's example of the Laconian proves otherwise. Aristotle, in his *Eudemian Ethics* (1248b36 – 1249a17) proffers the example of 'civic dispositions, such as the Laconians have'. He distinguishes these dispositions, rendering people 'merely' good (*agathos*) and those – who are motivated towards virtue for its own sake, and are hence both good and noble (*kalos kagathos*). Anthony Kenny, in his *Aristotle on the Perfect Life* (Kenny 1992) states the difference between *kalos kagathos* and Laconian as follows:

> The Laconian, like any virtuous man, performs virtuous actions for their own sake, because they are the acts that virtue requires; where he differs from the noble person is in the answer he gives to the second order question "What is the point of being virtuous?" The *kalos kagathos* gives the answer "Because virtue is splendid, fine, and noble" ; the Laconian gives the answer "Because virtue pays"
>
> (Kenny 1992: 12)

The Laconian may share some of the excellences that a *kalos kagathos* has. His virtue may be as *reliable* as that of the *kalos kagathos,* but this does not render them morally equivalent. On the contrary: it is better to be both good *and* noble than to be merely good.

Virtue ethics is, as a theory, more interested in aiming for the top than avoiding the bottom. An example of an extrinsically motivated reader might perhaps be, say, a literary critic who comes to insightful readings of given texts – but for an ulterior purpose. If his judgements stem *also* from external motivations (he may be interested in academic power, have certain political ambitions, or may be eager to please a certain 'in-crowd') his judgements are not thereby invalidated – but he is more properly considered a Laconian, and his reading practice is morally inferior to that of one who loves to read for its own sake. How do these insights relate to reading education? If this dissertation's thesis holds and literary intelligence is best approached as a virtue than there is no denying the motivational component of the virtue of literary intelligence. A reading education which results in readers being intrinsically motivated to read is much more preferable to a reading education which aims to elicit conformist reading patterns, and uses rewards and punishments to achieve this goal.

What is then the relationship between motivation and reading education? The research offers some fascinating observations. As Krashen (2004) puts it, educational research "offers no support for the use of rewards and suggests (…) that rewards may be harmful. If an activity (reading well and intensively) is good in its own right, than using rewards to bring children to do it may effectively undermine the pursuit of this activity. Smith (1988) puts it as follows:

> "Every child knows that anything accomplished by coercion, no matter how benign, cannot be worth doing in its own right"
>
> (Smith, F: 1988)

By implementing a structure reinforcing extrinsic motivations for pursuing activity *y* we may inadvertently undermine the development of intrinsic motivations. This has as a consequence that we render a kalokagathonic into a Laconic activity, effectively undermining the nobility of a virtue.

A programme of reading education, in order to do justice to the moral import of reading education, it ought to foster intrinsic motivation, and be dissuaded from imposing extrinsic rewards or punishments. It should not be thought a coincidence that when asked how to encourage reading, students rarely recommend rewards. Ivey and Broaddus (2001) asked 1,765 sixth graders what stimulated them to read. Only 7 percent mentioned extrinsic rewards.

Indeed, when teachers believe students to be 'reluctant readers' more often than not it is the case that "students were not reluctant to read but were only reluctant to read school-assigned material (Bintz 1993). There is little evidence that an appeal to extrinsic motivations does anything more than – grudgingly – elicit the desired behaviour. But the fostering of a virtue is an entirely different matter than an elicitation towards specified behaviour.

The notion that an appeal to extrinsic motivation may 'crowd out' the essential internal motivations rendering our activities truly virtuous is commented on at length in various publications by the American educationalist Alfie Kohn.

In his article "How Not to Teach Values" (Kohn, A. 1997), Kohn comments on programmes of 'Character Education' and unmasks them as "for the most part, a collection of exhortations and extrinsic inducements to make children work harder and do as they're told". This is not commensurable with a programme of character education in so far as character is understood in virtue-ethical terms.

Because intrinsic motivation is so fundamentally connected to real character education and the pursuit of virtue is cannot take place outwith the context of character development, it follows that extrinsic inducements are quite dangerous if it can be shown that the use of extrinsic inducements undermines intrinsic motivation. The claim is contentious, but would make sense from a virtue-ethical perspective. The claim that this 'overjustification-effect' exists is vigorously defended by – among others - Deci et.al. (2001) and there seems to be enough evidence for the statement to warrant carefulness when introducing extrinsic rewards or punishments.

Another argument against extrinsic motivations would be that the purpose of a literary education is a lifelong reading habit. This habit is unsustainable if not for people actually enjoying their reading activity. Focusing on an internal motivation is then much more promising.

§6.8 What, if literary intelligence is a virtue, is its reliability component?

If literary intelligence is a virtue, it is essentially not a skill and will function in a very different manner as would a skill. Because of its being a virtue, it cannot be proceduralized; it cannot be placed in a *schema* for it is the result of a sensibility, a fine awareness of social and moral particulars.

Such an awareness *cannot* be exhaustively codified. This means that the reliability component, the tangible result of *my* exercise of the virtue of *phronesis* will not be identical to the result of your exercise of the selfsame virtue. This is because every virtue is a deep quality, an excellence, of my character and hence in inalienable part of my selfhood. My exercise of the virtue of *phronesis* is also *my* exercise and in exercising it I advertise, so to speak, my moral individuality. So too when it comes to exercising my literary intelligence upon a given text – in reading it and interpreting it, I do so individually.

Different individuals' readings of a given text may be in agreement with each other, or they may differ , sometimes radically. The object of literary intelligence being *phronesis* , it is impossible to ascertain with total certainty how reliable a literary education is, but then this is impossible to ascertain for *any* education which has character traits as its object. As Maritain argued: the object of Art is an objectively perceptible work of art, the object of *Phronesis* however, is the mind itself which, though real, cannot be perceived as one would an inanimate object.

Also, because a virtue is tied to one's moral identity and is as such unlike a skill, it does not lead to identical responses with regards to the same literary texts. Indeed if it would, if all were in agreement that a literary text *a* could exhaustively be interpreted as *y, y* being the body of possible interpretations of *a,* than literary intelligence could not be a virtue.

It is in the exercise of literary intelligence that our individuality, our likes and dislikes, show. It is our individuality that renders our literary judgements unique, but literary intelligence being a virtue makes that our judgements are not merely instantiations of our personal likes and dislikes, but are in themselves reasoned judgements that ought to be able to stand up to inquiry.

§6.9 Why the aim of a literary education should be to lay the foundation for a lifelong reading habit

A virtue is a *habit.* It is an entrenched character trait, entwined with our selfhood and inseparable from it. If we conceptualize literary intelligence as a virtue, than it too must be a habit. Not only must it be merely a habit though. For it to be a virtue it must be a *lifelong* habit. Were it not than it would be the case that even though it were a virtue, it would be no serious matter or moral lapse if we were to lose this habit somewhere along life's way. But this is impossible. It is one of the hallmarks of a virtue that we do not willingly surrender it.

This insight has consequences for how we think about the acquisition of literary intelligence. We cannot separate it from having a lifelong reading habit. Literary intelligence is, after all, a mature response to literary texts which is dependent on this lifelong reading habit.

Reading well is ontologically dependent on reading much. There are no shortcuts to becoming a competent and intelligent reader, and even if we do become competent and intelligent readers, we are not thereby done. As in any virtue we can and must always strive to do better. Indeed we would not be good readers if did not regret the fact we cannot read as much as we would like to.

The goal of reading education ought to be at assist the pupil into acquiring a lifelong habit of reading. Nothing less will do. The habit must be maintained where any kind of external inducement is absent – it must be pursued voluntarily, or not at all. It follows therefore that much emphasis should be placed on the happiness that results from an extensive reading habit and – more contentiously perhaps – reading education in schools should be mostly *fun.* Pupils are themselves the best judges of what they *want* to read. Indeed, Krashen (2004) makes the case that any reading that pupils do is good, even reading comic books. Krashen mentions the following story of comic-book publisher Jim Shooter:

On a November day in 1957, I found myself standing in front of Miss Grosier's first grade class in Hillcrest Primary School, trying to think of a really good word. She had us playing this game in which each kid had to offer up a word to the class, and for every classmate who couldn't spell your word you got a point, provided of course that you could spell the word. Whoever got the most points received the coveted gold star.

"Bouillabaisse", I said, finally.

"You don't even know what that is," Miss Grosier scolded.

"It's fish soup."

"You can`t spell that"

"Can too"

"Come here. Write it," she demanded

I wrote it, she looked it up, and admitted that it was, indeed correct.

Easiest gold star I've ever won. And right here, right now, I'd like to thank, albeit somewhat belatedly, whoever wrote the Donald Duck comic book in which I found the word bouillabaisse. Also I'd like to thank my mother who read me that comic book and so many others when I was four or five (…) I learned to read from those sessions long before I started school. While most of my classmates were struggling with *See Spot Run,* I was reading *Superman.* I knew what indestructible meant, could spell it, and would have cold-bloodedly used it to win another gold star if I hadn't been banned from the competition after

(Shooter 1986: A85 quoted in Krashen (2004))

Apart from eliciting pleasurable reading experiences, research has also found that a steady diet of comic-book reading amounts to a large exposure to print matter. With a comic book averaging about 2,000 words, a comic book a day amounts to a print exposure of almost 750,000 words, a total approaching the yearly reading volume of middle-class children. (Krashen 2004: 97).

Krashen also mentions a number of studies which have found that pupils who read almost nothing but comic books still make significant gains in reading comprehension and "do not score significantly below average in reading comprehension (ibid: 102) but even so such reading habits are relatively rare and it is found that comic books serve as a conduit to book reading. (ibid: 110)

Light reading in itself may not be enough to develop reading comprehension to its widest possible extent – but its serving as a 'conduit' is understandable from a virtue ethical perspective: Literacy, understood as literary intelligence, is an instantiation of virtue of *phronesis.* Phronesis is a trait which we can only be said to *have* when we have achieved some level of psychological maturity. From the perspective of a mind well-versed in the highest achievements of the literary mind comic books or light reading may found to be inferior in quality – but such reading matter is nonetheless a necessary step in the *acquisition* of intellectual virtue.

Even so we should be careful not to dismiss light reading as 'inferior' as such – for excellence only exists in relation to our character traits superiority or inferiority are not transcendent qualities. They are always superior or inferior in relation to *someone.* For something to be *good* it must be *good for a concrete person.* The 'goodness' of reading matter must be understood first and foremost as appropriateness to the person reading. Dostoyevsky may be very good – but it is no good to someone who would already struggle with Stephenie Meyer's *Twilight* series.

Dostoyevsky must then wait until an ocean of reading matter has been consumed and the mind has been readied. 'Goodness' must be understood as a concrete 'good for me', or 'good-for-*a*', not as an abstract 'good-as-such'-ness. If we are consistently exposed to a pleasurable reading habit and many opportunities for gorging on reading matter we find enjoyable, it follows that we have greater chances of acquiring a lifelong reading habit, a love of the written word, and so may acquire a greater level of practical wisdom, of *phronesis*, than we otherwise would have.

The goal of literary education is then not exposure to a set canon of texts – indeed this may be entirely counterproductive – but rather the elicitation of a pleasurable habit.

For those able to master it, a taste for great literature will follow in its wake. This has consequences for the question whether or not literary education should focus on pupils being exposed to 'great' literature: in other words: whether or not the focus of reading education should be on being exposed to a 'canon' of great works.

§6.10 Literary intelligence is acquired through the practice of extensive personal reading.

For our literary intelligence to foster one must be exposed to as much reading matter as possible – and this reading matter must be in principle enjoyable. If it is not enjoyable we shall not develop a love for reading, without a love for reading we shall never acquire a lifelong reading habit, without such a habit it is nigh impossible to achieve literary intelligence to any great extent. The kind of texts we are capable of tackling depends on how we have developed as persons we are. The judgement that a certain literary work may be considered extremely valuable reading matter by those who have fostered their literary intelligence may be considered a trustworthy judgement. And in any given national literature there are books and authors which have been given pride of place, which are accorded accolades and honours on account of them being perceived as being especially powerful exemplars of the human condition, communicating great truths that transcend the merely here and now.

This may well be true, but in order for one to be able to come to a fruitful reading of these – often very complex – texts one must already have achieved a very high level of reading comprehension as well as a commensurate moral and psychological maturity. This is so because if literary intelligence is an instantiation of *phronesis,* then it is impossible for the young to possess it. If literary intelligence is ontologically related to *phronesis* than it follows that a certain kind of psychological maturity is needed for a reader to fruitfully read the most challenging – and rewarding – of novels.

A strictly canon-oriented curriculum, a course in literature where the choice of reading matter is made on the grounds of the cultural and historical prestige of certain authors and texts, may then well subvert the interest of the reader to that of a programme of cultural reproduction.

Whereas cultural continuity is in itself a good thing, even a condition of the continued functioning of civilization and our acquiring virtues, cultural continuity must not be confused with cultural reproduction. TS Eliot understood this when he stated that tradition can only be acquired through struggle, through meeting it as an individual, and cannot be understood as a corpus that can be transmitted whole to a passive new generation. English speakers may be properly proud of counting such authors as Shakespeare, Spenser, Donne, Milton, Pope, Dickens, Orwell and Rushdie, as well as many others as part of their heritage. It would be good for children to be introduced to their works at some level and have a grasp of literary history. However, being taught literary history does not equate having had a literary education.

The goal of literary education is a lifelong reading habit, it is acquiring the ability to live intimately with the written word. Knowing *about* literature is valuable – but also something completely different than actually acquiring a fruitful reading habit.

In so far as sixteen-year olds are capable of reading some Shakespeare, Dickens, Milton and Pope than by all means they ought to be introduced to it – but only because they can offer valuable reading experiences. There seems to be little merit in reading Shakespeare for Shakespeare's sake, for great literature cannot be so without a reader to consider him so. There is no merit in any text as such, the merit lies in its being read, in the active participation of the reader's mind with it. Whereas ideally people should read 'the best that has been thought and said' – it is also the case that the best is the enemy of the good.

Our reading habits ought rather be steered towards 'good things that have been thought and said' rather than the more exclusive and traditional Arnoldian literary *telos*. Here, too the perfect is the enemy of the good.

There is no denying that canons have been used to as tools for cultural dominance – after all: *quis judicabit?* Who gets to decide which work makes it on the list and which does not? Good, well-read teachers ought to be able to recommend books the pupil might enjoy on an individual basis. There are many thousands of great works to choose from. Consecrating a limited canon as a fulcrum of literary education, limiting the choice readers, and backed up by the ever-present external motivation of the exam system, may well result in having a deleterious effect on the intrinsic motivation of readers. Canons are part and parcel of a closed society – and a deep longing for lists of approved authors, reading lists and consecrated 'great' works which ought be studied to the exclusion of others may be considered according to Cyrille Offermans, a Dutch literary critic and author, as a symptom of cultural confusion, a restorative desire.

In an article published in NRC Handelsblad (10 September 2005) Offermans argues against moves to codify a 'canon' of Dutch literary works. His most persuasive arguments are twofold:

His first argument is that investing a text with a canonical status is to inhibit the reader to engage with it *as* a text. It makes it more difficult to read the text in question separate from the cultural authority with which it is imbued. The full force of a text cannot come to the fore unless we approach it as a text.

Furthermore, Offermans argues that the problem is not so much that pupils do not read 'high' literature and prefer reading Giphart (an up-market popular author) over Willem Frederik Hermans (one of the 'Big Four' of post-war Dutch writers), but rather that they do not seem to read much *at all.*

If there is a culture of illiteracy in schools – by which is meant a culture inhospitable to the practice of extensive reading. Imposing a list of 'canonical' literature will not serve its purpose. The goal of a literary education is the habituation of the literary intelligence. This has two consequences for the question of whether or not 'canons' of literature are suitable for use in education. A reading habit can only be acquired through extensive reading – a reading practice much wider than the reading of those works included in a 'canonical' list invested by cultural authority by prominent literary critics.

Also, if this list even were to truly encompass 'the best that has been thought and said', than it would follow that readers would only be capable of reading it with some level of fruition if they have already achieved a very high level of reading competence. This would make such lists of limited value of students who are yet to be imbued with a love for reading. Offermans suggests it would be a good thing if graduate students in the field of Dutch literature had read each and every work included in the proposed canon.

At the same time, there can be no awareness without there being something to be aware of. Indeed some kind of canonicity which imbues great literature seems to be a condition for moral communication to take place in any society. This, at least, is the position of Alasdair Macintyre. In his *Idea of an Educated Public* (Macintyre 1985) he states that the idea of an educated public presupposes that such a community can only exist where: "there is some large degree of shared background beliefs and attitudes, informed by the widespread reading of a common body of texts, texts which are accorded canonical status within that community" (Macintyre 1985: 19)

By a canon, Macintyre does not mean a body of texts that can be set up as a 'final court of appeal'. Indeed, such a thing would be impossible, for sound theoretical reason any text set up in such a role would immediately elicit an enormous variety of opposing interpretations[41] . However, Macintyre does advocate a canon to which one could make a certain sort of appeal, an appeal that 'has to be treated with a special seriousness, that to controvert requires a special weight of argument'.

What form does such a Macintyrean canon take? What makes texts, for Macintyre, so special that an appeal to them should be treated differently than other arguments? Canonical texts, in Macintyre's reading, are a shared possession, indeed a cultural heritage of a particular community but it is not merely the shared possession that makes these texts canonical, as Macintyre points out: there must also be an "established tradition of interpretative understanding of how such texts are to be read and construed." (Macintyre: 1985, 19)

[41] Examples of such a 'final canonicity' of texts are the Bible during the period of the English Commonwealth and the works of Marx in the former communist states.
Both regimes could not control the varied, sometimes highly subversive, readings that came into being. It could suppress them, but not control them. The Puritan and Communist canons in fact created characters as dissident, unruly and uncontrollable as George Fox and Ernst Bloch respectively.

Macintyre even goes so far as to strongly distinguish a 'literate and reading' public from an 'educated' public. For Macintyre it seems inconceivable that there can be a form of literary education which does not refer to canonical texts. And in doing so he makes a statement almost Leavisian in its stringency: "mass literacy in a society which lacks both canonical texts and a tradition of interpretative understanding is more likely to produce a condition of public mindlessness than an educated public" (ibid.) At the same time these remarks remain tentative: Macintyre does not elaborate on them, other than to muse that there is no more 'educated public' and indeed no more 'western culture' as he interprets it:

> I think the great disaster has already happened. I think the West is already gone. What we have to do is find means of constructing and sustaining local forms of community through which we can survive this age.
>
> (Pearson 1994:42)

On the other hand – it could be argued that arguments basing themselves on canonical texts and a received interpretative framework *are* so important for Macintyre because, in his view, there is no such thing transcendental or abstract moral reasoning. Indeed our very notion of rationality is historically – and therefore – culturally determined.

But even if we accept this latter assertion as true, need we go so far as to adopt Macintyre's notion of the canon? For both Aristotle and Macintyre, we cannot free rational debate cannot bring any resolution and cannot lead to progress unless its participants are educated through a particular moral tradition. In so far as we are successful human beings we need integration in a wider moral tradition. An appeal to a canonical work – to that extent – becomes an appeal to a cultural marker, a recognizable symbol. And such an appeal is an appeal made to *others*:

> Practical reasoning is by its nature (…) reasoning together with others, generally within some determinate set of social relationships. (…) The making and sustaining of those relationships is inseparable from the development of those dispositions and activities through which each is directed towards becoming an independent practical reasoner. So the good of each cannot be pursued without also pursuing the good of all those who participate in these relationships.
>
> (Macintyre 1999: 107)

Seen within this social context of practical reasoning Macintyre assumes a canon not because of any inherent superiority that these texts might have (although one might assume they must have been of a unique stature to have been recognized as canonical works) but rather because a reference to them would be understood as being of particular salience in the community we find ourselves involved in. And because the very structure of our human life is one of dramatic narrative, the narratives that are recognized as particularly meaningful over an extended period of time gain for themselves positions that are vital to the continued existence of the tradition and community we are members of:

> A living tradition then is a historically extended, socially embodied argument, and an argument precisely in part about the goods which constitute that tradition. Within a tradition the pursuit of goods extends through generations. Hence the individual's search for his or her good is generally and characteristically conducted within a context defined by those traditions of which the individual's life is a part and this is true both of those goods which are internal to practices and of the goods of a single life. Once again the narrative phenomenon of embedding is crucial: the history of a practice in our time is generally and characteristically embedded in and made intelligible in terms of the larger and longer history of that tradition through which the practice in its present form was conveyed to us; the history of each of our own lives generally and characteristically embedded in and made intelligible in terms of the larger and longer histories of a number of traditions.
>
> (id: 222)

At the same time, however, the argument for the canon seems to be undercut by Macintyre's insistence that the cultural catastrophe has already taken place. If this is true we cannot hope to educate anyone for membership of the 'educated public' for the very socio-cultural conditions for the existence of this group are lacking. Also, if there is no more 'educated public' and western culture has been essentially subverted, is it still sensible to speak in terms of a canon?

After all; if a canon consists of the symbolical literary texts serving as the foundational narratives of our community it is no longer certain that there is *still* a canon if the community has gone. The canon is not and cannot be a locus of transcendent culture. What essentially are canonical works is dependent on our social structure.

All in all, Macintyre's case for the canon contains valuable elements: the first being the identified need for some kind of commonality in our reading, the second being his postulated distinction between a reading public and an educated public.

What it does not presuppose, is the idea of a canon which is a closed list of consecrated works, a list which no longer allows for addition or subtraction. Macintyre's canon is fluid: If we assume a certain kind of commonality in reading matter, a certain corpus of literary works of special importance to a given cultural community, we need not assume this corpus will remain exactly the same in the passage of time.

Does the Macintyrean distinction between a reading public and an educated public stand up? I think not. I would argue that the distinction between a reading and educated public is too artificial and is dependent more on a notion of literary study as a study of literary content rather than a study of form.

If there is mass literacy, a reading culture, a widely held *practice* of reading among a populace it is difficult to see how this could lead – not to literary debate and public argument – but rather to a "condition of public mindlessness" [42]. Even if there were at the outset no canonical texts – it is unlikely that no texts should emerge which proved to be more popular than others – even if all literate members of society started out by reading different books – if such a thing were possible – would it not be a matter of time before enthusiastic readers started advising others to read their own favourites? A reading experience, being something that gives pleasure and insight in the human condition, is something that wants sharing. Nothing makes a text canonical but a devoted fan-base.

At the same time it seems unlikely there can be a mass literacy without there being – at the outset – canonical texts. But can there be mass literacy without 'a common interpretative understanding'? After all, this is the second condition Macintyre attaches to the fostering of an educated public. Here too, the question is one of degree, if a canon may be little more than a number of texts which are more commonly read and referred to than others, how common must a 'common interpretative understanding' be? Obviously a common interpretative understanding cannot be taken to mean that readers will necessarily produce identical interpretative outcomes of their reading.

---

[42] Ibid.

Even under the most restrictive of shared interpretative understandings – such as the Bible or the works of Karl Marx were subjected to in Puritan England or the former Eastern Bloc states, a variety of conflicting readings developed nonetheless. Obviously, if there would be *no* level of shared interpretative understanding at all there could be no communication about what was read *at all*. But we could argue on the basis of Wittgenstein's private language argument that if the idea of a private language is inconsistent and, indeed, the idea of a private *concept* is inconsistent than it would follow equally that there can be no such a thing as a private reading – an interpretative understanding of a text which is essentially incommensurable and incapable of comparison with another person's interpretative understanding. My reading of a text, in so far as it *is* a reading and not – say – a delusional and only marginally text-based fantasy, must be communicable to *some* extent at least.

There are of course degrees of communicability and it is obvious that a reading public becomes a more common reading public if our readings become more communicable, but communicability is already vouched for to the greatest extent by the rules of *genre*.

It is when *genres* are no longer understood, or positively subverted, as in the case of 'creationist' readings of the book of Genesis, that communication over a text is no longer possible. One cannot argue with a creationist who reads a religious poem as one would a eyewitness report – all we can say is that the creationist is mistaken in his choice to approach Genesis as *such* a text. If we have a common understanding that a historical document is one thing, a novel another, and epic religious poetry something else, we have already achieved a far-reaching commonality of reading.

It is surely the case that we can argue that text *a* is artistically superior over text *b* , it may also be argued that it is possible to hypothetically construct a canon of works that may be considered especially representative of a given literary culture, but even on the basis of a Macintyrean defence of the canon, it still seems inappropriate to focus exclusively on a limited number of canonical works in the course of a literary education. The moral salience of the literary experience is founded on the dialectical relationship between reader and text. Both must be present; we cannot privilege one over the other.

To give undue pre-eminence to a limited number of texts extolled for their 'intrinsic worth' is consequently to have misunderstood the nature of literary experience and literary intelligence.

At the same time, we may assume that some books are better, more appropriate, more worthwhile and more valuable than others. It is the task of teachers of literature to identify these texts and motivate her pupils to take them up. As with any advice, it is never a final word on anything – but rather an invitation to share a reading experience – or experiences – which the advisor has found worthwhile. To it, one could possibly add one's own, or register one's disagreement. So too, in an educational setting. The teacher might be aware of reading preferences of the pupil and may steer him or her towards more challenging – and possible even more rewarding – works.

The role of the teacher in fostering a reading habit will be explored in the next paragraph.

§6.11 The role of the teacher

Because the task of the teacher is to foster reading habits, and in literary intelligence, intrinsic motivation is most effective in bringing about success, it follows that teachers ought to be actively in interested in reading and possess active reading habits.

Because a virtue is acquired not only through virtuous action but also by example and emulation, it follows that aliteracy in a reading teacher (that is to say: being able to read well but not having an interest in doing so) is not an admirable trait in teachers. (Nathanson, Pruslow, Levitt 2008). It is found that an aliterate teacher will be generally less successful than one who is imbued with a love for reading.

Dispositions are not only of prime importance for students: we also need to assume that teachers *have* these dispositions before students can even begin to *acquire* them. One could go so far as to argue that someone uninterested in reading should not work in reading education. Dispositions in teachers and students are of prime importance for the realization of admirable character traits. Also because virtues are acquired through experience, action, and emulation, it would follow that literary intelligence is not only fostered by the school environment but that the home situation is of prime importance in the acquisition of literary intelligence.

Virtues are acquired first and foremost through imitation and example. A literary education cannot be pursued in total isolation, without any kind of support or facilitation. After all, what is good not so much the desired behaviour, but the acquired deep-seated habit. This is not just the case for reading, but for every virtue. Aristotle alludes to this when he writes:

> One swallow does not make a summer; neither does one day. Similarly, neither can one day, or a brief space of time, make man blessed and happy.
>
> (Aristotle 1995: 76)

Virtues are acquired as a result from habit and we learn them by doing them:

> We become just by performing just acts, temperate by performing temperate ones, brave by performing brave ones
>
> (ibid: 91-92)

And, one might add, literate through reading.

But because every person's disposition is different, this means only general rules of moral behaviour can be provided, as the acquisition of any virtue is so intimately tied to a person's selfhood that the influence of particular circumstances cannot be avoided. Neither, because they are particular, can their influence be predicted. Everyone becomes literate in slightly different ways then someone else. Broad generalities of our habituations towards being literate may be described, but it is theoretically impossible to devise a 'method' for unfailingly producing literate individuals

So which generalities of habituation can possible be identified? Much depends on the situation of the child or person in question, whether he or she is in school or not and so on. A number of different factors can be identified: the home-situation, the school situation, and general facilitation of the reading habit in society – in particular through the *availability* of print. These factors will be treated in paragraphs 12 to 14

§6.12 The habituation of reading praxis in the home environment.

Baker and Sher (2002) have found evidence for the thesis that the influence of the home situation with regards to literacy is mainly one of *motivation,* finding that "home experiences which promote intrinsic motivation to read are likely to be particularly critical for beginning readers" (Baker and Sher 2002).
A particularly noticeable finding of Baker and Sher was that parental reading motivation is not correlated with wealth or access to reading material (ibid: 201). This is commensurate with Rose's historical findings

> Parental endorsement of [reading for] pleasure uniquely contributed to children's reading motivation. (...) It appears that parents' focus on the pleasure one can derive from reading influences the pleasure that the child takes from reading
>
> (ibid: 262)

Most progress in literacy seems to be made when children are read to by their parents. This would make sense as any art is best acquired through imitation. This too seems to explain the difference in literacy between middle-income and low income parents. Children of both socio-economic groups were exposed to roughly the same amount of print material – but active involvement in reading by one of the parents made a large difference in the effectiveness of the exposition to print. The different level of reading involvement of the parent correlates according to Baker and Sher with how parents view reading.
It is tragic that even though lower-income parents recognize reading as an important skill, literacy as a desirable goal, hereby tend to over-emphasize the didactic importance of reading as a *skill,* thereby unwittingly acting to the detriment of the development of literary intelligence.

Lower-income parents, more than middle-income ones, generally provide pre-school children with skill books (say, ABC books) and conceive of the child's exposure to print as: "a teaching opportunities characterized by drill and practice" (ibid: 264) – with the concomitant deleterious effect on intrinsic motivation that has also been identified by Krashen (Krashen 2004).

Also, children who use skills books instead of storybooks are less likely to be read to by an expert – adult – reader. If we perceive reading as less of a skill and more of a virtue this would make sense – as virtues are acquired through habituation requiring an expert hand. A parent's love of reading may then be easily communicated to a child. A parent who only recognizes reading as a useful skill will not be as capable in fully habituating a child into this praxis.

Home reading, and then particularly reading to small children in the home environment is found to contribute up to 30% in the variance in motivation. It may therefore be considered a factor which ought not to be neglected.

Indeed, there is little hope for children to become intrinsically motivated readers, laying the foundation for a lifelong habit, if parental motivation is lacking. To borrow a phrase from Alasdair Macintyre, we are *dependent rational animals* and not in the least dependent on parental motivation to habituate us into habits of literacy. This is an important factor for our achieving rationality. The importance of shared book reading is also recognized by Yarosz and Barnett (2001) who refer to numerous other studies pointing out the very same factor (a.o.: Scarborough & Dobrich 1994; Bus et al. 1995; Teale 1981), The research shows that the *effect* of parent-preschooler reading is not dependent on socio-economic status. Indeed a large number studies confirm that there are many low-income provide rich literacy environments (Chall 1981; Taylor & Dorsey-Gaines 1988)

Yarosz and Barnett in their study analyzed data obtained from the 1995 (US) National Household Education Survey. They found that although the achieved level of education influences the frequency of parent-preschooler reading, ethnicity was found – at least in the US – to be a large factor.

Non-English speaking Hispanic mothers educated up to BA degree level or higher were 2.5 times less likely to read to their children as white mothers with fewer than twelve years of schooling.

Only a small minority (14%) of non-English speaking Hispanic mothers in the US with fewer than twelve years of schooling read to their child or children every day. It is to be expected that huge gaps of attainment in literacy may consequently have cultural causes as well.

This is not in itself surprising. Not every culture or subculture values literacy to the same extent – and dispositions towards reading will therefore vary. In the Netherlands it was found that ethnic minority children, especially those with a North-African background where very often not read to. One reason for this, apart from the generally low level of educational attainment in North-African families, was that most North African immigrants in the Netherlands are Tamazight (or more precisely: Tarrifit) – a Berber people with an oral culture.

In fact, because of contentious political reasons there has not so far been agreement about a generally accepted Tarrifit writing system. This situation is obviously inconducive to the fostering of a culture of literacy among the Tarrifit people.

The continued lack of educational attainment of second-generation Moroccan immigrants in the Netherlands may be part-attributed to the lack of a culture of literacy in the home, causing the pre-school child to lack an exposure to print and a habituation into literacy. A culture of literacy is beneficial to both the general facilitation of the pre-school's child access to print material and collaborative parent-child storybook reading, both of prime importance for the habituation into a habit of literacy.

§6.13 The habituation of reading praxis in school.

It is not merely the home environment that facilitates reading. The school environment ought to be conducive to the fostering of the reading habit – and in its wake the virtue of practical wisdom.

Here too, as in the home environment, the effect of *imitation* has been confirmed by a number of studies. Indeed if no influence of imitation could have been shown this would have constituted an argument against my thesis that deep qualitative literacy – literary intelligence – is a virtuous rather than a skilful trait. The role of the teacher here is paramount. Virtues are acquired through imitation and emulation, and it would follow that a teacher who does not himself values reading will be less efficient as a teacher of literacy.

There have been a number of studies focusing on the importance of the role of the teacher in fostering – or subverting – intrinsic motivation for certain activities. Brophy (1986) and Deci's (1971) work in the psychology of motivation suggested teachers play are focal points for the development for motivation. Schunk (1990a & b) found that teachers with low self-esteem tend to avoid opportunities for reflection and positive change, negatively affecting a classroom culture. Considering how important intrinsic motivation is for the acquisition of literary intelligence, it is a pertinent question to ask ourselves how the literary disposition of individual teachers consequently influences the fostering of literary education.

Nathanson, S., J. Pruslow, et al. (2008) have surveyed a group of 747 students enrolled in a graduate school of education and found a disconcertingly high level of what they term *aliteracy*. By 'aliteracy' they describe "the ability to read but a disinterest in personal reading." (Nathanson, S., J. Pruslow, et al. (2008): 1). If we approach literary intelligence in terms of an intellectual virtue than the notion of *aliteracy* is troublesome. It is possible to interpret it as an example of a situation where a subject is technically capable of reading but not given to instantiating this capacity.

The possibility of *aliteracy* denotes that the kind of *literacy* that Nathanson, Pruslow et al. are discussing is not structurally similar to literary intelligence. After all one who has literary intelligence – who has the intellectual virtue of literary intelligence – cannot choose to disregard this mental trait. By the very fact that they have literacy skills which are not instantiated it is highly likely that *aliterates* are not in the possession of literary intelligence.

The problem is not of a technical nature. After all: there is no *inability* to read. Rather, aliterates suffer from: "lack of engagement or intrinsic motivation to read, even when they are capable of successfully comprehending material" (ibid: 2)

After identifying aliteracy as a growing problem in the setting of the US educational system, Nathanson, Pruslow et al. ask themselves if the level of aliteracy prevalent among those in the teaching profession might be a possible cause of wider aliteracy found in society.

The research literature suggests that teachers are not by definition enthusiastic readers. Mueller (1973) found that many teachers did not value reading highly. Mour (1977) corroborated Mueller's findings. Smith (1989) found that typical undergraduates majoring in education "possess only moderately positive attitudes about reading" Powell-Brown (2003), too, found a prevalent culture of aliteracy among prospective educationalists. These conclusions were drawn as well by Applegate and Applegate (2004) who referred to the lack of reading enthusiasm as the 'Peter Effect' – describing the general impossibility that one cannot pass on what one does not possess.

Applegate and Applegate found that 51.5% of respondents (of a group of 379 undergraduate education majors) were unenthusiastic readers; this is a worryingly high level of aliteracy among those in the teaching profession or those aiming to enter it.

In turn, Nathanson, S., J. Pruslow, et al. (2008) surveyed a large number of graduate students of education as well as current full-time teachers. Some highly fascinating findings were that there were statistically significant differences between enthusiastic and unenthusiastic readers in the amount of discussion of literature in their high school classes:

> To put it another way, enthusiastic readers were more likely than unenthusiastic reading to report that high school teachers put a great deal of emphasis on discussing their reactions to and interpretations of literature. The most meaningful difference was noted among enthusiastic readers who reported a great deal of emphasis [on] discussions and interpretations of literature in their high school classes
>
> (Nathanson, S., J. Pruslow et al. 2008: 5)

Also, positive early reading experiences were found to be both meaningful and statistically significant with enthusiastic readers being more likely to rate their early reading experiences as positive (ibid: 6). Whereas 56% of unenthusiastic readers reported not having a teacher which exhibited a love of reading, 64% of enthusiastic readers did have such a teacher. Considering the consequences of these findings, it does not appear that Nathanson, Pruslow et al. are far off the mark when they state "teachers as a group [do not] have firmly ingrained reading habits. This is a sobering and unsatisfactory situation which, we believe, could have negative implications for the literacy of future generations." (ibid: 6) If one approaches literary intelligence as a virtue, it is not difficult to see why this is so.

Virtues are not taught as such, they are acquired through practice and emulation of those who already have acquired them. In the case of literary intelligence, when conceptualized as an intellectual virtue, this means that the student ought to be consistently be exposed to literary texts and a pedagogical environment supportive of a lively and active participation with them. An educator who lacks a love of reading cannot (for the lack of the intrinsic motivational component of a virtue) be in the possession of literary intelligence and here too it does not seem possible that one may pass on what one does not possess. Lacking an interest in reading may then well be a strong indication that a candidate in question is not necessarily suited to teach reading at any level beyond technical comprehension. The candidate may well be unsuited to provide an appropriate pedagogical environment where literary intelligence may flourish.

These research findings suggest that it may well be the case that policy-oriented solutions to increase positive reading habits and elicit enthusiasm with regards to reading may be wasted efforts if the professionals delivering these ambitious goals are themselves unattracted by the prospect of extensive reading.

§6.14 The general facilitation of the reading habit: print availability

Other forms of stimulation may be considered outwith the home and school environment. An obvious example would be the availability of reading material in society in general.

A number of fascinating experiments with 'book floods' – where schools and libraries have had a great number of books made available to them - have been undertaken in numerous places. The study of the Bradford Book Flood experiment was documented in Ingham (1981) and its finding were that mere *availability* of reading material having been found to correlate positively with reading habits.

These findings have been substantiated by a number of studies, as reported by Krashen (2004). He contends that simply providing access to large amounts of print material has a discernible positive effect on reading habituation. He mentions a large number of studies finding positive correlations between print availability in the home and amount of personal reading (Morrow 1983; Neuman 1986; Greany and Hegarty 1987; McQuillan 1998; Kim 2003; Lao 2003) Other research has been done into print availability in schools. Krashen mentions (Krashen 2004: 58) that a print-suffused learning environment is found to be generally conducive to a practice of increased reading and, eventually, the fostering of a reading habit.

Positive correlations between print availability and an uptake in the amount of reading were shown at the classroom level by Morrow (1982) and Morrow and Weinstein (1982). An increase in school library stocks were found to result in more reading by Cleary (1939), Gaver (1963), and McQuillan (1998) – the 'Book Flood' experiments as was undertaken in Bradford may also be taken as evidence for this hypothesis.

Also, it is not only increased stocks which correlate with increased reading by students: Krashen reports a number of studies (Houle and Montmarquette (1984); McQuillan and Au (2001)) which found that increased opening hours of school libraries also independently influences the amount of books students take out.

A third factor of influence, found by McQuillan and Au (2001) was the regularity with which teachers took students to the school library. A continuous exposure to a print-rich environment, within or outwith the school is beneficial to an acquisition of a reading habit.

These effects are found not only at the school level: better access to *public* libraries also affects how much students read. A number of studies mentioned by Krashen (2004) in support of this observation are Lance, Welborn and Hamilton-Pennell (1993); Krashen (1995); Worthy and McKool (1996); Ramos and Krashen (1998); Pack (2000). These studies have found, respectively that children are largely dependent on libraries for access to print material (Gaver 1963; Ingham 1981), library quality (in terms of both books and staffing) is strongly relates to students' reading achievement (Lance, Welborn and Hamilton-Pennell 1993), Heyns (1978) reported that children who live closer to public libraries consistently read more.

Ramos and Krashen (1998) report dramatic increases in library use if they occasionally visited the public library during school time and the study of Worthy and McKool (1996) suggested that many children who report to 'hate' reading find themselves more positively disposed to reading after having been introduces to public libraries.

The power of access is great, though not of course absolute. At the same time research findings seem to imply that access is a greater factor in reading stimulation than poverty. A number of studies have correlated poverty with access to print material (Smith, Constantino and Krashen 1996; Neuman and Celano 2001) which both found that affluence correlates strongly with access to print materials. Where children in the affluent Beverly Hills neighbourhood of Los Angeles had an average of 200 books available to them at home, children in the deprived Watts neighbourhood averaged 0.4 books per child. The deprivation of access to print also stretched itself out the wider print environment. Some of the findings of Neuman and Celano (2001) are particularly pertinent. For instance: high-income neighbourhoods have, on average, for more retail outlets selling print material. One studied low-income neighbourhood offered no place to buy young-adult literature, whereas one high-income neighbourhood featured three such outlets. High income neighbourhoods also stock a much wider variety of print material:

> The total number of children's book titles available in the two low-income neighbourhoods was 358 (one title for every twenty children) in one and 55 (one title for every 300 children) in the other. In one high income neighborhood 1,597 titles were available (0.3 per child). Comparing the print-richest and print-poorest, high-income children have 4,000 the times the number of titles available
>
> (Krashen 2004: 69)

Also, public libraries in poor neighbourhoods were found to offer fewer books, fewer opening hours and fewer staff. Krashen rightly points out that these terrifying findings suggest that the first priority of any policy which aims to overcome this vast discrepancy is not more 'instruction' – but rather providing access to print material. McQuillan (1998) found that the relationship between print material and reading achievement held even when the effects of poverty were controlled. This effect was also found by Roberts, Bachen, Hornby and Hernandez-Ramos (1984) and seems to fall in with the observations made by Jonathan Rose in his *Intellectual Life of the British Working Classes* (Rose, J. 2002) where a great many narratives are recorded of individuals who though living in poverty managed to gain some level of access to print materials and hence become successful and intelligent readers – even if their choice of literature was limited. Derek Davis, for instance, reports tapping into his father's collection of Western and detective novels.
In his own words he reported the reading experience as follows:

> Obviously nobody moulded my reading habits. I never had stories read to me at bedtime, and the children's classics remained for me to discover when my own children came along. In one unplanned leap I plunged into reading and found myself simultaneously reading voraciously on several widely differing levels.
>
> (Rose 2002: 377)

This is of course not to say that one ought not to read at bedtime, or not provide children's books – but in the very least providing access to print material may already set a young reader on the course to becoming an intelligent reader, providing a training which will serve him or her for the rest of their life. In the case of Derek Davies – it gave him a flying start at grammar school.

There is of course another reason why access to a wide variety of print material is so important – a large choice of reading matter, of all varying levels of quality activates the reader, makes students seek out what they find enjoyable – and allows for that psychological autonomy which the mature reader ought exhibit. Edward Blishen, writer and teacher, who managed a school library in the 1950s described his pursuit of print matter for his pupils as follows:

> Cheap annuals, poorly written children's novels – I needed to have such things on the shelves. Oh those school libraries that contained nothing but the best, or the very good! Could one expect boys like mine to reach out at once, in all their inexperience, for books so sophisticated and demanding? The presence of familiar bad books made them feel at home in the library...; and the more familiar, informal, boy-managed it seemed to be, the more likely they were to use it.
>
> If I wanted them to become real readers, I argued, then I must ask myself what made anyone whatever a real reader. And surely, part of the process was the discovery. For yourself, of bad, better, best. Literature, like life, was a mongrel business. That was the delight of it. So I must have a mongrel library.
>
> (Blishen 1971*:* 164)

A rich print environment therefore seems to be an important factor in reading stimulation, a virtue ethical theory of literary intelligence may go some way towards explaining this.

It is possible that the mere presence and availability of print material is effective because of its non-intrusiveness.

Indeed, as Zagzebski points out that a virtue is a state of the soul and *it is acquired by long-term consistent habituation.* Foundational to virtues are motivations, and a motivation is described by her as 'an emotion or feeling that initiates and directs action towards an end'. (Zagzebski 1996: 131) As Zagzebski rightly points out – motivations are continually operative and hence cannot be so powerful or present that we are even continually aware of them. Rather, they are persistent, but low-level emotions.

It follows that the guidance of these emotions, that is to say a facilitation of positive emotions towards print, should operate at the same level. There is little room for didacticism in the acquisition of virtues. A well-stocked, clean school library with liberal opening hours sends the message that literacy isn't simply a matter which is found 'important' - rather like washing your hands before dinner, learning your tables of multiplication, eating your greens and like worthy ambitions – but is something which is *natural,* something which is given a pride of place, something which doesn't need a utilitarian justification, because literacy and the acquisition of literary intelligence, are good *in themselves.* For a print-access based stimulation of reading to work it is indeed the naturalness, the normalcy of it, is paramount.

If reading is not considered 'normal' in the society or subculture in which the pupil lives, it is difficult to perceive how it may ever become a natural, indeed 'normal' part of his or her future life. Derek Davies reported that he read because there were books around the house and though his parents did not as such overtly stimulate reading, consumption of print matter – even in the form of the sports paper or the Western novel – was a more or less accepted part of household life. Derek Davies could not have developed into a successful reader, and would have missed out on a valuable and morally relevant form of intellectual development if reading had been *ab*normal in his household.

We may conclude therefore that a variety of social and educational factors influence the acquisition of a reading habit. On the other hand it may also be expected that a view of reading education as is contained in this dissertation will have far-reaching consequences on how literary education is dealt with in the classroom. Some of these consequences will be analysed in the following paragraphs.

It will be argued that, most importantly, literary education may not be considered as one subject among many, but rather as the humane centre of the curriculum, being of value to pupils of all backgrounds and varying intellectual capabilities. The most important immediate consequence of the above considerations is that literary education cannot flourish in the context of a utilitarian 'outcome-based' educational system.

§6.15 The fostering of literary intelligence implies an alternative to 'outcome-based education'

How does treating literary intelligence as a virtue affect educational provisions and structures? For literary intelligence to be considered a virtue, it must have a component of intrinsic motivation. On the contrary, an emphasis on testing is an emphasis on external motivation which may well positively inhibit the development of intrinsic reading motivation. Because fostering literary intelligence is primarily a moral exercise it cannot sit well in educational systems which are primarily outcome-based .

Scrutiny in its day wrote strongly against the then-Labour government's outspokenly technocratic educational policy. Regardless of the contemporary political outlook of *Scrutiny* contributors, it can scarce be argued that their criticism was aimed more at the increasing amount of central planning – fuelled intellectually by a intellectual commitment to utilitarianism. (Bocock and Taylor 2003a & 2003b)

The concept of literary intelligence as an intellectual virtue demands a model of educational praxis unhampered by an ethos of box ticking or immediately measurable 'results'. The growth of virtue cannot be exemplified or discerned in a utilitarian fashion. This is not to say that a literary education does not allow for discernible 'results' – on the contrary – a virtue is a success concept with effects that are not only mental states but rather activities 'in' the world.

This is exactly what makes a deep literary understanding much more than a luxurious or elitist ornamentation – it is important because it fosters practical reason, which is a trait that is important to have, not only for the individual involved but for society as a whole. Martha Nussbaum describes practical reason, *phronesis,* not merely as a mental trait but also as one the basic and universal human capabilities. Indeed, it is probably *the* capability which makes us most recognizably human:

> All human beings participate (or try to) in the planning and managing of their own lives, asking and answering questions about what is good and how one should live. Moreover, they wish to enact their thought in their lives – to be able to choose and evaluate, and to function accordingly. This general capacity has many concrete forms, and is related in complex ways to the other capabilities, emotional, imaginative, and intellectual. But a being who altogether lacks this would not likely to be regarded as fully human, in any culture.
>
> (Nussbaum 1990: 222)

Not only is practical reason needed for *ourselves,* we need it to function socially or in the context of a wider polity. As such, though a theory of literary intelligence is not in itself a *political* theory. It has political ramifications and has consequences for the foundations of educational policy but it would be erroneous to treat it as one –ism among many. It treats with virtues, and virtues are good in themselves and regardless of the social position of them that possess it:

> [The] virtues are virtues, not modes of class oppression: the compassion and gentleness by shown by Jesus to Mary Magdalene, Cordelia to Lear, Bonnhoefer to his Gestapo captors, are themselves virtuous. They are not class property, any more than they are only Christian; they recur in classical Greece, primitive East Africa, contemporary Buddhism. Courage is courage in the battle of Bataan, before Agincourt, at the Hot Gates.
>
> (Inglis 1985: 124)

In Aristotle, as is recognised by Curren and Nussbaum, the viability of the polity is intimately related to the moral functioning of its citizens. A polity in which its citizens are deprived of essential goods, who lack basic levels of sustenance or indeed are poorly educated, cannot be called a stable, let alone a flourishing, polity. At the same time the relationship between individual and social functioning works the other way round as well. It is difficult to come to an actualization of our individual potentials in a dysfunctional state.

The aim of government is then, for Nussbaum: "to produce capabilities to function". Because practical reason is a basic capability, government has a basic responsibility to foster it, and foster it widely.

As Holbrook has shown, a literary education, an education that fosters literary intelligence and practical wisdom may take many forms and is applicable too to those society would rather discard. Virtues admit of degrees, and some will be better at actualizing these traits than others but while excellence may only be achievable to some, the pursuit is relevant and pertinent for all. Nussbaum recognizes this in her analysis of the role of the polity in the pursuit of virtue: because capabilities are basic human potentials, the role of the state is *broad* and *deep*. Deep, because they do not admit to resolution as if they were mere questions of distributive justice: broad, because the fostering of capabilities is not a minority pursuit.

The capability government should be most concerned with is practical reason (Nussbaum 1990, 214) because the pursuit of virtue, culminating in living a good, happy, and moral life, is not something which can be achieved by some *for* others. Indeed, David Carr in his *Educating the Virtues* seizes on this point when he says that: "a morally sound life is a matter of *personal* effort." (Carr 1991: 8)

A virtue is admirable in a person because he or she has acquired them voluntarily or in the very least could have rejected them. He too considers the virtues to be good for more people than their possessors and emphasises the social, and hence, the political importance of developing the virtues:

> [The] moral virtues (...) adapt us to successful social relations with others and renders us an asset rather than a liability in a civilized human community.
>
> (ibid: 48)

We cannot be virtuous without practical reason; we cannot be moral without the deep, practical, contextual, culturally-laden awareness of self and other, the moral know-how that is acquired slowly over the course of a lifetime. A literary education, fostering literary intelligence and practical wisdom may be an important part of a student's moral development.

It will not be the beginning of moral growth, and hopefully it will not be the end either. There can, of course, be no such thing as a 'curriculum for morality', for what it is to be moral can only be learned through moral experiences – and either way morality is not a case of rule-following, or even has much to do of propositional moral knowledge.

It is only after having acquired moral experiences, of which literary experiences may be some, that we acquire these settled traits of characters called virtues, and we only come to a level of moral knowledge, necessarily, deep, contextual, unpredictable, that we may come to some form of moral knowledge:

> It is precisely the moral dispositions called virtues which give content and substance to moral thought, and in the absence of which moral deliberation would hardly be possible.
>
> (ibid: 254)

It would not do to defend the thesis that an intensive literary education 'makes people good' as such. That would be a gross simplification. However, literary education does provide students with a wealth of morally relevant experiences and trains the intellect in a fashion so as to make students more liable to making correct moral choices. For literary education to be morally relevant, it should not be tempted into didacticism. Moral knowledge is not propositional and for literary education to be morally relevant it should not base itself on a model of imparting and acquiring information as such. (cf. (ibid:259))

What would a literary 'curriculum' look like? This question is not easy to answer because this theory does not extend to, and in fact questions the worth of, technical questions concerning the curriculum. It is likely however that a lot can be learned from the critiques levelled against educational schemes by those critics and educationists who have been influenced by this Leavisite notion of 'literary intelligence'. By extension the notion of literary intelligence offers powerful arguments against exclusively "skills-based" approaches to education.

Chapter 7: A deontology of reading education

If virtues are more fundamental than acts, acts are than morally derivative from virtues. Zagzebski has shown how the notions of right and wrong acts, moral duty, justified act, justified belief and unjustified belief might be derived from the aretaic concepts. The moral definitions she provided are also useful for determining whether or not a literary education can be morally defended. In consideration of the fact that beliefs are more fundamental than acts (for certainly we φ because, at some level we have beliefs about φ)

Using the formal definitions of deontic concepts, the following questions will be treated:

1: Is it a justified belief to think an extensive reading habit beneficial to the flourishing life?

2: Is it a justified belief to think an extensive reading habit ought to be promoted and fostered?

3: Is it a belief of epistemic duty to believe an extensive reading habit beneficial to the flourishing life?

4: Is it a belief of epistemic duty to think an extensive reading habit ought to be promoted and fostered?

5: Is it consequently a right act to acquire an extensive reading habit?

6: Is it consequently a right act to promote and foster an extensive reading habit?

7: Is it, *a fortiori,* a moral duty to acquire an extensive reading habit?

8: Is it, *a fortiori,* a moral duty to promote and foster an extensive reading habit?

§7.1 Is it a justified belief to think an extensive reading habit beneficial to the flourishing life?

A *justified belief* is, according to the definition offered by Zagzebski: "what a person who is motivated by intellectual virtue, and who has the understanding of his cognitive situation a virtuous person would have, might believe in like circumstances." (Zagzebski 1996: 241)

The question, then, may be rephrased as: "Would a person who is motivated by intellectual virtue, and who has the understanding of his cognitive situations a virtuous person would have, might believe in like circumstances." Given that there are strong arguments that literary experiences may be considered closely related to real-life experiences, and both may be treated as phenomenological instances of witnessing, it is not difficult to accept that where real-life experiences may be morally salient; this is also the case for literary experiences.

Also considering that there appears to be a strong correlation between the concept of literary intelligence as discerned by Leavis, Bantock and Harding and the Aristotelian faculty of practical wisdom, or *phronesis* we would be, in the very least, *justified* to believe an extensive reading habit beneficial to the flourishing life in the sense that a person with *phronesis may* believe that an extensive reading habit is beneficial to the flourishing life.

§7.2 Is it a justified belief to think an extensive reading habit ought to be promoted and fostered?

Considering that the belief that an extensive reading habit is beneficial to the flourishing life, it follows that it is equally justified to believe it ought to be promoted and fostered. After all, to have a trait *x* which is both admirable desirable is itself an admirable and desirable state. Given that it is desirable to have trait *x* we should endeavour that such traits are promoted and fostered in our societies.

§7.3 Is it a belief of epistemic duty to believe an extensive reading habit beneficial to the flourishing life?

The difference between an epistemic duty and a justified belief is straightforward. Whereas a justified belief is defined as a belief which a virtuous person "might believe" under the circumstances an epistemic duty is a belief which: "is what a person who is motivated by intellectual virtue, and who has the understanding of his cognitive situation a virtuous person would have, would believe in like circumstances." (**ref**) The difference is then that we may be justified to believe various different things we have a moral duty to believe certain other things. For instance; we may be justified to believe that (...) whereas someone else me be equally justified that this is not the case. However we would not consider anyone justified to believe that the world was flat or the Holocaust did not take place.
Beliefs of moral duty do, however, allow for two different senses in which they can be understood.

> A belief is an epistemic duty (strong sense) in certain circumstances, if and only if it is unjustified not to believe it. A belief is an epistemic duty (weak sense) in certain circumstances if and only if it is wrong to choose to reject it
>
> (Zagzebski 1996: 241)

The epistemic duty to believe *x* entails *x* may not be disbelieved without incurring a level of culpability – how much culpability is in fact incurred depends on whether or not a belief is an epistemic duty in the weak sense or in the strong sense. The question then, must be rephrased as follows: "Is it a belief of epistemic duty to believe an extensive reading habit beneficial to the flourishing life and, if so, is this belief an epistemic duty in the strong or in the weak sense?".

A belief that is considered an epistemic duty is obviously a stronger belief than one that is merely 'justified'. In the very least one would have to argue that, for the belief that an extensive reading habit is beneficial to the flourishing life to be an epistemic duty, it must be shown that it is, in the least wrong to choose to reject it. But what does it mean to say that one rejects a belief x? In the very least, to reject a belief x is to believe it to be substantially untrue – and thereby to consider an opposing belief ($\neg x$) true. To reject a belief x is then to affirm a belief $\neg x$. In the case of the belief that "extensive reading is beneficial to the flourishing life" this means, effectively, a substantial denial of this belief; to state then that extensive reading has no discernible effect on the flourishing life or, indeed, may be said to be harmful.

The statement that "extensive reading has no or negative influence on the flourishing life' is then a substantial rejection of our belief. Now, consequently, it must be shown that this statement cannot be justified. If this belief can be justified then the original belief, that "an extensive reading habit is beneficial to the flourishing life", cannot possible be a belief of epistemic duty: there is, after all, then a possibility of rejection.

So is the belief that "extensive reading has no, or negative, influence on the flourishing life" justified. For a belief to be justified it must be shown that "a person who is motivated by intellectual virtue, and who has the understanding of his cognitive situation a virtuous person would have, might believe [this belief] in like circumstances." (Zagzebski 1996: 241)

Now, would a person, who is motivated by *phronesis,* give his assent to this belief? There are reasons to assume this to be unlikely. One attempts at a coherent criticism of the relationship between an extensive reading habit and a development of moral sensibility is John Carey's *What Good are the Arts?* (Carey 2006) but this does not detract from his making a powerful case for the moral and political power of literature itself – and indeed his critique of the ameliorating power of literature is itself fuelled by a moral understanding of what literature is. He fiercely criticizes notions of a 'transcendental' culture – the consumption of which would automatically 'civilize' us.

On the other hand, he actively affirms both the mind-expanding power of literature and the fact that that literary experiences, though different from real-life experiences, do allow us to witness a variety of human situations which in turn challenges us and enlarges our mental life:

> Like drugs, drink and antidepressants, literature is a mind-changer and an escape, but unlike them it develops and enlarges the mind as well as changing it.
>
> (Carey 2006:210)

From the context it is obvious that the development and enlargement of which Carey writes are morally relevant. An extensive reading praxis is a valuable factor towards fostering an insight, intelligence and sensitivity, as well as an imaginative eye for detail and an increased self-esteem which are all necessary for what in this thesis would be described as *eudaimonia.*

Still, it could be argued that we can only consider the belief that an extensive reading habit is beneficial to the flourishing life an epistemic duty if and only if we have previously accepted virtue theory as a convincing philosophical perspective. This is, however, only true to a very limited extent. To refuse to countenance virtue theory as a stronger philosophical perspective than utilitarianism or deontological ethics does not automatically mean to reject some of its conclusions. A utilitarian may properly withhold his judgement vis-à-vis the belief that an 'extensive reading habit is beneficial to the flourishing life' our judgement if he does not believe there is such a thing as *eudaimonia.*

Nonetheless if one is of the opinion that a theory of virtue is unpersuasive and concepts such as intellectual virtue, practical wisdom, and the good life are fundamentally meaningless one does not so much *reject* this belief in the sense that one considers it *untrue* , rather one considers it meaningless. A deontologist might not, as such, reject the belief outright, but rather consider the statement devoid of meaning. As such, he would not be in a position to either affirm or deny, for to hold a statement devoid of meaning is neither. To believe that reading is a good thing is not necessarily to be forced to assent to a theory of virtue.

However, it must be considered an inescapable conclusion that a virtue ethicist ought to give his unqualified assent to this belief, for he has an epistemic duty to believe an extensive reading habit beneficial to the flourishing life.

It may thus be concluded that the belief that "an extensive reading habit is beneficial to the flourishing life" may properly be considered a belief of epistemic duty in the sense that it is wrong to reject it. This belief is therefore an epistemic duty in the weak sense.

Is it however also an epistemic belief in the strong sense? A belief is an epistemic duty in the strong sense if it is unjustified *not to believe it* – which is a stronger condition than merely thinking a substantial rejection of a given belief unjustified.

Strictly speaking it is possible to disbelieve the belief that an extensive reading praxis is beneficial to the flourishing life on theoretical grounds: someone might withhold assent from this belief on the grounds that he or she does not think a philosophical concept such as the 'flourishing life' tenable. Because virtue theory itself is not a belief of epistemic duty, the belief that an extensive reading habit is beneficial to the flourishing life can at most be a belief of epistemic duty in the weak sense.

However, we may find correlate beliefs which *are* beliefs of epistemic duty in the strong sense. Though someone who rejects virtue theory would be justified to withhold assent to the belief that an extensive reading habit is beneficial to the flourishing life, he or she would not be in a position to withhold such assent to the belief that an extensive reading habit is beneficial *simpliciter*. This, it seems, is difficult to deny. Few have actively attempted to limit or frustrate students' reading out of any sense of moral responsibility. (Although of course parents or teachers may attempt to steer pupils away from certain books – this does not usually happen out of a belief that reading *as such* is not beneficial, but that rather reading *certain* books may not have the desired moral effect. Indeed most attempts to control children's reading stems from a deep-seated belief in the efficacy of texts in influencing moral behaviour – for better or worse.)

So even those who seek to limit and control children's reading do not do so out of either a rejection or a disbelief that reading, *in se,* is not beneficial. Indeed the few examples that can be found of people purposely and knowingly rejecting literature are to be found among extreme religious movements – some of which categorically reject the reading of *any* fiction. This notion is more often than not based that fiction, not being a factual report, is because of this lack of empirical veracity no more than 'untruth' , or even 'lies'. However, this position has never been cogently defended. In Christianity, even Tertullian, who was not noted for his tolerance towards secular activities, in the very least accepted the study of pagan literature, if with qualifications. The outright denial of reading being beneficial seems impossible – even a complete withholding of judgement with regards to the beneficial effects of reading does not seem warranted. Consequently, it must be affirmed that the belief that reading is beneficial is a belief of epistemic duty in the strong sense.

§7.4 Is it a belief of epistemic duty to think an extensive reading habit ought to be promoted and fostered?

If a habit *x* is found beneficial for the good life then, by definition, habit *x* ought to be promoted and fostered as an aid to the good life. As the belief that an extensive reading habit is a belief of epistemic duty, we can be said to have a moral duty to promote the fostering of such a habit.

§7.5 Is it consequently a right act to acquire an extensive reading habit?

Yes, if we have a belief that habit *x* is good, then by definition this implies a belief in the desirability of acquiring *x*, therefore we ought, all things being equal, acquire *x*.

§7.6 Is it consequently a right act to promote and foster an extensive reading habit?

This is to be answered in the affirmative.

§7.7 Is it a moral duty to acquire an extensive reading habit?

If we have an epistemic duty to believe that a habit *x* is a good thing to have, we also have – all other things being equal – a moral duty to acquire this habit. In the same way one could state that in so far as that we believe that truthfulness is a virtue, we should strive towards being truthful, and acquire the virtue of truthfulness. We all have duty to become – or stay – truthful. So too do we have a duty to acquire practical wisdom, or the virtue of *phronesis* ; for we cannot become successful moral knowers without this virtue. Indeed, considering that every virtuous act holds an exact mean between two vices, and we must always determine this mean in a state of sensitivity to concrete socio-cultural particulars we cannot be said to be truly moral without the virtue of practical wisdom. We can be said, without ado, that we have a moral duty to become practically wise. But is it possible to infer from this a duty to acquire an extensive reading habit?

Of course, reading intelligently is but one of many ways through which one may acquire practical wisdom. Moral goodness is not, of course, circumscribed to the literate. At the same time, knowing what we know about reading is that being in the possession of an extensive habit of reading is pleasurable, has many social and academic advantages and is undeniably of great moral import. It would be an evil to knowingly and willingly deprive oneself of these goods. The question whether or not we have a moral duty to acquire this habit is than a qualified yes. Yes, we have a duty to acquire this habit, on the condition that we cannot be said to be culpable if we do not acquire such a habit out of ignorance.

The only reason why someone would not willingly foster such a habit is then out of an acquired ignorance, which may be due to a less than successful exposure to print materials or a lack of positive reading examples and experiences in his environment.

This leads us to the question whether we – when we are aware of the positive cognitive and moral effects of a reading habit – we have a duty to foster this habit in others in general, and in pupils in particular.

We may consequently, a contrario, also conclude in this matter that, if we have a moral duty to acquire an extensive reading habit, we also have a moral duty to avoid being aliterate. We could rephrase Zagzebski's definition of a moral duty with regards to habits it as: "It is a moral duty to have a *habit* (strong sense) in certain circumstances if and only if it is wrong not to have it. It is a moral duty to have a *habit* (weak sense) in certain circumstances if and only if it is wrong to choose to reject it".

It is doubtful that we are under a moral duty (strong sense) to avoid aliteracy. This would mean, after all, that not having a reading praxis would be morally wrong under all circumstances. However aliteracy in the sense of being able to read but generally avoiding to read seems to be difficult to conceptualize if we leave out a certain element of wilfulness. This raises the question whether or not aliteracy is a vice (a character trait we have a moral duty to avoid) in the weak sense. *Aliteracy* stems from a positive *dislike* to read, and in its strongest form a *wilful* rejection of a reading praxis.

Whether or not *aliteracy* is a vice, i.e. a habit of character that we have a moral duty to avoid would consequently depend on individual circumstances. If we define aliteracy as an ability to read and a failure to maintain a reading praxis, the 'ability' is generally described as a purely technical reading competence. However, even though technical ability to read is a *necessary* condition it is hardly a *sufficient* condition of a wide-reaching praxis of reading. We may be perfectly capable of reading a phone-book or the sports-paper and yet lack any practice in intelligent qualitative reading.

Only in so far a pupil has been sufficiently introduced to this praxis and yet still rejects it, we can speak of a level of culpability and, indeed, a level of viciousness. At any rate, aliteracy, as a dislike of reading, is hardly an admirable habit and possibly a vice. In so far as it is a (weak) epistemic duty to accept the belief that an extensive reading practice is good to have, we are under an obligation not to reject this praxis. Aliteracy is a vice in so far as it consists of such a wilful rejection. Aliteracy is therefore a moral, and hence educative, problem.

§7.8 Is it justified to believe literary education ought to be promoted?

If we are justified in believing that an extensive reading practice is a good to have, are we also justified in believing that a programme of literary education, with the aim of eliciting such a habit, is good?

If we believe some habit to be virtuous, we believe it to be both admirable and desirable. Even if the possession of a virtue is not immediately desirable for ourselves, it is in a greater social context. For instance: I may be disadvantaged by returning a large cash find because I have the virtue of honesty. At the same time, from a social point of view, it is desirable for as great a number of people that could possibly acquire it. And it is, as a virtue, admirable in all.

Literary intelligence, as a form of *phronesis,* is also both desirable and admirable. Indeed, more than other virtues *phronesis* is desirable to have because of its architectonic nature. It is difficult to conceptualize whether anyone can be virtuous at all without having recourse to this virtue and, like all virtues, it is admirable in all. As Zagzebski puts it:

> A person *A* is praiseworthy (justified) for doing an act (having a belief) *S* (…) in case *A* does what a virtuous person would (probably) do (believes what a virtuous person would [probably] believe) in the same circumstances and is motivated by virtuous motives.
>
> (Zagzebski 1996: 236)

No one who has *phronesis,* or is motivated by intellectual virtue, could possibly deny that the virtue of *phronesis* ought to be facilitated and fostered as widely as possible. The belief that literary education, with the aim of eliciting literary intelligence at all levels ought to be promoted is then, a strong epistemic duty if we take the previous belief (that an extensive reading praxis is good to have) for true, regardless of whether or not we are card-carrying virtue ethicists. If some praxis or habit is good, then it ought be promoted.

If then, we reach the conclusion that a literary education is a good thing, we have a criterion with which to pass judgement on at least some schemes of education. Many fields of knowledge and many disciplines are good, and worthy of a place in the tightly-packed schedules of the contemporary primary and secondary school, but in the very least we have here a scheme of normative ethics which can explain why a literary education is important, and why attempts to suppress it for whatever reason are, indeed, vicious. Also it allows us to look critically at a number of schemes designed to promote reading. After all, a virtue is of the mind but works beyond it. A virtue is not a good intention or pious wish-thinking, it is an acquired excellence of character working in the world – it is properly a success concept.

Virtues would need structural and social support for their fostering. Following Alasdair Macintyre, we cannot postulate the existence of virtues (or moral excellences which are transferable across varying human practices[43]) without support of institutions:

> Institutions are characteristically and necessarily concerned with what I have called external goods. They are involved in acquiring money and other material goods, they are structured in terms of power and status, and they distribute money, power and status as rewards. Nor could they do otherwise of they are to sustain not only themselves, but also the practices of which they are the bearers. For no practices can survive for any length of time unsustained by institutions – and consequently of the goods external to the goods internal to the practices in question – that institutions and practices characteristically form a single causal order in which the ideals and the creativity of the practice are always vulnerable to the competitiveness of the institution.
>
> (Macintyre 1985: 194)

[43] After all, a virtue, unlike a skill, cannot *not* be exercised whenever appropriate. I can choose to speak Dutch when I like to, or choose not to speak Dutch when I like to. I cannot however choose to exercise the virtue of justice whenever I like to. If I have the virtue of justice I am bound to exercise it whenever circumstances demand it and if I do not exercise it when needed, I cannot be said to have the virtue, or at least not have it to the full.

Institutions are necessary for the flourishing of practices (Macintyre 1984) but must at the same time be *sustained* by the practices they nurture. An institute lacking such support becomes nothing more than a manipulative tool. Macintyre states: "In this context the essential function of the virtues is clear. Without them, without justice, courage and truthfulness, practices could not resist the corrupting power of institutions." [44]

> The novel insists that the humanities, including the study of excellent works of literature and art, are a central and ineliminable part of a good education. They cannot and should not be *replaced* by books of a more technical or social-scientific sort, though such books may have their own usefulness. This is the central curricular idea that I see the novel as putting forward; and I support it.
>
> (Nussbaum 1990: 219)

---

[44] Ibid. The dialectical relationship between *eudaimonia,* the good consisting of the exercise of acquired excellences, and *good government* sustaining *eudaimonia* with the provision of external goods and itself only being kept from corruption if not checked by the public exercise of the virtues citizenry is a theme already expounded on by Aristotle in his *Politics* (bks. III & VII)

§7.9 Is it a moral duty to promote and foster an extensive reading habit?

The capacity to be able to read complex literary texts intelligently, having a love of reading and an extensive reading habit are not simply skills, or morally irrelevant preferences. On the contrary, to be an intelligent reader, to be in the possession of literary intelligence, is to be in the possession of a form of intelligence with deep moral salience. This form of intelligence, practical wisdom or *phronesis,* is the architectonic intellectual virtue tying together the cognitive and practical aspects of our moral life. In a very real sense, the intellectual virtue of *phronesis* is the most fundamental virtue of all, as all other virtues depend on it.

As such, we have a moral duty to become practically intelligent or, at least, as practically intelligent as we may become. Reading extensively is one way, but one very powerful and proven way to acquire practical wisdom. Reading changes lives for the better. It is conducive to psychological states of happiness, widens boundaries of personal experience, and allows us to reflect on situations we would never have considered possible. Reading extensively may not be the panacea for all social and educational problems, but it is a great aid towards personal development and we have no reason for not valuing it as such and to promote extensive habits of reading in our children and pupils.

Also, a virtue, understood in a broadly Aristotelian framework, never exists in splendid isolation; it does not exist in isolation to other virtues and it does not exist ultimately for the individual sake of an isolated individual. The *telos* of *any* virtue is necessarily social. As David Carr says:

> Aristotle is arguing for the quite reasonable view that what count as the kinds of qualities or virtues apt to promote the well-being or flourishing of human beings as such, are those that fit them for a life of harmonious and co-operative relations with their fellows in some sort of civil human community
>
> (Carr 1991: 47)

Virtues then are always social, and are an object of social concern; and acquisition of virtues is an eminently practical matter, and because of this we need to be initiated in the practice of virtue. Much like we become skilled musicians by practicing music – so too we become virtuous – and eudaimonic – human beings by practicing the virtues. We become practically wise by practicing our sensitivities, practicing our social and cultural awareness, by practicing our faculties of moral judgement. Reading extensively is one very important way of practicing practical wisdom, for to have literary intelligence is to be practically wise. As we can only acquire the virtue of practical wisdom through practice, literary education is a decidedly practical endeavour.

The practice one aims to initiate children in is good-in-itself. Its goodness is not dependent on whether or not children at every point in their life understand why the practice is good for them; for understanding is a hallmark of maturity and children are not, by definition, mature. As Carr puts it:

> [Those] acts which we properly call just and courageous are acts such as would be done by a truly just and courageous man, not those only superficially similar acts that we might encourage a small child to perform in the course of his moral education in order that he may eventually grow up to be a just, courageous or unselfish person. As yet the small child might only have the foggiest idea why he is being encouraged not to cry when he falls down and grazes his knee or why against his inclinations he being encouraged to share his sweets with the hated little sister., but it is only by practising these aspects of virtue that he will acquire a grasp of the practicalities of moral life that may in time lead to his being a reflected and committed practitioner of it – in short, a just, courageous, and temperate person.
>
> (ibid: 52)

The duty to promote the virtue of practical wisdom exists independently from any inclination that the future agent (for it is difficult to argue that children are moral agents in their own right) may or may not have. 'Not feeling like it' has never been an excuse for not acquiring any virtue – or for not engaging in virtue-practice.

It may well be that in many households there is little access to print and the practice of reading. This may make for little forehand interest in either books or reading. Nonetheless it would be grotesque to refuse to expose children to books because they 'are not interested in them' – indeed it would be as grotesque as pandering to every inclination that a child may bring to muster. It is, indeed, to abdicate from one's responsibilities as a parent and as an educator.

All things put together, we can be said to have a moral duty to promote and foster an extensive reading habit. To not do so is to deprive a future generation of the joys and riches of reading, it is to deprive them of a multitude of perspectives on the human conditions, it is to deprive them of a great good. Such deprivation would itself be a great evil. There would not be anyone who is knowledgeable about the advantages and pleasures of reading who would not want to foster and promote this pleasurable and morally relevant activity. There exists therefore a moral duty to promote and foster habits of extensive reading. As citizens, educators, and parents we are all called to promote reading in whatever way we can.

§7.10 Moral Intelligence and Moral Education

Literary intelligence is a moral quality or disposition that I have identified as a form of *phronesis* or practical wisdom. Practical wisdom as a disposition is oriented towards the search for the good life. Although the disposition is by definition the disposition of an *individual* it cannot be acquired in isolation. Macintyre (1999) states that: "We become independent practical reasoners through participation in a set of relationships to certain particular others" (Macintyre 1999: 99). Also, because the exercise of practical wisdom is always *towards* some evaluative good it seems difficult to conceptualize a *phronesis* that can be exercised in perfect isolation. Even if we exercise *phronesis* in the form of literary intelligence we do not do so in isolation, but we enter into a relationship – albeit an indirect one – with other minds through the means of a literary text. This is also pointed out by Harding 1967:

> [Whether] it takes the form of play with companions, of drama, or of fiction. Imaginary spectatorship now occurs in a social setting.
>
> (Harding 1967: 137-8)

The perceived 'isolation' of the solitary reader is a misconception; the reader is through his reading intimately involved in a social existence which the author communicates through content and form of the novel. We are, if we wish to see ourselves as successful human beings, to conceptualize ourselves in a network of mutual obligations and relationships. It is part of our human condition that we are part of 'institutionalized networks of giving and receiving'. This is not to say that this educational network cannot be criticized, or that the contingent makeup of the institutionalized network leads to disparities of power or even grave injustices. The irony of the social relationships that are 'constitutive means to the end of our flourishing' (Macintyre 1999: 102) is that they – at the same time – 'give expression to established hierarchies of power (…) [and] as instruments of domination and deprivation, often frustrate us in our movement towards that good' (ibid: 103)

Rather like in Macintyre (1984) we find that the internal goods of virtues (such as *phronesis*) need the support of social institutions (a healthcare system, educational institutions, the family) for their sustenance. But social institutions have – at the same time – the power to corrupt and inhibit the fostering or exercise of these virtues.

It follows that institutions may serve to foster the virtue of *phronesis,* indeed an educational system may through a sustained programme of reading education, but it is also possible for such an educational system to pervert reading education – and make it serve ulterior motives.

To some extent, an example of such a perversion would be a certain trend in what is commonly described as 'character education'. Alfie Kohn (Kohn 1997), for one, suspects much of "what goes by the name of character education nowadays is, for the most part, a collection of exhortations and extrinsic inducements designed to make children work harder and do what they're told". Whereas Kohn readily admits that 'character education' does not necessarily entails moral drills – and schools have a role in helping pupils become good persons – he derides its perversion into drill and moralism.

One example proffered in Kohn (1997) pertinent to this subject is the example of an African American school in Chicago that uses a framework created by the US-based 'Character Education Institute':

> Periodic motivational assemblies are used to "give children a good pep talk," as the principal puts it, and to reinforce the values that determine who will be picked as Student of the Month. Rule number one posted on the wall of a kindergarten classroom is "We will obey the teachers." Today, students in this class are listening to the story of "Lazy Lion," who orders each of the other animals to build him a house, only to find each effort unacceptable. At the end, the teacher drives home the lesson: "Did you ever hear Lion say thank you?" (No.) "Did you ever hear Lion say please?" (No.) "It's good to say always say …. What?" (Please.) The reason for using these words, she points out, is that by doing so we are more likely to get what we want.
>
> (Kohn 1997)

Kohn then continues to analyse examples of what he calls the 'narrow conception' of character education and concludes that they are, in effect, examples of an attempt to transfer conventional morality: "acculturating students to conventional norms of 'good' behaviour" (ibid.). This transfer may be partially successful, at least temporarily "buying a particular behaviour" but, as Kohn points out: "[They] are unlikely to leave children with a *commitment* to that behaviour, a reason to continue acting that way in the future." (ibid.)

Virtue theory offers a sound reason why this is so: virtues cannot, by their nature, be acquired either through bribes or by training, drill, or moral exhortation.

It is rather by being put in real-life social and ethical situations that one acquires the experience needed for a moral disposition to grow. Although this experience can only be understood within a given social and historical context we cannot fool ourselves into thinking that the job of moral educators is done when conventional morality has been dutifully Xeroxed on a worksheet for classroom use. Virtues cannot be acquired through drill because the very notion of a character-trait (*hexis*) as it is understood by Aristotle implies by definition personal initiative and action.

Macintyre, too, points out that virtues are not acquired through mimicking social conventions (Macintyre 1984) and the definition of a virtue used by Zagzebski, a virtue being a "deep quality of a person, closely identified with her selfhood" (Zagzebski 1996 : 104) does not allow either for passive acquisition. Virtues are acquired through active experience. Kohn's argument is also redolent of Denys Thompson's critique of 'Education for Citizenship':

> Education in Citizenship is subordinate to the main ends of education. In a mature developed person the virtue of citizenship is comparatively a by-product. A mere good person may be an incomplete and in many ways undesirable person.
>
> (Thompson 1934)

Kohn, as an alternative to a narrow approach to character education, suggests among others, that character education ought, on the contrary, better be concerned with activities which: "provide children with explicit opportunities to practice "perspective taking" – that is, imagining how the world looks from someone else's point of view". Literature, according to Kohn, can play an important role in value education. Like Nussbaum, he rejects "simplistic morality tales" but sees the moral value of "rich, complex, literature" (Kohn 1997). In his view, we should:

> "[rather] than employ literature to indoctrinate or induce mere conformity, we can use it to spur reflection. Whether the students are 6-year-olds or 16-year-olds, the discussion of stories should be open-ended rather than relentlessly didactic. Teachers who refrain from tightly controlling conversations are impresses again and again by the levels of meaning students prove capable of exploring and the moral growth they exhibit in such an environment. Instead of announcing "This man is a hero; do what he did," such teachers may involve the students in deciding who (if anyone) is heroic in a given story – or in contemporary culture – and why. They may even invite students to reflect on the larger issue of whether it is desirable to have heroes." (ibid.)

This, of course, is not to say that good children's literature does not at the same time illustrate character traits. Indeed it would be odd if literature did not do so at all. Humans by the virtue of their humanity are endowed with characters and hence character-traits. Literature allows us to see these traits 'in action' in the fictional world evoked by the text. Leal (2000) argues persuasively that character-illustration in children's literature does not necessarily equate moral exhortation, but instead can lead us to In her study of 77 prize-winning[45] children's books she analyzes works on the basis of their literary excellence – the Newbery Medal being awarded for "distinguished writing" (ibid.), which is a "contribution to literature" (ibid.). She aligns herself with Lynch-Brown and Tomlinson (1999) in her stating "Moral reasoning in the form of reading and discovering whether the reader's decisions about certain situations match the character's actions is recognized as a personal value of literature for children" (Leal 2000)

Her analysis of Newbery Medal awarded books shows that the children's books in question depicted positive character traits far more often than negative ones. From an ethical point of view this is not surprising – goodness is acquired through the emulation and example of goodness. Goodness - philosophically speaking - is much more than an absence of evil. The correlation between perceived literary worth and the preponderance of positive character traits is interesting. It is unlikely that the mere presence of positive character traits is itself constitutive literary worth – but apparently literary worth and positive moral content need not be in conflict with each other but indeed books of literary worth may offer "a compelling vision of the goodness of goodness itself" (ibid.)

A possible point of criticism would be that a study such as this one is essentially a reductionist approach to individual virtues and character-traits. Such an approach has theoretical problems as noted above.

It may well be the case that original motivations for introducing literary education had ulterior motives not unlike contemporary character education.

---

[45] The 77 books in question had won the Newbery Medal, a prize for excellence in young people's literature awarded by the Association of Library Service to Children of the American Library Association.

This, at least, would be the position that authors such as Baldick (1983), Hunter (1988) and Viswanathan (1989) take. But even if these historical claims were proven true, it does not change the essential moral nature of literary education and neither can it serve as an argument against the position that literary intelligence is best described as a virtuous trait.

Literary education having been concretely used for ulterior purposes does not invalidate the claim that literary education correctly understood is of great moral importance: a*busus non tollit usum*: The moral dimension of reading pedagogy does not lie in the communication of some moral truth, but is to be found in the *act* of reading; an entering into a dialogue with a specific literary text. This makes the moral import of reading a far wider-reaching notion than the mere transfer of a 'moral message' embedded in the material read.

A reading pedagogy centring on the reading of 'moral narratives' or 'virtuous stories' is in fact instruction under the guise of reading pedagogy and consequently does not do a great service to either. Because *phronesis* is acquired through experience – there are no shortcuts. Moral instruction is no substitute for moral experience – both philosophical and psychological insight bears this out.

If government ought to promote reading education for moral reasons – for aiding pupils acquire the virtues needed for the pursuit of *eudaimonia,* or the good life, is reading education than a subset of moral education? The answer to that question depends on what one means by 'moral education'. Strictly speaking *all* education is has a moral component because the end-goal of all education is – or rather ought be – some good. Such a good is *either* a good which is to serve as a means to a good end *or* some good which is good in its own right. In the very least then, literary education is moral as all education is moral.

However, literary education however cannot be used fruitfully – as has sometimes been attempted - as a form of moral instruction. The reasons for this are easy to grasp:

Phronesis, being a virtue, can only be acquired through experience, exposure, imitation and initiation. It is impossible that it is acquired through instruction. It is, after all, not a technique or a matter of rule following.

If to read intelligently is a form of virtuous knowledge, a morally salient form of intelligence, it cannot possible be acquired through instruction. To aim to do so is a self-defeating exercise.

Also, if our notions of moral formation through the reading of 'moral' literature is unduly didactic and places an undue emphasis on the *content* of the reading matter we may be lead to absurd situations. An example of such a situation could be witnessed recently when the AQA Exam board demanded schools destroy volumes of poetry containing Carol Anne Duffy's poem *Education for Leisure* after three complaints had been made, two referring to a recent moral panic concerning knife-crime and one finding the depiction of a gold-fish being flushed down the toilet unpalatable.

That being said, as was pointed out earlier even books and literary works distributed because of their perceived social message of conformism can well have exactly the opposite effect. There is no compelling evidence that social control through control of a literary canon is in any way efficient.

Once again: *moral instruction is a self-defeating exercise*; indeed it is a philosophical impossibility. For literary education to be morally efficacious, the emphasis ought to be on creating a reading culture through which to foster the poetic function.

This makes the 'canon' of works a rather less important factor in reading education.

It is possible for one to have literary intelligence without it ever having been exercised on canonical works , indeed this is the problem with Leavis – his understanding of literature of 'worth' is far too narrow. Also if the exercise of one's literary value judgement is a virtue, and a virtue is a deep personal quality of a person, closely entwined with one's selfhood, than it follows that the exercise of a literary value judgement must always be personal. As Leavis said: "a judgement is one's own or it is nothing".

Chapter 8: Conclusion

§8.1 What good is reading?

Does reading have any use? Can a literary education be justified by an appeal to philosophy or ethics? This dissertation has so far argued that that is, indeed possible. Starting off from the influential positions and ideas voiced by FR Leavis and members of his circle it is argued that it is especially their concept of "literary intelligence" which allows for the cognitive underpinning of this essentially ethical claim. This dissertation argues that the concept of literary intelligence as used by Leavis, Bantock, Harding and eventually Holbrook is no product of theoretical idiosyncrasy but may rather be interpreted as a form of Aristotelian practical wisdom: *phronesis*: the intellectual virtue of being, roughly said, 'in touch with reality'. This allows to make the case for the relationship between reading and positive personal development.

Both fiercely defended as vilified, Leavis and those influences by him have had a great influence on literary education in Great Britain and beyond. They were not the first to point out the relationship between literature and ethics – but few have pointed it out with more intelligence and greater urgency. Without compromise they have defended the idea that a literary intelligence must by necessity be a moral intelligence. The urgency with which they stated their case was needed then as it is needed now.

However, a more decidedly philosophical approach to how we are to understand the moral salience of such a literary intelligence was called for. In this dissertation it is argued that virtue ethics offers such an approach, and that this approach was already alluded to by Geoffrey Bantock, when he sought to use J.H. Newman's epistemology as a foundation for the Leavisian notion of literary intelligence. As a consequence, this theoretical approach opens up new ways of looking at reading and reading education.

It ought to be clear that reading is not simply another skill to be added to a 'skills set', or yet another morally neutral and technical 'competence' which can be trained. On the contrary: a literary education properly understood is an education in the fullest sense of the word, it is necessarily preoccupied with values and the discernment of value. Its close relationship to *phronesis* or the virtuous discerning of salient moral details makes it a 'competence' which is *intrinsically good* , that is to say a character trait which cannot be used for ill purposes but is, by its very nature, always admirable and desirable. As such, it ought to be fostered, promoted and stimulated. To fail to promote an intrinsic good is itself evil. It is therefore impossible to come to an intellectually coherent opposition to literary education *as such.*

A literary education, rightly understood, is a leading-out from the straight-forwardness of our workaday lives – is an avenue through which we find our minds expanded, through which we may come to recognize the moral nuances of our existence and ultimately through which we may learn to live well. Not because trough reading we imbibe morally laudable messages but because literary experiences are isomorphic to real-life experiences to the extent that they too have moral salience. Learning to read well helps us to get in touch with reality, without which we cannot hope to become morally successful human beings.

A literary education is then the opposite of training and literary intelligence cannot be acquired by training. It is only by reading much that we can hope to read well, rather like we need to live much in order to live well.

If to read well means to increasingly reason well, to increasingly acquire practical wisdom, then it is a fundamentally important insight that reading well may only be achieved by reading much, reading widely, indeed perhaps even reading indiscriminately. A literary education must therefore be, by its very nature, open-ended. One can never claim to be 'done'. There is no end point and no set course. In a very real sense, the journey itself is the destination.

A literary education is then, consequently, a necessarily moral education. But the morality of a literary education is not of a tidy, conventional or didactic nature. On the contrary – a book is moral in so far as it expands our consciousness and trains our faculties for practical wisdom, *not* by communication some or other socially approved sentiment.

To read well, then, is a great gift. It is to have acquired one of the most important mental traits. This trait cannot simply be acquired in isolation – it must be promoted, one must be exposed to it, one must be initiated into it, one must become motivated to pursue it. Because intrinsic motivations are vital to the development of any virtue and motivations are properly understood as emotions, a literary education must also be a schooling of the sentiments, a training of the emotions. This alone would set literary education apart from other subjects. By its nature it must be the humane centre of a curriculum.

To undergo literary education is then to be involved in the lives of others. Practical wisdom, of which literary intelligence is an instantiation, is a *communal* matter as well as a personal one. Indeed: one cannot be said to live in a healthy society if there are only a few individuals who can be said to be *phronimoi*. In so far as a literary education properly understood is a training in *phronesis,* it has a direct social relevance that must not be underestimated. There can be no good society without good people. If a literary education is one way through which people may develop practical wisdom they are more capable of acquiring admirable character traits. It follows that literary education should then be stimulated to the furthest possible extent.

Reading *much* is the one key to reading well – and parents and educators should not stop at any opportunity to enable their pupils and children to access print material, promote a habit of reading and foster a love of books which will last a lifetime: a lifetime which, hopefully, will be spent in search of the good life.

§8.2 Desiderata for further research

Any dissertation must be limited in scope and the distinct emphasis on explaining and analysing literary intelligence in virtue-theoretical terms means that numerous tangential questions must be left untreated here. Some of the questions which would merit additional research are the following:

§8.2.1 Concerning Philosophical Questions

The tantalizing theory of literary experience as given by Harding demands to be put to a more fundamental philosophical critique. In particular, his idea of literary experience being structurally isomorphic to 'real-life' experiences could do with more elaborate philosophical treatment. Strong arguments have been proffered for the phenomenological relationship between literary and real-life experiences but the precise nature of the relationship remains not entirely clear and more work may need to be done to come to a proper understanding of these experiences.

§8.2.2 Concerning Social Theory

A reappraisal of the undeniably moral and ethical importance of literacy in society, may also lead to a reappraisal of the role of print in society: It would be advisable if efforts were made to foster a society-wide culture of reading. A lifelong reading habit may benefit all members of society, and not merely its children. What does it mean for a society to lose its literate class? What does it mean for a society to suffer through a continuous decrease in literacy? What does it mean for a society when high-end literacy becomes increasingly confined to an ever decreasing group of people? If the well-being of society as a whole depends on the moral and intellectual well-being of individuals, then it is to be expected that a decline in voluntary free reading will have discernible and negative social effects. It would be fruitful to try and come to an analysis of such effects.

§8.2.3 Concerning Literary Studies

Arguments such as proffered in this dissertation may go some way towards reappraising Ethical Criticism and the schools of thought associated with this branch of literary theory. In general it would be interesting to reread the literary-critical and literary-theoretical works of Leavis, Wayne C. Booth and others. In this dissertation the relationship between philosophy and literature is almost exclusively treated from the philosophical perspective. However fruitful such an approach may be, it must remain incomplete without a concomitant study from the perspective of literary studies well.

§8.2.4 Concerning Ethics

The moral dimension of literary education is quite specific. It may be defended cogently, but only by taking recourse to virtue theory. This does, however, also imply that virtue theory may well be a stronger ethical theory than either utilitarianism or deontology.

This research may well be used as stepping stone to the further analysis of the concept of intellectual virtue in particular, and the concept of virtue in general. The concept of intellectual virtue in itself provides for renewed credence in more refined forms of ethical cognitivism. We do not seem to be able to escape from the conclusion that in order to *be* good we have to *know* the good. Consequently this dissertation may form a stepping stone towards the reappraisal of moral cognitivism, with 'literary intelligence' then being a morally salient form of knowledge which should, as such, be fostered.

Appendix

Jan-Jaap van Peperstraten was born in Soest (NL) in 1978. He attended the Breskens Public Elementary School and the Zwin School in Oostburg, sitting his university entrance exams in 1996.

He attended the University of Nijmegen where he graduated MA in Philosophy in 2004. He consequently took teaching degrees in Philosophy and Social Sciences from Utrecht University in 2004 and 2006 respectively, and has worked in a number of Dutch secondary schools at a variety of levels. In 2006 he was awarded a research stipend by the University of the West of Scotland.

This doctoral dissertation was successfully defended on May · 2010.

Bibliography

Abbs, P. (1978). "An existentialist approach to education." Times Educational Supplement. 19 May 1978

Abbs, P. (1995). The Tradition of Poetic Humanism and the Teaching of the Arts. Powers of Being: David Holbrook and His Work. E. Webb. London, Associated University Presses: 112-124.

Applegate, M.D., & Applegate, A.J. (2004) "The Peter Effect: Reading habits and attitudes of preservice teachers". The Reading Teacher (**57**): 554-563.

Aristotle (1976). Ethics. London. Penguin Books

Armstrong, A. E. (2006). "Towards a strong virtue ethics for nursing practice." Nursing Philosophy 7: 110-124

Armstrong, I. (2000). The Radical Aesthetic. Oxford, Blackwell.

Armstrong, M. and M. Young (1964). New Look at Comprehensive Schools. London, Fabian Society.

Bailin, S. (2003). "The Virtue of Critical Thinking." Philosophy of Education: 327-329.

Baker, L. and D. Scher (2002). "Beginning Readers Motivations for Reading in Relation to Parental Beliefs and Home Reading Experiences." Reading Psychology **23**(4): 239-269.

Baldick, C. (1983). The Social Mission of English Criticism. Oxford, Clarendon Press

Bantock, G. H. (1956). L.H. Myers, a critical study. London, University College Leicester Jonathan Cape.

Bantock, G. H. (1963). The Education of the Less Able Child. Education in an Industrial Society. London, Faber & Faber: 200-223.

Bantock, G. H. (1965a). Education and the Literary Intelligence. Education and Values: Essays in the theory of education: 33-52.

Bantock, G. H. (1965c). Freedom and Authority in Education: A Criticism of Modern Cultural and Educational Assumptions. London, Faber & Faber.

Bantock, G. H. (1965d). Newman and the possibility of 'order'. Freedom and Authority in Education. London, Faber & Faber: 106-132.

Bantock, G. H. (1970). T. S. Eliot and Education. London, Faber.

Bantock, G. H. (1981a). Discovery methods. The parochialism of the present. London, Boston, Henley, Routledge & Kegan Paul: 52-64.

Bantock, G. H. (1981b). Equality and education. The parochialism of the present. London, Boston, Henley, Routledge & Kegan Paul: 107-132.

Bantock, G. H. (1981c). Literature and the social sciences: with particular reference to the sociology of education. The parochialism of the present. London, Boston, Henley, Routledge & Kegan Paul: 24-51.

Bantock, G. H. (1981d). The arts in education. The parochialism of the present. London, Boston, Henley, Routledge & Kegan Paul: 80-94.

Bantock, G. H. (1981e). The death of Bazarov. The parochialism of the present. London, Boston, Henley, Routledge & Kegan Paul: 95-106.

Bantock, G. H. (1981f). The idea of a liberal education. The parochialism of the present. London, Boston, Henley, Routledge & Kegan Paul: 65-79.

Bantock, G. H. (1981g). The parochialism of the present, Contemporary issues in Education. London, Boston, Henley, Routledge & Kegan Paul.

Bantock, G. H. (1981h). The parochialism of the present: some reflections on the history of educational theory. The parochialism of the present. London, Boston, Henley, Routledge & Kegan Paul: 7-23.

Bantock, G. H. (1981). The parochialism of the present, Contemporary issues in Education. London / Boston, Henley, Routledge & Kegan Paul.

Begley, A. M. (2005). "Practising Virtue: A Challenge to the View that a Virtue Centred Approach to Ethics lacks Practical Content." Nursing Ethics **12**(6): 622-637

Berlyne, D. E. (1971). Aesthetics and Psychobiology. New York, Appleton.

Bilan, R.P. (1979). The Literary Criticism of F.R. Leavis. Cambridge. Cambridge University Press.

Bintz, W. (1993). "Resistant readers in secondary education: Some insights and implications." Journal of Reading **36**(8): 604-615.

Blishen, E. (1971). This Right Soft Lot London, Panther

Bocock, J. and R. Taylor (2003a). "The Labour Party and Higher Education." Higher Education Quarterly **57**(3): 249-265.

Bocock, J. and R. Taylor (2003b). "The Labour Party and Higher Education: The Nature of the Relationship." Higher Education Quarterly **57**(3): 220-238.

Booth, Wayne C. (1988). The Company We Keep: An Ethics of Fiction. Berkeley, Los Angeles, London, University of California Press.

Bousted, M. (2002). "Personal Growth through English - policy and practice." Changing English **9**(2): 185-196

Brophy, J. and N. Kher (1986). Teacher socialization as a mechanism for developing student motivation to learn. Social Psychology applied to education. R. Feldman. New York, Cambridge University Press: 257-288.

Bruner, J. (1996). The Culture of Education. London, Harvard University Press.

Bus, A. G. and M. H. van IJzendoorn (1995). "Mothers reading to their 3-year olds: The role of mother-child attachment security in becoming literate." Reading Research Quarterly **30**(4): 998-1015.

Carey, J. (1992). The Intellectuals and the Masses: pride and prejudice among the literary intelligentsia, 1880-1939. London, Faber & Faber.

Carr, D. (1991). Educating the Virtues, An essay on the philosophical psychology of moral development and education. London / New York, Routledge

Casey, J. (1966). The Language of Criticism. London, Barnes & Noble

Chall, J. S., C. Snow, et al. (1981). Families and literacy: The contribution of out-of-school experiences to children's acquisition of literacy., National Institute of Education.

Church, R., G. Davies, et al. (1938). "Claims of Politics." Scrutiny **8**(2): 130-166.

Clark, C. and K. Rumbold (2006). Reading for Pleasure: A research overview. London, National Literacy Trust.

Cleary, F. (1939). "Why children read." Wilson Library Bulletin **14**(119-126).

Code (1987). Epistemic Responsibility. Hanover NH, University Press of New England

Costall, A. (2001). Pear and his peers. Psychology in Britain: Historical Essays and Personal Reflections. G. C. Bunn, A. D. Lovie and G. D. Richards. Leicester, BPS Books: 188-204.

Cox, C. (1994). The significance of F. R. Leavis: the philosophical and educational context of the critic as "anti-philosopher". Educational Studies. London, Institute of Education - University of London. **Ph.D.:** 194.

Cunningham, A. E. and K. E. Stanovich (2001). "What Reading Does for the Mind." Journal of Direct Instruction **1**(2): 137-149.

Curren, R. R. (2000). Aristotle on the Necessity of Public Education. Oxford, Rowman & Littlefield.

Darling, J. (1999). Scottish Primary Education: Philosophy and Practice. Scottish Education. W. Humes and T. Bryce. Edinburgh, Edinburgh University Press: 27-36.

Deci, E. L. (1971). "Effects of externally mediated rewards on intrinsic motivation." Journal of Personality and Social Psychology **18**: 105-115.

Deci, E. L., R. M. Ryan, et al. (2001). "The Pervasive Negative Effects of Rewards on Intrinsic Motivation: Response to Cameron (2001)." Review of Educational Research **71**(1): 43-51.

Dixon, J. (1975). Growth through English, set in the perspective of the seventies. Oxford, National Association for the Teaching of English

Duffy, E. (1994). The Stripping of the Altars: Traditional Religion in England 1400-1580. New Haven, CT, Yale University Press.

Dunne, J. (1993) Back to the Rough Ground: 'Phronesis' and 'Techne' in Modern Philosophy. Notre Dame / London, University of Notre Dame Press

Dymoke, S. (2002). "The Dead Hand of the Exam: the impact of the NEAB anthology on poetry teaching at GCSE." Changing English **9**(1): 85-93

Eagleton, T. (1983). Literary Theory, an Introduction. Oxford, Basil Blackwell

Eagleton, T. (2007). Only Pinter Remains. Guardian. 7 July 2007

Edwards, E. A. (1934). "Ideals and Facts in Adult Education, *Adult Education in Practice, English in Australia,* and *Reading and Discrimination,* reviewed by W.A. Edwards." Scrutiny **3**(1): 91-100.

Entwistle, H. (1979). Antonio Gramsci: Conservative Schooling for Radical Politics. London / Boston / Henley, Routledge & Kegan Paul.

Fisher, Walter R. (1987). Human Communication as Narration: Toward a Philosophy of Reason, Value, and Action. Columbia, University of South Carolina Press

Furlong, J. (2002). "Ideology and Reform in Teacher Education in England: Some Reflections on Cochran-Smith and Fries." Educational Researcher **31**(6): 23-25.

Gallie, W. B. (1956). "Essentially Contested Concepts." Proceedings of the Aristotelian Society **56**: 167-198.

Gallie, W.B. (1964) What is a Story? in Philosophy and the Historical Understanding, London, Chatto & Windus

Gaver, M. (1963). Effectiveness of centralized library service in elementary schools. New Brunswick, N.J., Rutgers University Press.

Greany, V. and M. Hegarty (1987). "Correlations of leisure time reading." Journal of Research in Reading **10**: 3-20.

Green, A. (1990). Education and state formation: the rise of education systems in England, France and the USA. London, Macmillan.

Harding, D. W. (1937a). "The Cultural Background of Intelligence Testing." Scrutiny **6**(2): 144-154.

Harding, D. W. (1937b). "The Role of the Onlooker." Scrutiny **6**(3): 247-258.

Harding, D. W. (1962). "Psychological Processes in the Reading of Fiction." British Journal of Aesthetics **4**(2): 133-147.

Heyns, B. (1978). Summer learning and the effects of schooling. New York, Academic Press.

Holbrook, D. (1962) Llareggub revisited: Dylan Thomas and the State of Modern Poetry. London, Bowes and Bowes.

Holbrook, D. (1967). English for Maturity, Cambridge, Cambridge University Press.

Holbrook, D. (1968). English for the Rejected: Training Literacy in the Lower Streams of the Secondary School. Cambridge, Cambridge University Press.

Holbrook, D. (1969). "The wizard and the critical flame" Journal of Moral Education **1** (1)

Holbrook, D. (1975). Reading and Discrimination. Bookmarks: Writers on their Reading. F. R. Raphael. London, Quartet Books: 76-90.

Houle, C. R. and C. Montmarquette (1984). "An empirical analysis of loans by school libraries." Alberta Journal of Educational Research **30**: 104-114.

Hume, D. (1967). Treatise on Human Nature. Oxford, Clarendon Press.

Humphreys, A. R. (1939). "A Classical Education and Eighteenth Century Poetry." Scrutiny **8**(2): 193-207.

Hunter, Ian (1988). Culture and Government. Basingstoke, Macmillan

Hursthouse, R. (1991). "Virtue Theory and Abortion." Philosophy and Public Affairs **20**: 223-246.

Ingham, J. (1981). Books and Reading Development: the Bradford Book Flood Experiment. London, Heinemann Educational Books Ltd.

Inglis, F. (1985). The Management of Ignorance: a political theory of the curriculum. Oxford / Cambridge MA., Basil Blackwell.

Kermode, F. (2000). The Sense of an Ending: Studies in the Theory of Fiction. Oxford, OUP

Kim, J. (2003). Summer reading and the ethnic achievement gap. American Educational Research Association Conference, Chicago.

Knights, L. C. (1933a). "Scrutiny of Examinations." Scrutiny **2**(2): 137-162.

Knights, L. C. (1933b). "Good Intentions in Education, *The Educational Frontier,* reviewed by L.C. Knights." Scrutiny **2**(2): 215-218.

Knights, L. C. (1945). "On the Social Background of Metaphysical Poetry." Scrutiny **13**(1): 37-52.

Knulst, W. and G. Kraaykamp (1997). "The decline of reading, Leisure Reading Trends in the Netherlands (1955-1995)." Netherlands Journal of Social Sciences **33**(2): 130-50.

Kohn A. (1997). "How Not to Teach Values: A Critical Look at Character Education." Phi Delta Kappan (February 1997)

Kraaykamp, G. (2003). "Literary socialization and reading preferences. Effects of parents, the library and the school." Poetics **31**: 235-257.

Krashen, S. (1995). "School libraries, public libraries, and the NAEP reading scores." School Library Media Quarterly **23**: 235-238.

Krashen, S. D. (2004). The Power of Reading: insights from the research. Portsmouth N.H., Heinemann.

Lao, C. Y. (2003). "Prospective teachers' journey to becoming readers." New Mexico Journal of Reading **32**(2): 14-20.

Lahtinen, A.-M. (2003). Learning to understand through reading fiction. EARLI, Padua.

Lance, K. C., L. Welborn, et al. (1993). The impact of school library media centres on academic achievement. Castle Rock Co., Willow Research and Publishing.

Leal, D. J., C. H. Glascock, et al. (2000). "Reading Character in Children's Literature: A Character Trait Study in Newbery Medal Books." Ohio Reading Teacher **34**(1): 49-56.

Leavis, F. R. (1932). "'The Literary Mind'." Scrutiny **1**(1): 20-32.

Leavis, F. R. (1943a). "Education and the University: considerations at a critical time." Scrutiny **11**(3): 162-167.

Leavis, F. R. (1943b). "Literature and Society." Scrutiny **12**(1): 2-11.

Leavis, F. R. (1948). The Great Tradition. London, Chatto & Windus.

Leavis, F. R. (1961). Education & the University: A Sketch for an English School. London, Chatto & Windus.

Leavis, F. R. and D. Thompson (1964). Culture and Environment. London, Chatto & Windus

Leavis, F. R. (1965). James as Critic. Selected Literary Criticism: Henry James. M. Shapira. New York, McGraw-Hill Book Company: xiii-xxiii.

Leavis, F.R. (1972). Nor Shall My Sword. London, Chatto & Windus

Leavis, F.R. (1977) The Living Principle: "English" as a Discipline of Thought. London, Chatto & Windus

Leavis, F. R. (1982). New Bearings in English Poetry. London, Penguin Books.

Lipsett, A. (2008). No novels necessary for new look English GCSE. The Guardian. (Friday June 2008)

Macintyre, A. (1973). "The Essential Contestability of Some Social Concepts." Ethics **84**(1): 1-9.

Macintyre, A. (1984). After Virtue. South Bend, University of Notre Dame Press

Macintyre, A. (1985). The Idea of an Educated Public. Education and Values. G. Haydon. London, Institute of Education: 15-36.

Macintyre, A. (1999). Dependent Rational Animals: Why Human Beings Need the Virtues. Chicago, La Salle / Open Court.

MacKillop, I. (1995). F.R. Leavis: A Life in Criticism. London, Allen Lane / The Penguin Press.

Maritain, J. (1965). Art et Scolastique. Bruges, Desclée de Brouwer.

Marx, K. and F. Engels (2005). The Communist Manifesto. London, Penguin Books.

Mason, A. (1993). The Notion of an Essentially Contested Concept. Explaining Political Disagreement. A. Mason. Cambridge, Cambridge University Press: 47-68.

Mathieson, M. (1975). The preachers of culture: a study of English and its teachers. London, Allen & Unwin.

Mcguinn, N. (2005). "A place for the personal voice? Gunther Kress and the English curriculum." Changing English **12**(2): 205-217.

McLuhan, m. (1944). "Poetic versus Rhetorical Exegesis" Sewanee Review **52** (April)

McQuillan, J (1998). The literacy crisis: False claims and real solutions. Portsmouth, N.H., Heinemann.

McQuillan, J. and J. Au (2001). "The Effect of Print Access on Reading Frequency." Reading Psychology **22**: 225-248.

Moore-Gilbert, B. J. (1994). The Arts in the 1970s: Cultural Closure? London, Routledge.

Morrow, L. (1983). "Home and school correlates of early interest in literature." Journal of Educational Research **75**: 339-344.

Morrow, L. and C. Weinstein (1982). "Increasing children's use of literature through program and physical changes." Elementary School Journal **83**(131-137).

Mour, S. L. (1977). "Do teachers read?" The Reading Teacher **30**: 397-401.

Mulhern, F. (1979). The Moment of Scrutiny. London, NLB.

Murdoch, I. (2001). The Sovereignty of Good. London & New York, Routledge

Mueller, D. L. (1973). "Teacher attitudes towards reading." Journal of Reading **17**: 202-205.

Nathanson, S., J. Pruslow, et al. (2008). "The Reading Habits and Literacy Attitudes of Inservice and Prospective Teachers." Journal of Teacher Education **20**(10): 1-9.

Nell, V. (1988a). Lost in a book: the psychology of reading for pleasure. New Haven / London, Yale University Press.

Nell, V. (1988b). "The psychology of reading for pleasure: Needs and gratifications." Reading Research Quarterly **23**(1): 6-50.

Neuman, S. (1986). "The home environment and fifth-grade students' leisure reading." Elementary School Journal **86**: 335-343.

Neuman, S. and D. Celano (2001). "Access to print in low-income and middle-income communities." Reading Research Quarterly **36**(1): 8-26.

Newbolt, H. (1921). The Teaching of English in England. London, HM Stationery Office

Newman (1948). The Uses of Knowledge. Wheeling IL, Harlan Davidson

Newman, J.H. (1955). An Essay in Aid of a Grammar of Assent. Garden City NY, Image Books

Newman, J. H. (1962). A Letter Addressed to His Grace the Duke of Norfolk on Occasion of Mr. Gladstone's Recent Expostulation. Newman and Gladstone: The Vatican Decrees. Notre Dame, University of Notre Dame Press.

Newman, J.H.(1973). Letters and Diaries (vol. 24), C. S. Dessain et al., Oxford, Clarendon Press

Nozick, R. (1974) Anarchy, State and Utopia, New York, Basic Books

Nozick, R, (2007) "The Experience Machine," in Ethical Theory: Classical and Contemporary Readings , ed. Louis Pojman Wadsworth, Belmont (146-147).

Nussbaum, M. (1990). Love's Knowledge, essays on Philosophy and Literature. New York / Oxford, Oxford University Press.

Nussbaum, M. (1997) Cultivating Humanity: A Classical Defense of Reform in Liberal Education

Oakeshott, M. (1932). "The New Bentham." Scrutiny **1**(2): 114-131.

Oakeshott, M. (1935). "Thomas Hobbes." Scrutiny **4**(3): 263-277.

Oakeshott, M. (1937). "The Modern Mind." Scrutiny **6**(2): 208-210.

Olsen, D. R. (1986). Intelligence and literacy: The relationships between intelligence and the technologies of representation and communication. Practical Intelligence. R. J. Sternberg and R. K. Wagner. Cambridge, Cambridge University Press: 338 - 360.

Pack, S. (2000). "Public library use, school performance and the parental X-factor: A bio-documentary approach to pupils' snapshots." Reading Improvement **37**: 161-172.

Pearson, T.D. (1994). 'Interview with Professor Alasdair Macintyre' in Kinesis **20:42**

Pincoffs, E. L. (1986). Quandaries and Virtues. Lawrence, University Press of Kansas

Poole, R. (1995). England's Only Existentialist Philosopher. Powers of Being; David Holbrook and His Work. E. Webb. London, Associated University Presses: 211-227.

Powell-Brown, A. (2003). "Can you be a teacher of literacy if you don`t love to read?" Journal of Adolescent and Adult Literacy **47**: 284-288.

Pradl, G. M. (1995). A Moral Approach to English. Powers of Being: David Holbrook and his Work. E. Webb. London, Associated University Presses: 93-111.

Ramos, F. and S. Krashen (1998). "The impact of one trip to the public library: Making books available may be the best incentive for reading." The Reading Teacher **51**(7): 614-615.

Rane-Szostak, D. and K. A. Herth (1995a). "Pleasure reading, other activities and loneliness in later life." Journal of Adolescent and Adult Literacy **39**(2): 100-108.

Rane-Szostak, D. and K. A. Herth (1995b). "A New Perspective on Loneliness in Later Life." Issues in Mental Health Nursing **16**(6): 583-592.

Roberts, D., C. Bachen, et al. (1984). "Reading and television: Predictors of reading achievement at different age levels." Communication Research **11**(1): 9-49.

Robinson, J. and G. Godbey (1997). Time for Life, the Surprising Ways in Which Americans Use Their Time. University Park, University of Pennsylvania Press.

Rose, J. (2002). The Intellectual Life of the British Working Classes. New Haven London, Yale University Press.

Scarborough, H. S. and W. Dobrich (1994). "On the efficacy of reading to preschoolers." Developmental Review **14**: 245-302.

Schunk, D. H. (1990a). "Introduction to the special section on motivation and efficacy"
Educational Psychology, **82**, 3-6.

Schunk, D. H. (1990b). "Goal setting and self-efficacy during self-regulated learning" Educational
Psychologist, **25**, 71-86.

Schwartz (1962). Der konservative Anarchist: Politik und Zeitkritik Ernst Jüngers. Freiburg, Rombach.

Smith, C., R. Constantino, et al. (1996). "Differences in print environment for children in Beverley Hills, Compton and Watts." Emergency Librarian **24**(4): 4-5.

Smith, F. (1988). Joining the literacy club. Portsmouth, N.H., Heinemann.

Smith, M. C. (1989). "Reading attitudes of pre-service education majors." Reading Horizons **29**: 230-243.

Stotesbury, R. (2008). Reply to Ian Robinson. Leavis and Philosophy. Bishopstone, Edgeways Books: 34-37

Taylor, D. and C. Dorsey-Gaines (1988). Growing up literate: Learning from inner-city families. Portsmouth, N.H., Heinemann.

Teale, W. H. (1981). "Parents reading to their children. What studies of early readers tell us." Language Arts **55**: 902-910.

Thomas, D. (1992) On the Air With Dylan Thomas: The Broadcasts Maud, R. (ed.) New York, New Directions

Thompson, D. (1933). "A cure for amnesia." Scrutiny **2**(1): 2-11.

Thompson, D. (1934). "Progressive Schools, reviews by Dennis Thompson." Scrutiny **3**(2): 208-215.

Ulanov, A. and B. Ulanov (1995). Looking: Subjectivity and the True Self. Powers of Being: David Holbrook and His Work. E. Webb. London, Associated University Presses: 173-190.

von Wright, G. H. (1963). The Varieties of Goodness. New York, Humanities Press

Viswanathan, G. (1989). Masks of conquest: literary study and British rule in India. New York, Columbia University Press

Wallace, J. D. (1978). Virtues and Vices. Ithaca, Cornell University Press

Williams, R. (1958) Culture and Society, 1780-1950, New York, Columbia University Press

Witte, T. (2002). "Op zoek naar een 'gezond' curriculum voor het literatuuronderwijs". VON Cahier 2002.

Worthy, J. and S. McKool (1996). Students who say they hate to read: The importance of opportunity, choice, and access. Literacies for the 21st century: Research and practice. D. Leu, C. Kinzer and K. Hinchman. Chicago, National Reading Conference: 245-256.

Yarosz, D. J. and W. S. Barnett (2001). "Who Reads to Young Children? Identifying Predictors of Family Reading Activities." Reading Psychology **22**(1): 67-81.

Zagzebski, L. T. (1996). Virtues of the mind: an inquiry into the nature of virtue and the ethical foundations of knowledge. Cambridge, Cambridge University Press.

Printed in Dunstable, United Kingdom

91342997R00154